The Challenge of International Business

Edited by
Susan Segal-Horn

Titles in the Cranfield Management Research Series include:

The Challenge of Strategic Management
Corporate Strategy and Financial Decisions
Strategic Marketing Planning
Strategy Planning in Logistics and Transportation
Making Sense of Competition Policy
European Developments in Human Resource Management
Executive Redundancy and Outplacement
The Challenge of International Business
The Future of Services Management
Advances in Consumer Marketing

These books are available from all good bookshops or directly from Kogan Page Ltd, 120 Pentonville Road, London N1 9JN.
Tel: 071 278 0433 Fax 071 837 6348

First published in 1994

Kogan Page Limited
120 Pentonville Road
London N1 9JN

British Library Cataloguing in Publication Data

A CIP record for this book is available from the British Library.

ISBN 0 7494 1163 5

Typeset by Books Unlimited (Nottm), Sutton-in-Ashfield, NG17 1AL
Printed and bound in Great Britain by Biddles Ltd, Guildford and Kings Lynn

CONTENTS

LIST OF FIGURES

LIST OF BOXES

LIST OF TABLES

THE CRANFIELD MANAGEMENT RESEARCH SERIES

The Cranfield Management Research Series represents an exciting joint initiative between the Cranfield School of Management and Kogan Page.

As one of Europe's leading post-graduate business schools, Cranfield is renowned for its applied research activities, which cover a wide range of issues relating to the practice of management.

Each title in the Series is based on current research and authored by Cranfield faculty or their associates. Many of the research projects have been undertaken with the sponsorship and active assistance of organisations from the industrial, commercial or public sectors. The aim of the Series is to make the findings of direct relevance to managers through texts which are academically sound, accessible and practical.

For managers and academics alike, the Cranfield Management Research Series will provide access to up-to-date management thinking from some of Europe's leading academics and practitioners. The series represents both Cranfield's and Kogan Page's commitment to furthering the improvement of management practice in all types of organisations.

THE SERIES EDITORS

Frank Fishwick
Reader in Managerial Economics
Director of Admissions at Cranfield School of Management

Dr Fishwick joined Cranfield from Aston University in 1966, having previously worked in textiles, electronics and local government (town and country planning). Recent research and consultancy interests have been focused on business concentration, competition policy and the book publishing industry. He has been directing a series of research studies for the Commission of the European Communities, working in collaboration with business economists in France and Germany. He is permanent economic adviser to the Publishers Association in the UK and is a regular consultant to other public and private sector organisations in the UK, continental Europe and the US.

Gerry Johnson
Professor of Strategic Management
Director of the Centre for Strategic Management and Organisational Change
Director of Research at Cranfield School of Management

After graduating from University College London, Professor Johnson worked for several years in management positions in Unilever and Reed International before becoming a management consultant. Since 1976, he has taught at Aston University Management Centre, Manchester Business School, and from 1988 at Cranfield School of Management. His research work is primarily concerned with processes of strategic decision making and strategic change in organisations. He also works as a consultant on issues of strategy formulation and strategic change at a senior level with a number of UK and international firms.

Shaun Tyson
Professor of Human Resource Management
Director of the Human Resource Research Centre
Dean of the Faculty of Management and Administration at Cranfield School of Management

Professor Tyson studied at London University and spent eleven years in senior positions in industry within engineering and electronic companies.

For four years he was a lecturer in personnel management at the Civil Service College, and joined Cranfield in 1979. He has acted as a consultant and researched widely into human resource strategies, policies and the evaluation of the function. He has published 14 books.

CONTRIBUTORS

Alan Braithwaite BSc (Hons) MBA has worked for the last ten years as a consultant in logistics and physical distribution. He founded LCP four years ago and the practice is now a partnership with Richard Spooner. He has specialised in the area of strategic planning, developing new methods for preparing strategies and relating logistics to commercial issues for his clients. Recent projects have been with both multi-nationals and with prestigious UK retailing and mail order companies. He has also worked extensively for the professional distribution sector. He has written widely on the subject of logistics and distribution and contributes to specialist courses on logistics at Cranfield University School of Management. Before entering consultancy he spent four years in the furniture industry and six years in the food industry, including three years with HJ Heinz Co Ltd where he was Department Head of Industrial Engineering.

Chris Brewster BA (Econ) PhD MIPM is a Professor of European Human Resource Management and Director of the Centre for European Human Resource Management at Cranfield University School of Management. He has consulted and taught on management programmes throughout the world and was responsible for the Cranfield research project on expatriate managers. His publications, as well as numerous articles, include *The Management of Expatriates, Employee Relations, Cost Effective Strategies in Industrial Relations, European Community Social Policy, The European Human Resource Management Guide, European Developments in Human Resource Management* and *A Different Tack*. The latter was based on comparative research into Swedish and British management styles. He is also supervisor to four PhD students in the area of expatriation.

Adrian Buckley BA MSc FCA FCCA FCT is Professor of International Financial Management at Cranfield University School of Management and a past Director of its MBA programme. He qualified as a chartered accountant and his industrial experience embraced five years of management consultancy, two years in banking, and six years' work in financial planning and corporate treasury. He was the first group treasurer at Redland plc. He has written extensively in his field and has contributed over 100 articles to professional journals and is author of two books on international finance.

Sally Butler ACIB MBA is a Teaching Fellow in Strategic Management at Cranfield University School of Management. She joined the Cranfield Management Development Unit after completing the full-time MBA programme. She has several years' experience in the financial sector, particularly in international corporate banking, during which time she worked in a variety of industries. She is an Associate of the Chartered Institute of Bankers. Sally Butler's interests are in the areas of cross-cultural management, leadership and the development of international managers. She is currently conducting doctoral research into the influence of national culture on organisational culture within multi-national organisations.

Martin Christopher is professor of Marketing and Logistics Systems at Cranfield University School of Management, where he is Head of the Marketing and Logistics Faculty and Chairman of the Cranfield Centre for Logistics and Transportation. His interests in marketing and logistics strategy are reflected in his many published articles and books. He is Co-Editor of *The International Journal of Logistics Management*. Martin Christopher has held appointments as Visiting Professor at the University of British Columbia, Canada, the University of New South Wales, Australia and the University of South Florida, USA.

James Cooper is Director of Cranfield Centre for Logistics and Transportation at Cranfield University School of Management, where he is also Exel Logistics Reader. Having worked in the distribution division of Kodak, he returned to academic life at the Transport Studies Group, Polytechnic of Central London. Professor Cooper has extensive research, consultancy and teaching experience in both freight transport and logistics. He has led a number of major studies on these topics for both the UK government and many companies and he participates in the DRIVE 2 programme of the European Commission as a partner in the COMBICOM consortium. He is a Visiting Lecturer at the University of Linköping in Sweden and the Catholic University of Brabant in the Netherlands. As UK representative on the OECD expert group on advanced logistics and communications, he has contributed to establishing a wider appreciation of the importance of logistics.

Liam Fahey is Adjunct Professor of Strategic Management at Babson College (USA) and Visiting Professor of Strategic Management at Cranfield University School of Management. He has previously taught at Northwestern University's JL Kellogg Graduate School of Management and at Boston University. His area of specialisation is strategic management. His research has appeared in numerous periodical publications and he is author and editor of several books including *Winning in the New Europe* (Editor, 1992) and *The Portable MBA in Strategy* (Co-editor, 1993). Professor Fahey has acted as consultant to various organisations, both national and multinational.

David Faulkner Bsc (Bcon) MA, D Phil FIMC Lecturer in Strategic Management at Cranfield University School of Management. Prior to this he had a long career in strategic management consultancy first with McKinsey and subsequently with Arthur D Little. He also has experience as an entrepreneur, having built up and run his own leisure goods company. David Faulkner is an Oxford-trained economist by background. His interests in the strategy field include issues of strategy formulation and, in particular, the development of cross-border strategic alliances, a field in which he completed his doctorate. He also continues to be an active management consultant, working with senior executives on issues of business and corporate strategy.

John Hailey is a Lecturer at Cranfield University School of Management. He has extensive international experience of working with entrepreneurs, managers, development workers and policy makers. He has worked in a number of different countries in the Asia/Pacific region, and prior to coming to Cranfield was a Fellow of the East West Centre in Hawaii. Currently he teaches international management courses on Cranfield's MBA programmes, with a particular interest in cross-cultural management issues and managing in developing countries. He regularly undertakes consultancies and runs training programmes for government and international agencies in Africa and the Asia/Pacific region.

VK (Veekay) Narayanan is currently Professor of Strategic Management and Associate Dean of Academic Affairs at the School of Business, University of Kansas, where he is also Director of the Centre of Technology. He has worked with several organisations, both private and public, including multinational corporations and social service institutions. He has previously taught at the University of Pittsburgh, and the Graduate School of Management at Rutger University, New Jersey. He has published over 30 articles and book chapters and three books including most recently, *Organization Theory: A Strategic Approach*.

David Parker has held academic posts at a number of UK universities and is currently a Lecturer at the University of Birmingham Business School. He has also acted as a consultant at the University of Naples. He has researched and published widely in the area of public sector and private sector efficiency.

Juana Pickard from Chile, is in her final year of research into the management of expatriate personnel, supervised by Dr Chris Brewster at Cranfield University School of Management. Her main interest is in the re-integration of personnel into their home-based organisation after expatriate postings. She is coordinator of a joint project with The Centre for International Briefing and is conducting a major survey of UK expatriates.

Collin Randlesome BA MA is a Senior Lecturer in European Management at Cranfield University School of Management. Before this, he spent seven years in Europe, lecturing at the Universities of Erlangen-Nuremberg and Basle prior to joining the English Institute in Zurich as Senior Interpreter and Translator. He has contributed to numerous books and reports on management and business cultures in Europe and is the author of a book entitled *The Business Culture in Germany*, due to published in the spring of 1994. His research and consultancy work focus on companies with interests in Germany, Switzerland and Austria.

Susan Segal-Horn BA(Hons) MA, MBIM, Sloan Fellow is Lecturer in Strategic Management at Cranfield University School of Management. She teaches international business strategy across a range of MBA and corporate programmes. Her research focuses on strategy in international service industries, particularly international growth and globalisation issues, on which she is a regular speaker at international conferences. Her publications include work on the internationalisation of retailing, managing professional service firms, strategies for coping with retailer buying power, strategic groups in the European food industry, managing services across borders and global service delivery for international service firms. From 1986 to 1988 she was Adjunct Associate Professor of Corporate Strategy at the Graduate School, University of Notre Dame, USA. She was previously Principal Lecturer in Corporate Strategy at Brighton Business School, University of Brighton.

Introduction

Susan Segal-Horn, Cranfield University School of Management

International business matters. It matters not only to the planning departments of large multinational companies, or to governments trying to attract the investment of such companies to create jobs for their people. It matters also to the managers of small and medium-sized firms, and to corner shops, trying to retain the business of their local customers. Whether they know it or not, they are competing in an international marketplace for goods and services. Every initiative taken by an international firm has an impact in a local market and on the market share of local firms and their ability to satisfy their customers.

INTERNATIONAL BUSINESS AND INTERNATIONAL INTEGRATION

International trade has a long history. Most of the great expeditions and famous explorers of the past, most wars and conquests, were about discovering new trading routes and sources of wealth to be traded, or protecting them once found. The world balance of power has always been dominated by the strongest trading nations, their political power directly linked to their economic power.

Until the last century, international trade was dominated by trading companies or investment houses. Within the last century, international trade has increasingly become dominated by multinational companies. The difference between the former and the latter is that the activities of multinationals were based on foreign direct investment (FDI) and, further, that these investments were actively managed as a single operational entity. This has in itself influenced the nature of international trade, since much of it is now internal to these international corporations, carried out between its own business units and operating divisions, either importing goods produced in their overseas subsidiaries, or exporting products to be sold by these subsidiaries. Multinationals are therefore responsible for overseeing immense resources and many have assets that exceed those of all but the richest national governments. This combination of factors means that such firms play an important role not only within their domestic economies, but also in the economies of the many host nations in which they have a presence. It is also the source of their impact on the conditions of local competition for the small and medium-sized firms within these various national markets. The competence and quality of management in multinational corporations is therefore an issue not just for the firms themselves, but also for the health of the world economy.

Over time however, the task of international managers has changed. The early emphasis was on learning to manage large-scale technologies of production and distribution. These required continuous high flows of inputs to achieve maximum benefit from scale efficiencies of output. This drove companies to international expansion beyond the domestic market, mainly to develop markets of sufficient size to absorb the new high levels of output and to provide continuity of supply. Chandler's seminal work *Strategy and Structure* (1962) describes these developments in detail. However, gradually overseas subsidiaries became more independent, often in response to protectionist barriers erected by national governments against foreign exports. The task of managers became more one of planning, control and administration of large autonomous overseas operations. From the 1960s onwards, another set of trends began a new pattern of convergence. Gradual economic integration via international trade agreements such as the General Agreement on Tariffs and Trade (GATT), plus the transformation of international communication and transportation systems, together with technological advances in the miniaturisation of products and components, transformed the cost structures of many industries and necessitated a complete rethink of the economic assumptions of supply and demand on which they were based. It became possible, indeed mandatory, to deconstruct the whole chain of activities of production and supply and redesign them again from first principles. This rebuilding usually included much broader options and choices of where to locate business activities world wide, in order to maximise both efficiency-seeking by the firm and responsiveness to shifting patterns of demand in all its markets.

Clearly the management skills in this latest phase of international business are for high levels of integration and coordination across borders. That is the capability being emphasised in much current corporate advertising, for example that of ABB (Asea Brown Boveri) the

Swedish/Swiss engineering company, throughout its 1993 campaign which featured captions such as 'The art of being local world wide'. This means local presence, local roots and local services combined with international reach and resources, which can be brought to bear for local customers' benefit. Additionally, the resources do not have to be directly owned by the company but may be available through an alliance or partnership with another firm. The rapid growth of such cooperative ventures as a common feature of international business, means that international managers at most levels must have the ability to adapt and learn from collaboration, as well as from competition, to be effective in the changing world arena.

THE CHALLENGE OF INTERNATIONAL BUSINESS

When a company first decides to expand outside its domestic market, it faces a step change in the complexity attached to every business decision. For all businesses, operating internationally is much more challenging than operating solely within their domestic market. In every facet of managerial decision-making it creates greater risks and problems. For example, geographic market selection for international expansion is far more complex than expansion within a firm's domestic market. Although domestic expansion certainly requires careful judgement of relative market attractiveness, potential competition, adaptation to local market conditions and coping with the problems of managing the business over the larger geographic area, wider challenges of a different order arise with selection of markets for international expansion.

International markets often contain barriers to trade, both tariff and non-tariff such as import quotas, or foreign ownership rules. Other obvious but daunting challenges include different laws, different planning regulations, different transportation infrastructure and distribution systems, different languages, different currencies, different climates, different consumer preferences and any number of varieties of differences in individual and social behaviour, political systems and religious or ethnic norms. As a result, operating internationally involves decisions about how, and to what extent, to adapt products, managers and investment plans to take account of these national and cultural differences. All this means fine judgements about degrees of political risk, financial risk and commercial risk in every international business decision, which do not arise within the domestic home market.

The body of knowledge encompassed by the field of international business is also very wide. It includes a whole range of subject areas that each have their own long-established research traditions and histories, such as theories of international trade, exchange rate theory, theory of the multinational enterprise, the structure of international investment and a whole set of conceptual approaches governing the evolution of internationalisation. In addition, each separate management function, R & D, production, information systems, finance, marketing, human resource management and strategic management, all contain international specialisms and approaches of their own. Given such richness and diversity, how is the practising manager to make sense of it all?

Perhaps it is best to begin by recognising that there are many different ways of being international. These different approaches to international strategy suit different companies in different industries at different times. Indeed, a company may pass through many stages in its own approach to being international. The company may pursue strategies that are widely different in the different countries in which it has a presence. These differences may weaken the company by loading it with a bloated cost structure, riddled with unnecessary duplication, inconsistent and poorly controlled quality, a confused image to its customers and poor bargaining power with its suppliers world wide. Or, by contrast, it may be that the duplication of dedicated overheads and the variegated positioning in each of the national markets in which it operates, is precisely the reason for the success of the company in those sectors and markets in which it competes.

In the above example, both the strategies are viable. What is important of course, is that they are each viable in a different context, for a specific product, in a specific market, at a specific point in time. Therefore international management must, above all, be understood as contingency management par excellence. The three main approaches to being international which firms have most frequently adopted, are summarised in Table I.1. It distinguishes between *multinationals* which treat each country market as independent and best serviced by a subsidiary dedicated to meet its local needs and conditions. *Global* firms emphasise world-wide strategies to benefit from operational scale. They are heavily centralised, with direction and control emanating mainly from central headquarters. The third type, *international* firms, are probably less effective than the two other more extreme types, since they will achieve lower levels of efficiency than the global firm but also lower levels of responsiveness to local conditions than the multinational.

However, more recently an approach to international business which most closely resembles the contingent, conditional view of international management, has become known as the *transnational*. Developed first

Table I.1 Three approaches to being international

Organisational characteristics	Multinational	Global	International
Configuration of assets and capabilities	Decentralised and nationally self-sufficient	Centralised and globally scaled	Sources of core abilities centralised; others decentralised
Role of overseas operations	Sensing and exploiting local opportunities	Implementing parent company strategies	Adapting and exploiting parent company's abilities
Development and diffusion of knowledge	Knowledge developed and retained within each unit	Knowledge developed and retained at centre	Knowledge developed at centre and transferred to overseas units

Source: Bartlett and Ghoshal 1989

in the work of Bartlett & Ghoshal (1989), the transnational is probably best understood as a state of mind rather than an organisation structure. It is a state of mind which is adaptable and which sees efficiency, across international boundaries, as something that companies achieve through responsiveness and the ability to learn. Thus decision-making is approached at whatever level, and in whatever geographic context, is most appropriate for the international objectives of the firm. Achievement of goals, rather than protection of turf, country managers' pet assumptions, or the historical traditions of the firm, is what should influence decisions.

The notion of contingency theory as a framework for making sense of the management of international companies, has a deep appeal, given the permanent fluidity and changeability of the international business context. It is, however, an approach which rejects certainties and prescriptions and thereby places great strains on international business managers. It is natural to seek for certainty as the reassuring basis for action, and deeply disconcerting to find only continuous uncertainty. But to seek to impose certainties where few exist is a recipe for failure in any business context. It remains more helpful therefore to accept the discomfort and try to find more and better ways of interpreting and acting within it.

None of the contributions in this book attempts to oversimplify. Yet each tries to show how the traditional problems faced by managers in international corporations may be interpreted in new ways. Like new light in old windows, the core problems remain the same, but the ways of addressing them evolve all the time. What the reader should find in this book are syntheses and perspectives which help them to be more effective as managers. It should help them make more informed decisions not only with regard to their own specific area of responsibility, whether it be the training of managers for international assignments or the rethinking of long-term international distribution needs, but perhaps more importantly, by dipping into and thinking about what *all* the chapters have to say, to see how their functional responsibilities affect and are affected by, all the others. If that is achieved, then this book will genuinely have met its objective – the development of truly international managers.

THE BOOK IN OUTLINE

The subject of international business is extremely wide. This book represents a selection of themes and issues in areas which, in the judgement of the editor, have particular importance for international managers in the 1990s. Inevitably, there will be gaps. Nevertheless, the contributions given here do address both the traditional big themes of international business such as the international environment, consumers, markets and finance, together with many relatively recent influential developments such as deregulation, privatisations, strategic alliances and international logistics planning. The book is designed to be read as a book, so that the cumulative sum of its parts may influence the thinking of all managers participating in, and affected by, international business.

Across the chapters, some international business themes resonate throughout the book. The reader should expect to note and think about:

- The Triad: the emerging 'hub-and spoke' structure of international trade
- The paradox of simultaneous cultural, political and economic convergence and divergence, integration and fragmentation
- Global, regional and local: achieving the balance.

The structure of the book

The book is divided into three parts. Part 1 deals with the international business context. Liam Fahey and V K Narayanan provide an overview and an integrated synthesis of how to scan, monitor, forecast and assess the changing international business environment. The emphasis is on how external environmental issues impact on different aspects of management and how to use their framework to make international strategies work better. Susan Segal-Horn debates the contentious issue of consumer convergence, giving particular attention to the effect of regional trading blocs on the homogenisation of markets. She looks at the conditions under which standardised global strategies or adapted local strategies are likely to be more effective, taking the internationalisation of the retail sector as an illustration.

Part 2 focuses particularly on some of the most important international management challenges involving people, culture and learning. The different contributions explore the importance of transferring learning: between national cultures and international managers; between national cultures and organisational cultures; and between different international corporate cultures. Sally Butler and Collin Randlesome introduce a model which helps to make sense of one of the most widespread general issues facing all companies operating across borders – the impact of national cultures on international businesses. Their concept of 'cultural fluency' is a simple and perceptive means of clarifying the confusions at the heart of many cross-cultural interactions, which make doing business across borders so difficult. The next two chapters deal with different aspects of the same problem, the international transfer of managers. Chris Brewster and Juana Pickard highlight the inadequacies of the preparation that companies provide for those managers whom they wish to send on overseas assignments. Their research shows a clear correlation between prior training of expatriate managers and their performance in their overseas assignments. Both amount and type of training were relevant, not only for the managers themselves but also critically for their spouses. By contrast, John Hailey looks at the problems encountered by international firms in their long-term attempts to 'glocalise' their international operations by using a much greater number of local managers to fill senior positions. However, the process of localising senior management, rather than importing expatriates, appears to be a cyclical one, with problems occurring in the second generation. Hailey uses the experience of the international drinks firm Guinness, in Nigeria, to illustrate some of the pitfalls in the transfer process. Finally, in his chapter on strategic alliances, David Faulkner uses the alliance between the two automobile companies Rover (UK) and Honda (Japan) to illustrate the importance of organisational learning from cross-border alliances. His research has shown that the most successful long-term alliances are those in which the partners learn to learn from each other, so that their mutual agenda shifts and develops as the alliance matures.

In Part 3 of the book are grouped together innovatory research contributions on some of the most challenging international resource issues. These concern the utilisation and deployment of major assets, including finance, investment and the international supply chain. Each of the chapters in this section addresses issues of improved performance, efficiencies and flexibility. Adrian Buckley provides a new perspective on international investment decisions. He demonstrates how corporations can maintain flexibility, and enhance shareholder value, through structuring their investments as options, rather than as discrete financial decisions. In his chapter on international trends and comparisons in privatisations, David Parker shows that privatisations alter both the internal (national) and the external (international) business environments, and thus change the agenda for management. Basing his conclusions on original data from the UK, Malaysia and the Czech Republic, he explains the conditions under which privatisation is, or is not, likely to generate the greater levels of efficiency expected of it, in the industries in which it occurs. The final two chapters in the book deal with the changing pattern of international logistics and the significance of these changes for the strategies and structures of international firms. James Cooper appraises the continuing complexity of European markets, with rationalisation and fragmentation continuing side by side. He provides a powerful and detailed analysis of the changing relationships between buyers and suppliers down the supply chain of manufacturing, distribution and retailing, as some products and markets remain local, while others have already become global. Alan Braithwaite and Martin Christoper look at the implications of global convergence for managing the global supply chain. They conclude that the high level of coordination required to manage complex global supply chains may result in higher costs. Such additional costs must be weighed against the cost savings resulting from standardised global production, as firms plan and implement their international strategies. Both these final chapters provide plentiful illustration of the themes that recur throughout the book: the paradox of simultaneous trends of integration and fragmentation, within which international business has to be conducted.

The range and choice of topics covered in the chapters which follow, reflects the diversity and complexity of international business. Most readers will have a natural interest in their own area of responsibility, each of which has its own specialist books, journals and magazines. This book has been compiled in the belief that successful cross-border management requires managers who are at ease across functions and across cultures, and are sympathetic to the contribution of each to the whole.

All the chapters in the book are based on research carried out at Cranfield University School of Management by the contributors.

REFERENCES

Bartlett, C and Ghoshal, S (1989) *Managing Across Borders: the Transnational Solution*, Harvard Business School Press, Boston, Mass

Chandler, A D (1962) *Strategy and Structure*, The MIT Press, Cambridge, Mass

PART ONE

THE CHANGING CONTEXT

1

Global Environmental Analysis

Liam Fahey, Babson College, USA, and Cranfield University School of Management, and V K Narayanan, University of Kansas

INTRODUCTION

Few firms can afford to depend on their home country market for their future growth and prosperity. Increasingly, firms of all sizes are venturing into marketplaces thousands of miles from their homeland. European, North American and Asian products can be found in almost every country in the world. Even small firms that sell predominantly if not exclusively in their home country find themselves competing against firms headquartered in distant countries. All large corporations, irrespective of their origins, must now compete in Europe, Japan and North America, commonly referred to as the Triad, if they wish to sustain their competitiveness on the global stage (Kotler et al 1985, Fahey 1993). Increasingly, they must also develop a presence in developing regions of the world such as China, Central and Eastern Europe and South America, if they wish to be among the winners in global competition.

Few industries in any one region of the world are immune to what happens in other regions. In fact, the importance of countries as sources of advantage in firms' global strategies and the interconnectedness of industries across national and regional boundaries has recently been discussed by Porter (1990). What takes place in the electronics industry in Japan affects many related industries in Europe and North America. What happens in the shoe industry in China and other Far Asian countries dramatically affects the shoe industry in Europe and North America. Development of the European Airbus was largely ignored in the United States until it began to affect the sales of Boeing and McDonnell Douglas. In short, there is simply no escape from the reality of global competition.

This introductory chapter is intended to illustrate the importance of understanding the global macroenvironment (ie the political, social, economic and technological milieu *outside* the bounds of an organisation's industry) in setting and executing strategy. Global demographic shifts, movement toward an integrated global economy, changes in governments and technological developments, all have significant implications for the evolution of industries' and organisations' strategies. Unfortunately, strategy analysis as practised in many organisations often gives short shrift to global macroenvironmental change beyond cursory economic considerations. This chapter argues that an analysis of the macroenvironment is essential for crafting and executing sound strategy. It aims to provide the framework and methodology that will permit an organisation to capture and analyse the key global macroenvironmental changes relevant to its business.

Managers need to pay attention to the global macroenvironment for at least three reasons:

1. Many transformations and discontinuities experienced by industries are caused by changes in the global macroenvironment. Regulatory change in the US and Europe has unleashed a torrent of change in the global airline and telecommunications industries. A sole focus on industry structure or current competitors will obfuscate the threats and opportunities that may be emerging in and around the global marketplace.
2. Perceiving and exploiting macroenvironmental changes, as many of the examples in this chapter demonstrate, can be the source of competitive advantage.
3. Finally, to strike a more sombre note, organisational scholars have long reminded us that if organisations don't pay attention to environmental changes, they may not survive at all (Narayanan and Nath 1993).

Before getting into the details of how to conduct and use macroenvironmental analysis, it is also important to understand what its objective is and what it is not. Like any form of forecasting or assessment of the future, its intent is not to foretell the future. That is an impossible task. What global macroenvironmental analysis can do, however, is the following:

- Provide an understanding of current and potential changes taking place in the broad global environment external to any given industry. Understanding current changes is an important guide to anticipating the future and, hence, choosing strategic actions. Analysis of the macroenvironment should thus cover a timeframe from short run to long run. The role of current changes is often emphasised in practice at the expense of potential changes; however, both are important.

- Provide critical inputs to strategic management. Understanding change is not enough. Unfortunately in some companies, analysis of the macroenvironment too often degenerates into the provision of nice-to-know information and descriptive details of what is taking place rather than information that is useful in determining and managing the firm's strategies.
- Facilitate and foster strategic thinking in organisations. An understanding of current and potential social, economic, political and technological change can challenge the prevailing wisdom by bringing fresh viewpoints into the organisation. An analysis of changing demographics and lifestyles has challenged and changed key market segmentation premises underlying many firms' global strategies.

However, these benefits of macroenvironmental analysis are only realised when those doing the analysis are willing to assume the difficult, but necessary, task of making judgements. As the many examples cited in this chapter illustrate, the role of the international manager is to interpret and make sense of change in the global macroenvironment. In particular, the implications of macroenvironmental change for an organisation's current and future strategies is never self-evident; it is always the product or outcome of the judgements of those doing the analysis.

This chapter begins by addressing what the macroenvironment is, detailing its social, political, technological and economic segments. It then shows how to capture macroenvironment change – how to scan, monitor and forecast change. Finally, it describes the process of integrating macroenvironmental analysis into strategy development and execution.

UNDERSTANDING WHAT THE MACROENVIRONMENT IS

To understand the concept of macroenvironment, it is helpful to visualise a firm's environment, as shown in Figure 1.1. The firm is portrayed as enclosed within several layers or levels of environment.

The *task environment* refers to the set of customers, suppliers and competitors that constitute the most proximate or immediate environment. Thus, a global firm actually faces multiple task environments when it competes in many national marketplaces. Much of the day-to-day operations of a firm involve activities or decisions related to its task environment. Thus, a firm may negotiate a new source of capital with

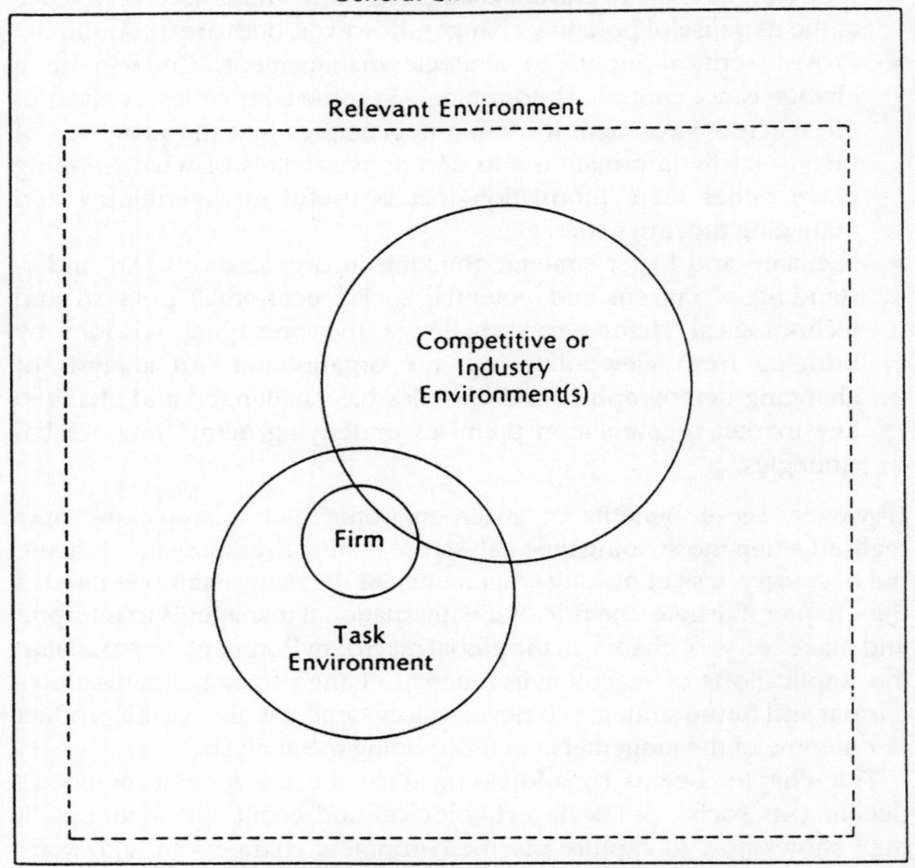

Figure 1.1 Levels of environment

potential investors, enter into a component co-development agreement with a supplier, or attend to a customer complaint. The task environment is more or less specific to a firm, and is not necessarily shared by its competitors. The customers are often loyal to a brand; the suppliers may have granted preferred customer status to a firm. Such factors as brand loyalty or preferred customer status ensure that the task environment of a firm is generally distinct from that of its competitors.

The *competitive or industry environment* surrounds the local task environment. A global industry thus may have:

- Competitors that compete against each other in many national markets as well as many local competitors

- Suppliers in many different countries that provide raw materials, components and supplies to the major and local competitors
- Distribution channels that are most often specific to each country or region
- End-customers or consumers that are typically specific to a country or region.

Increasingly, however, firms in many industrial and service industries now find themselves facing global customers, that is, it is the same customer (eg IBM, Unilever, Toyota) that is purchasing in different countries around the world. Needless to say, these firms are now adopting an integrated approach to global procurement.

At the broadest level lies the *general environment* or macroenvironment – the focus of this chapter. Before detailing the segments that constitute the macroenvironment, it is important to note the *relevant environment* indicated in Figure 1.1. Rarely will any organisation need to analyse every facet of the global, social, political, technological and economic environments. In any case, it would be well nigh impossible to do so. Relevant environment thus refers to the boundaries of the general environment drawn by an organisation for some analytical purposes. In short, the manager needs to focus on the key aspects of the environment that are most relevant to the organisation. A consumer goods firm may define its relevant environment quite differently from an industrial products firm. All definitions of the relevant environment require judgement; yet such judgements are necessary for engaging in worthwhile analysis.

Segments of the macroenvironment

To facilitate analysis, four major segments of the global macroenvironment are identified: social, economic, political, and technological. The principal elements of each segment are briefly noted in Box 1.1. Each will be briefly discussed. (For more detail see Fahey and Narayanan 1986.)

The *social* segment consists of demographics, lifestyles, and social values. From this segment managers seek to understand shifts in the structure of the population within countries and regions and mobility across national boundaries, how lifestyles are changing and whether social value change is taking place within countries and regions.

The *economic* environment includes the general set of economic conditions facing all industries. It includes the stock of physical and natural resources and the aggregation of all the markets where goods and

Box1.1 Key elements of the macroenvironmental segments

THE SOCIAL ENVIRONMENT

The social environment consists of demographics, lifestyles and social values.

Demographics may be segmented into a number of elements:

- *Population size*: the total number of people in a given geographic area
- *Age structure*: the number of people within different age bands such as 0 – 10 years and 11 – 20 years
- *Geographic distribution*: growth rates within and shifts of population across geographic regions
- *Ethnic mix*: the mix, size and growth rates of ethnic groups
- *Income levels*: the amount and growth rates of income across demographic/lifestyle groups such as family types, age levels, geographic regions etc.

Lifestyles may also be segmented into a number of elements:

- *Household formation*: the composition, type, rate of change and size of households
- *Work*: whether people work, what type of work; where they work; expectations about work; how long they work
- *Education*: type and level of education
- *Consumption*: what people purchase or consume (or do not purchase and consume)
- *Leisure*: how people spend their spare or non-working time

Societal values may be broken into a number of types of values:

- *Political values*: reflected in how people vote; how they feel about major political and social issues such as support for the military, abortion and preservation of the environment
- *Social values*: reflected in attitudes toward work, leisure, participation in organisations, acceptance of other groups, acceptance of social habits (such as smoking) etc
- *Technological values*: reflected in acceptance of new technologies, choices between costs of technologies and their benefits etc
- *Economic values*: reflected in pursuit of economic growth, tradeoffs between economic 'progress' and its social costs etc.

THE ECONOMIC ENVIRONMENT

The economic environment refers to the nature and direction of the economy in which business operates. Two types of change are especially worthy of emphasis:

1. *Structural change*: This refers to change within and across sectors of the economy such as movements in economic activity from some types of industries to others (such as a decline in steel industry and growth in a number of the electronics industries) and movements in the relationships among key economic variables such as the relative levels of imports and exports as a percentage of GNP.
2. *Cyclical change*: Refers to upswings and downswings in the general level of economic activity such as movement in GNP, interest rates, inflation, consumer prices, housing starts and industrial investment.

THE POLITICAL ENVIRONMENT

The political environment may be segmented into formal and informal systems.

- *Formal system*: The formal system consists of the electoral process as well as the institutions of government: the executive branch, the legislatures, the judiciary and the regulatory agencies.
- *The informal system*: This refers to the arenas outside government in which political activity occurs. It includes local community settings and the media.

THE TECHNOLOGICAL ENVIRONMENT

The technological environment involves the development of knowledge and its application in 'how to do things'. It can be broadly segmented into the following domains:

- *Research*: fundamental or basic research that seeks the principles and relationships underlying knowledge, often termed invention.
- *Development*: transforms knowledge into some prototype form, often termed innovation.
- *Operations*: puts the knowledge to use in a form that can be adopted by others, often termed diffusion.

services are exchanged for payment. Economic activity is reflected in levels and patterns of industrial output, consumption, income and savings, investment and productivity within and across nations and regions.

The *political* segment incorporates all electoral processes, and the administrative, regulatory and judicial institutions that make and execute each society's laws, regulations and rules. This is perhaps the most turbulent segment of the macroenvironment.

The *technological* segment is concerned with the technological progress or advancements taking place within and across societies. New products, processes, or materials; general level of scientific activity; and advances in fundamental science (eg physics) are the key concerns in this area.

A simple way of remembering the four segments is by the acronym PEST (political, economic, social and technological). The model is presented in Figure 1.2 which shows multiple linkages among the segments: every segment is related to and affects every other segment. The purpose of this figure is to highlight that the global macroenvironment ultimately can only be understood as an interrelated system of segments. However, the model does not specify the types of linkages; these are deemed to be the output of a process of analysis. In other words, the linkages depend upon managers' judgements in their efforts to scan, monitor and forecast macroenvironmental change.

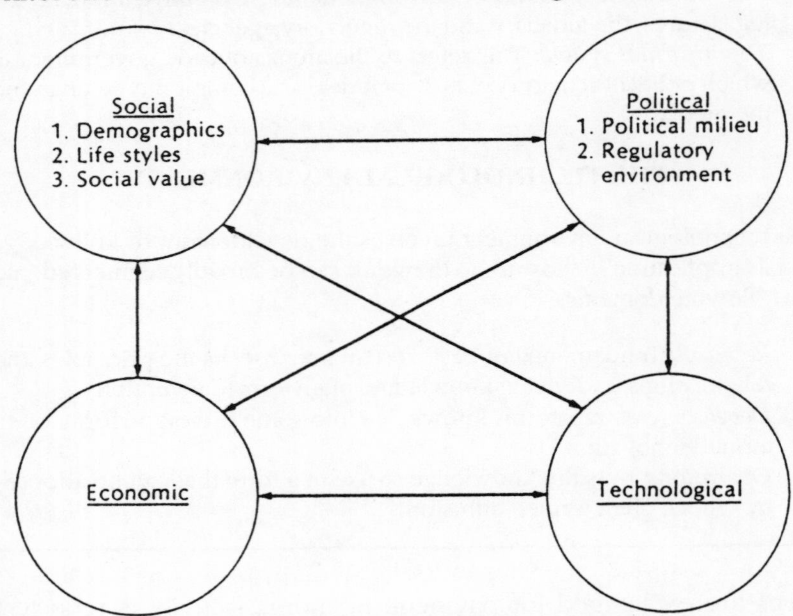

Figure 1.2 A model of the macroenvironment

ANALYSING THE MACROENVIRONMENT

It is one thing to identify the key segments of the macroenvironment and their interrelationships. It is another to analyse them. This section offers a framework of analysis for identifying, tracking, projecting and assessing change in the global macroenvironment. It consists of four analytical stages:

1. Scanning the environment to detect ongoing and emerging change
2. Monitoring specific environmental trends and patterns to determine their evolution
3. Forecasting the future direction of environmental changes
4. Assessing current and future environmental changes for their strategy and organisational implications.

Scanning

The scope and purpose of scanning can be simply stated: to alert the organisation to potentially significant macroenvironmental effects before they have fully formed or crystallised so that the organisation will have as much time as possible to consider its actions. To do so requires that the firm identify indicators or precursors of current and potential change and issues in the social, political, technological and economic environments. Indeed, successful scanning draws an organisation's attention to possible changes and events well before they have revealed themselves in a discernible pattern.

To cite merely one obvious global example: many firms have only in the last two years begun to scan what is happening in and around China. One large US firm now scans as a matter of course all publications pertaining to China emanating from various global institutions such as the United Nations and the World Bank, leading business publications such as *The Economist*, *The Asian Wall Street Journal* and the *Financial Times*, a small number of newsletters devoted primarily or largely to Asian affairs and the general business electronic databases. The avowed purpose of this scanning effort is to detect signals of emerging and potential political, social and economic change in different parts of China. The firm is interested in China because if China decides to massively upgrade its physical and telecommunications infrastructure, it will represent a significant business opportunity.

As illustrated in the China example just noted, scanning involves a systematic search of primary (ie individuals) and secondary (written) data sources. Many organisations now regularly scan an extensive array of electronic databases for items that might be of relevance. Some firms even outsource this activity to specialists. For example, a number of consulting organisations in the Triad regions specialise in providing updates and forecasts on social and political change in individual countries. Some firms use panels of experts and others so that they can receive regular input about change in one or more of the macroenvironmental segments. For example, some large corporations regularly draw upon their own panel of economists for global economic analysis and projections. Many European and US firms now use panels of technology experts for evaluation and projections of technological change in different regions of the world.

Ideally, scanning feeds into monitoring and forecasting early signals or indicators of potential macroenvironmental change. Such scanning is especially useful when macroenvironmental change takes time to unfold. This gives an organisation lead time to work out the implications for its actions. For example, many scans of individual countries often pick up the early signs of civil unrest. Such signs may be statements by local community leaders or so-called 'fringe group' spokespersons. Various actions such as marches, parades, localised disturbances and riots may indicate political and social discontent. Local election results sometimes also foreshadow civil and political unrest and potential upheaval. Once an organisation has become aware of a specific potential change, it can then begin to monitor its development, project its evolution and examine its implications. In short, the immediate action implications for an organisation may not be clear without further tracking and careful assessment of specific trends.

However, scanning also often has direct and immediate action implications. It sometimes results in the detection of macroenvironmental change that is already in an advanced state: a change that has evolved to the point where it is actual or imminent rather than potential at some, as yet, unspecifiable date. For example, one consumer goods firm which had very few sales in South America did a scan of demographics and lifestyles in every country in the region. It discovered, much to its surprise, significant pockets of unmet demand in its target market segments. As a consequence, it launched a large-scale market research study in each of the major national markets. Scanning is more likely to unearth actual or imminent global macroenvironmental change when it explicitly focuses an organisation's antennae on geographic areas that previously may have been neglected, or it challenges the organisation to rethink areas to which it had paid attention.

Monitoring

Monitoring involves tracking macroenvironmental change over time. Specifically, the focus is upon the evolution of trends such as demographic and economic indicators, sequences of events such as technological developments or political election results, or streams of activities such as the actions of regulatory agencies. The trends, events and activities that are tracked may have been unearthed during scanning or the organisation may accidentally become aware of them or they are brought to the organisation's attention by outsiders.

The intent of monitoring is very different from that of scanning. Its purpose is to assemble sufficient data so that the manager can discern whether certain patterns are emerging. It is important to note that these patterns are likely to be a complex of discrete trends. For example, an emergent lifestyle pattern in any single country may include changes in entertainment, education, consumption, work habits, and domicile-location preferences. The emergence of 'singles' or single individual households as the most prevalent form of household in the US reflects a pattern among these trends. A pattern in political opinion shifts might be discerned from a series of election results, referenda or special ballots or propositions held at various levels of the political process as well as opinion polls.

Monitoring ensures that the hunches and intuitive judgements about weak signals that emanate during scanning or the judgements and opinions of others that are brought to the attention of the organisation are tracked for confirmation, elaboration, modification and (in)validation. For example, many European firms are now carefully monitoring the evolution of political, economic and social developments in Central and Eastern Europe. How these developments unfold in individual countries will largely determine the extent of the potential market for the products of these firms.

In monitoring, the data search is focused and much more systematic than in scanning. Signals are used, usually derived during scanning or brought to the organisation's attention by outsiders. For example, in monitoring political developments in foreign countries, many firms track the following: local, state and national election results; actions and activities of emerging local, state and national leaders; emergence of new legislation and its progress through the relevant legislatures.

As monitoring continues, trends accumulate into patterns. What may have been hazy and uncertain in scanning is imbued with details and clarity. For example, in tracking the emergence of social and political issues, the first indicators (often picked up through scanning) are feelings of discontent or loosely distributed concerns expressed by a few individuals. These sentiments begin to attract the attention of others and gradually what is often referred to as a social movement begins to evolve. Such has been the evolution of the consumerism movement in many developed countries and the environmentalist or Green movement in Germany.

The outputs of monitoring are threefold.

1. It details specific descriptions of macroenvironmental patterns to be forecast
2. It provides the identification of trends and patterns for further monitoring
3. It identifies patterns requiring future scanning.

Thus, the outputs of monitoring go beyond simply providing inputs to forecasting. Monitoring may identify trends or apparent trends that were not included in the scope of the original monitoring programme. Also, it is not unusual for monitoring activities to indicate areas where further scanning may be desirable.

Forecasting

Strategic decision-making requires a future orientation: it needs a picture of what is likely to take place in the external environment. The analyst must therefore confront the difficult task of laying out possible evolutionary paths of anticipated change in the social, political, economic and technological environments and connections among them. Many of the typical foci of forecasting global macroenvironmental change are shown in Table 1.1.

The intent of forecasting is to develop plausible projections of the scope, direction and speed of macroenvironmental change. Scope refers to the substance of what is being forecast: whether it is economic growth and development in China or the Far East in general, demographic shifts in Mexico and Central America, the evolution of political union within the European Community or future developments within NAFTA (the North American Free Trade Area). Direction refers to which direction the specific trend and pattern is moving: interest rates and inflation in South American countries may move up or down; more or fewer individuals may follow a particular lifestyle in any region. Speed refers to how quickly or slowly a trend or pattern is projected to move. Frequently, political

Table 1.1 Sample foci in global macroenvironmental forecasting

1. The Social Environment

a) What will the age structure look like in Japan in the first decade of the next millennium?
b) What lifestyle changes in terms of household formation, work, leisure, education and consumption will take place in the major South American countries in the next two decades?
c) What shifts will take place in political values around a united Europe within and outside the European Community?
d) What will the governmental structure look like in Russia five years from now?

2. The Economic Environment

a) Which countries in Asia will experience the highest growth rates over the next ten years?
b) What economic interdependencies will emerge between countries in the European Community and countries in Central and Eastern Europe?
c) What will be the average inflation rate in key South American countries during the rest of this decade?
d) How will the flow of exports and imports between the Triad regions change over the next years?

3. The Political Environment

a) What direction will political union take in the European Community?
b) What key legal and regulatory changes will occur in Japan and other Asian countries that will affect exporting to these countries?
c) What influence will such global bodies as the World Bank and the United Nations have on the newly developing countries?
d) What political struggles are likely to occur between the so-called developed countries and the so-called newly developing countries?

4. The Technological Environment

a) What new governmental assistance will be provided by Asian and European countries to support specific R & D and technology development programmes?
b) What new materials or compounds are likely to result from research programmes underway in different countries?
c) What shape might a 'data highway' take that would provide linkages between countries?
d) What new technology development networks or consortia might be formed by whom and for what purpose?

change in the form of movement toward democracy is projected to move quickly only to have forces unleashed that retard its development.

There are two distinct types of forecasting. The first involves projections based on trends that are evident (ie they are reflective of data over some time period) and can be expected with some margin of error to continue unabated over some future period of time. For example, many demographic trends such as the numbers of children entering high school or the number of people reaching retirement age may be projected reasonably accurately for five to ten years irrespective of the country or region. Some lifestyle trends may also be projected such as rates of household formation. Some technological trends may also be projected such as the rates of diffusion of new products.

The second type of forecasting relates to alternative futures. They may be predicted not just as a product of current trends but as judgements regarding events that may take place or that may be made to happen by an organisation or other entities such as competitors, customers, suppliers, social and community groups and governmental agencies. Alternative futures are thus brought about by the interaction of many different social, political, technological and economic trends and patterns.

Alternative futures are more complex and more uncertain than projections. As a consequence, they are considerably more difficult to envision and construct. Scenarios serve as the analytical means by which many organisations conceive and elaborate alternative futures. Scenarios may be simple or elaborate. Many firms now construct reasonably elaborate scenarios involving future states of individual countries or regions. For example, scenarios are often developed around the economic futures of countries or regions. These scenarios are built around projections of economic growth, interest rate and inflation movement, exports and imports, rate of public and private investment and distribution of economic development within and across countries. A number of such scenarios have been constructed with regard to Central and Eastern Europe by European Community institutions, consulting firms, investment banks and individual corporations. (See Schwartz 1991; *Planning Review* 1992a, 1992b.)

In forecasting global macroenvironmental change, it is critical to understand the importance of the distinctions between projections and alternative futures. Projections reflect a largely predetermined future: the trends and patterns will continue for some period of time. Alternative futures, on the other hand, represent possible futures; they recognise that there are many potential pathways to the future; they reinforce in managers' minds that the future is likely to hold many surprises. Scenarios provide one powerful means of picturing such possible futures. Without a willingness to consider alternative futures, an organisation is likely to find itself constrained and victimised by its implicit presumption that the future is going to be largely a replication of the past.

As with scanning and monitoring, there are a number of key tasks and challenges that are central to forecasting. First, analysts have to understand the forces that drive the evolution of trends and patterns. This is a prerequisite to charting out the evolutionary path of global macroenvironmental change. For example, the groups endeavouring to craft alternative political futures around Central and Eastern Europe must identify and assess some of the underlying forces such as the desire of individual ethnic groups to establish their own 'nations', the extent to which central authorities in Russia may be able to exert influence over former members of the old USSR, the dynamics of rivalry among the various factions within each country, the influence of events in one country on its neighbours, and the impact of different rates of economic progress.

Second, analysts must decide the nature of the evolutionary path; that is, its scope, direction, speed and intensity. Often, analysts must determine whether the projected change is a temporary phenomenon or of some duration, or cyclical or systematic in character. For example, many firms have failed to appreciate the scope, direction and intensity of many emerging so-called social movements and social value shifts until they have evolved into widespread, unmistakable patterns. Staying with the example of Central and Eastern Europe, many firms (and other types of institutions) badly failed to appreciate the strength of the forces propelling change within the old USSR in the mid and late 1980s.

Third, the analyst has to delineate the evolutionary path or paths leading to projections and alternative futures. This is the essence of forecasting.

It is both impossible and unnecessary for an organisation to forecast all trends and patterns. In line with the earlier discussion of relevant environment, emphasis should be placed on macroenvironmental changes of importance to the organisation. Forecasting thus requires that the organisation identify what it is that it wishes to forecast and why it needs to do so. Before it invests time and effort in forecasting, the organisation needs to identify likely organisational implications of the potential macroenvironmental change. Forecasting and assessment are intimately linked.

Assessment

Assessment endeavours to identify and evaluate how and why current and anticipated macroenvironmental changes (will) affect strategic management of the organisation. During assessment therefore the frame of reference moves from understanding the macroenvironment – the focus of scanning, monitoring and forecasting – to identifying what that understanding of the macroenvironment means for the organisation.

In linking macroenvironmental analysis and strategic management the critical question is: what are likely to be the positive or negative impacts of global macroenvironmental change on the organisation's current and future strategies? Many of the specific types of questions typically asked in assessment are shown in Table 1.2. These questions compel the linking of macroenvironmental change and the organisation's more immediate industry and task environments.

Those macroenvironmetal changes or patterns judged to have already had an impact on the organisation's strategies or to possess the potential to do so are deemed to be issues for the organisation. The more important of these issues become the centre of attention in forecasting.

Typically, global macroenvironmental analysis generates a host of issues – far more than any organisation can systematically analyse. If an organisation attempts to analyse too many issues, it becomes bogged down in analysis, with the result that action becomes muddled and less decisive. Moreover, some issues are simply more important than others; that is, they have more serious implications for the organisation's current and future strategies.

Emphasis must therefore be placed on the judgement required to identify issues: to determine which trends and patterns are affecting or will affect the organisation. Judgement involves assessing and prioritising macroenvironmental change against the specific questions noted in Table 1.2.

Issues can be conveniently arrayed on a probability-impact matrix (Figure 1.3), with a separate matrix being prepared for each of the three planning periods: short, medium and long term. Although the scoring system for this assessment of probability and impact can be simple or complex, a general categorising of high, medium or low is usually sufficient. The merits of the matrix display are that it provides a comprehensive, at-a-glance array of issues, orders them in a manner that facilitates discussion and planning, and places them in timeframes appropriate to the allocation of resources and management attention. The issues arrayed on a temporal basis then should be fed into various

Table 1.2 Assessing macroenvironmental analysis implications: sample questions

---

1. **How might each change affect the firm's industry?**
- general expectations about the industry?
- emergence of new products?
- sales of existing products?
- entry and exit of competitors?
- emergence of new suppliers?
- entry and penetration of substitute products?
- intensity of rivalry among competitors?
- the propensity for alliance formation?

2. **How might each change affect the firm's more immediate task environment?**
- demand by existing customers?
- changes in existing competitors' strategies?
- changes in suppliers' strategies?
- relationships between the firm and its suppliers and distribution channels?

3. **What might be the implications of each change for the firm's current strategies?**
- what geographic markets are underserved?
- what geographic markets may decline?
- in what ways will customers be affected?
- to what extent is the firm's strategies vulnerable to changes in specific geographic markets?
- what assumptions underlying current strategies may need to be changed?
- what are the consequences of changing specific assumptions?

4. **How might each change affect the firm's future strategy choices and their execution?**
- what product-market opportunities might be generated?
- are these opportunities specific to regions?
- how might the risks and returns pertaining to existing businesses be reduced or enhanced?
- how might synergies across businesses be affected?
- what new vulnerabilities might be created?

---

strategic analyses; these linkages will be portrayed in detail in the next section.

Timing and Probability of Events	Event 1	Event 2	Event 3	Event 4
Event 1 (Prob., Timing)	///			
Event 2 (Prob., Timing)		///		
Event 3 (Prob., Timing)			///	
Event 4 (Prob., Timing)				///

Figure 1.3 Cross-impact matrix: an illustrative structure

Linkages among the analysis stages

It is important to keep in mind that although scanning, monitoring, forecasting and assessment are conceptually separable analysis activities, they are inextricably intertwined. Each one can and does influence the others. For example, scanning often generates signals of emerging change that lead directly into assessment: the manager at least implicitly assesses its impact upon the organisation's industry and the firm's future strategies. If warranted by the potential impact, further scanning, monitoring and forecasting may be deemed necessary. As noted previously, forecasting requires some initial assessment in order to ensure that the organisation expends its efforts upon the most critical issues. It is to the linkage between macroenvironmental analysis and strategic management that we now turn.

LINKING MACROENVIRONMENTAL ANALYSIS TO STRATEGY DEVELOPMENT AND EXECUTION

Three major points affecting the role of macroenvironmental analysis in strategic management should be noted. First, global macroenvironmental analysis, although intrinsically interesting, is useful only to the extent that it results in strategy-related actions and decisions. Second, integration does not just happen, it is made to happen: the specific linkages to various actions need to be thought through and not left to evolve in a happenstance manner. Third, integration needs to take place for short, medium and long-run horizons.

Corporate strategy

Global macroenvironmental analysis can directly impact corporate level strategy in at least three ways. It can affect the preferred pattern of diversification, how the corporation's resources are allocated, and the risk-return tradeoffs necessarily involved in corporate decision-making.

Patterns of diversification

Diversification represents the intent of an organisation to move into product-market segments unrelated to its existing businesses. An organisation can pursue a number of distinct approaches to diversification, each of which is influenced both by the global opportunities confronting the firm and by its own resource profile.

There are at least three ways in which macroenvironmental change can influence an organisation's pattern of diversification. First, corporations differ with regard to the synergies they try to exploit across their business units. These synergies could be upset or enhanced by global macroenvironmental change. For example, a number of leading consumer product and food firms such as Procter & Gamble and Heinz are now experiencing difficulties in maintaining and leveraging the marketing synergies that historically have been central to their corporate strategies. Changing demographics, lifestyles, social values and a persistent downturn in the leading economies have left many consumers increasingly price conscious, thus rendering it ever more difficult for these firms to build and sustain an image of superior 'value for money' around their brand names.

Second, different patterns of diversification are susceptible to different vulnerabilities. Change in the macroenvironment may amplify these vulnerabilities. For example, a diversification thrust that centres upon linkages across certain types of technologies is especially vulnerable to technology change that may emanate in countries to which the firm has historically paid little attention. Some pharmaceutical firms did not heed research and development advances in Japan until the products were almost in the marketplace. Many defence industry firms in both Europe and the US that diversified around their core technological capabilities now find many of the businesses they developed in the last decade suffering from the same difficulties as their historic core business: a lack of demand due to the end of the Cold War.

Third, macroenvironmental change may open up or close out existing patterns of diversification. This is particularly so when the pattern of diversification is not conglomerate. Political change in the form of a new administration either at the individual country level or that of regional institutions such as the European Community often affects application of the relevant law on mergers and acquisitions. Thus, mergers that might have been frowned upon or even disbarred by one administration may be allowed by a later administration.

Resource allocation

Global macroenvironmental change has important implications for corporate resource allocation; that is, the allocation of resources across business units. This is so for at least two reasons. First, as noted above, macroenvironmental change gives rise to differential product opportunities across business units. For example, many telecommunications firms facing high degrees of market penetration in the Triad are now seriously committing resources to enter many less developed countries. Thus, some business units facing emerging opportunities in countries or regions in which the firm has little experience may need an extensive infusion of resources. Second, global macroenvironmental change is increasingly affecting where opportunities exist. For example, in the early 1990s, compared with the 1980s, a number of corporations have dramatically added to the resources they have committed to 'dipping their toe' in China.

Risk-return tradeoffs

Political, economic, technological, and social shifts impact the returns and risks of existing and potential portfolios of business units. Anticipated changes in economic growth and development critically affect projected returns in both existing businesses and potential new businesses. For example, the downturn in the economies of Western Europe has led to a dramatic downturn in the overall performance of many US firms. Many firms now do extensive political risk assessments of foreign countries as an input to initial or continued investment. For example, some firms have recently announced they plan to re-enter South Africa as a consequence of its efforts to move toward democracy.

Business-unit strategy

Global macroenvironmental analysis impacts business-unit strategy in two distinct but related ways. First, its effects on industry structure and evolution need to be assessed. Second, its implications for various inputs to strategy development can then be assessed.

Implications for industry analysis

At the level of industry or competitive analysis, changes in the global macroenvironment may affect:

1. The boundaries of the industry
2. The forces shaping industry structure, such as suppliers, customers, rivalry and product substitution, and entry barriers
3. Strategic groups
4. The key success factors
5. The general expectations within the industry.

These elements provide the competitive context within which business-unit strategy is developed.

Global macroenvironmental change directly impinges upon the survival of an industry or specific industry segments. This is perhaps most evident in the way that technological change can make substantial segments of an industry obsolete. For example, technology advances underlying frozen foods have reshaped major sectors of the food industry. The technology developments facilitating linkages among voice, data and images are now reconfiguring what used to be distinct industry sectors (called telecommunications, television receivers and optics) into what is now referred to as the multimedia business.

Macroenvironmental change directly influences each of the forces shaping the industry structure: suppliers, customers, new entrants and substitute products. It can affect the number, type and location of suppliers, the products they offer customers, supply costs and the competitive dynamics of supplier industries. Global macroenvironmental change has dramatically shifted the supply sector in many industries. To cite merely one example: the political, economic and social change that has occurred in Korea and other Asian countries has spawned many new competitors for American and European firms that previously dominated many raw material and component businesses.

Changes in demographics, lifestyles and social values can affect the size, characteristics, and behaviour of the customer base in an industry or industry segment. For example, changes in lifestyles and related social values such as greater emphasis upon personal health and fitness in all the more advanced regions generated the necessary consumer base for the array of products now associated with jogging, tennis and fitness equipment for use in the home.

Product substitution and new entrants are most often driven by technological change. A variety of technology advances propelled the development of 'mini-mills', led by Italian and Korean firms, resulting in products that have displaced much of the product line emanating from old, large steel mills, so representative of the United States, the United Kingdom and Japan.

Global macroenvironmental change differentially impacts various strategic groups within an industry. This is especially so to the extent that strategic groups are geographically based. Changes to the extent that they affect customers' preferences, suppliers' capabilities, substitute products and so forth could potentially enlarge or decimate the product-market arenas in which different strategic groups operate. For example, many mid-size German firms, long dependent upon a buoyant German economy, have increased their emphasis upon export markets, in the wake of the recent major downturn in the German economy. Perhaps more importantly, macroenvironmental changes may afford opportunities for firms in a specific strategic group to overcome mobility barriers; that is, the barriers inhibiting a firm from moving from one strategic group to another. For example, deregulation of the airline industry in the United States in the 1980s and changes in the regulatory climate in the European Community has given impetus to alignments between European and US airlines, most recently evidenced in the alliance consummated between British Airways and US Air.

Global macroenvironmental change can potentially affect the key success factors in almost any industry or industry segment. At a minimum, such change needs to be assessed in terms of its impact on factors such as desired product quality, product functionality or performance criteria (such as reliability and durability), relative cost positions, image and reputation, and resource commitments for major product-market segments.

The discussion above suggests that macroenvironmental change potentially affects the general expectations about an industry and about the firms within it. For example, many industry sectors in a number of countries that depended on door-to-door sales have suffered severely due to a rapid increase in the number of women in the full-time workforce.

One useful means of integrating the above analysis is to develop issue-impact matrices. These matrices detail the effect of each one of the selected set of macroenvironmental issues on industry-level factors. Matrix displays of the type shown in Figure 1.4 facilitate assessments of these impacts. These assessments should include not only the general direction of change but its timing and intensity. Such assessments form much of the industry backdrop against which business strategies are formulated.

Impact on Industry

	Industry boundaries	Forces shaping industry	Strategic groups	Key success factors	General Expectations
Issue 1					
Issue 2					
Issue 3					
Issue 4					
Issue 5					
Issue 6					
Issue 7					
Issue 8					
Issue 9					

Figure 1.4 Issue-impact matrix: Linking issues industry analysis

Linkage to business-unit strategy

At the level of business-unit strategy, global macroenvironmental analysis together with industry and competitor analysis needs to be assessed for their impact on business-unit strategy in terms of:

1. Business definition
2. Assumptions
3. General strategic thrust.

Few concepts are more central to business-unit strategy determination than business definition. Abell (1990) has noted three critical elements in any firm's business definition:

- What customers does the business serve?
- What customer needs are satisfied?
- What technologies are employed to satisfy these customer needs?

Each of these elements can be affected directly or indirectly by macroenvironmental change. Many businesses have found that demographic and lifestyle change has altered not just their served or target customer base but also customer needs. The growth in the 'elderly' market (ie individuals over 65 years of age) has caused all kinds of businesses from insurance and financial services to food and entertainment businesses either to introduce new product offerings or to reshape significantly existing products. In short, as the population in many advanced countries ages, its needs and wants from many different industries shifts.

As noted by Yip (1992), business definition in the global arena adds an obvious fourth dimension – geography – to the three identified by Abell. As more countries and regions are included, greater variety is likely to be added to the customer, competitor and technology mix confronting any individual business. In short, a business definition that may historically have been appropriate for the United Kingdom, may lead to poor strategic decisions when it is applied without change to strategy development in the case of Asia.

Since strategy is about winning in the future marketplace, assumptions about the current and future environment always underlie any strategy. For example, key macroenvironmental assumptions (as distinct from industry assumptions) might include expectations about shifts in governmental policies, changes in technology developments and demographic and lifestyle shifts. These assumptions need to be anchored in a thorough analysis of the global macroenvironment surrounding the industry if they are to be realistic and hence useful for strategy formulation. For example, many firms now making initial investments in China and other Asian countries need to identify carefully the economic and political assumptions underlying these investments. Many North American and European firms that entered the Japanese market in the 1960s and 1970s learned the hard way that when assumptions about changes in governmental policies (ie policies more favourable to market penetration by foreign firms) and lifestyle changes (ie the propensity to buy foreign products) do not pan out, the best-laid plans will go awry.

Because of the importance of assumptions, the merits of identifying and challenging global macroenvironmental assumptions need to be emphasised. First, attention to assumptions compels a critical assessment of macroenvironmental change. It is not merely enough to identify prevailing change. Assumptions emphasise the importance of projecting and assessing the future direction of change. Second, consideration of assumptions facilitates and fosters sensitivity analysis. Every strategy alternative is always vulnerable to environmental change. Consideration of assumptions necessarily entails asking what macroenvironmental changes, as noted earlier, might most negatively affect each strategy alternative. Third, stemming from the first two points, assumption analysis frequently serves to heighten awareness of macroenvironmental change and its importance to strategic management.

Finally, global macroenvironmental analysis must be linked to the business-unit's strategic thrusts. This linkage is of course related to business definition and assumptions discussed above. For example, a market-share-building thrust presumes some relevant business definition as well as assumptions pertaining to customers, suppliers, new entrants, substitute products. Thus, macroenvironmental change through its impact on industry elements just noted may signal the need for a change in strategy thrust.

LESSONS FOR MANAGERS

The global macroenvironment affects the industry setting within which firms compete. It is not sufficient merely to conduct a conventional industry analysis: macroenvironmental forces can shape the industry for better or worse. And, the direction of the impact can change over time and is often highly variable across countries or regions. The following is a summary.

- Global macroenvironmental change has multiple impacts on any industry. It shapes the general expectations about the industry; it affects the industry's boundaries; it can enhance the strategic position of some competitors and detract from that of others; it can alter dramatically the key success factors. Macroenvironmental analysis must be guided by the intent to identify and assess these linkages; it should never be allowed to degenerate into the provision of merely nice-to-know information.
- Analysis of the global macroenvironment requires consideration and assessment of the social, political, economic and technological environments within and across countries and regions. These are not independent milieux; rather they are intertwined in multiple ways. However, it is useful to analyse them independently as a means to understand better how they interrelate.
- Macroenvironmental analysis hinges upon the execution of four distinct though related activities: scanning, monitoring, forecasting and assessment. Change in any of the macroenvironmental segments can be detected by identifying and monitoring key indicators or signals of emerging and potential change. Extensive data sources exist, both primary and secondary, to facilitate this phase of the analysis.

- Forecasting macroenvironmental change involves either simple projections or the development of scenarios that address possible futures. Scenarios serve the critical function of challenging the implicit pictures of the future that are often widely shared within organisations but which are rarely explicated and challenged. Unless these embedded views of the global context of business are exposed and critiqued, global strategy development is highly likely to be based upon unfounded assumptions.

REFERENCES

Abell, D F (1980) *Defining the Business: The Starting Point of Strategic Planning*, Prentice-Hall, Englewood Cliffs, N J

Fahey, L (1993) *Winning in the New Europe: Taking Advantage of the Single Market*, Prentice-Hall, Englewood Cliffs, N J

Fahey, L and Narayanan, V K (1986) *Macroenvironmental Analysis for Strategic Management*, West Publishing Company, St Paul, Minneapolis

Kotler, P, Fahey, L and Jatustripitak, S (1985) *The New Competition: What Theory Z Didn't Tell You About – Marketing*, Prentice-Hall, Englewood Cliffs, N J

Narayanan, V K and Nath, R (1993) *Organization Theory: A Strategic Approach*, Richard D Irwin Inc, Homewood, Ill

Planning Review, (1992a) special issue, Mar–Apr

Planning Review, (1992b) special issue, May–Jun

Porter, M E (1990) *The Competitive Advantage of Nations*, The Free Press, New York

Schwartz, P (1991) *The Art of the Long View*, Doubleday, New York

Yip, G S (1992) *Total Global Strategy*, Prentice-Hall, Englewood Cliffs, N J

Global Markets, Regional Trading Blocs and International Consumers*

Susan Segal-Horn, Cranfield University School of Management

This chapter discusses the development of international products and services for international markets. The discussion is placed in the context of what has become known as the standardisation/adaptation debate in international business strategy. The core of this debate is the question of how far, if at all, it is appropriate to design, market and deliver standard products and services across national market boundaries, or the extent to which adaptation to local market requirements is mandatory. These issues will be reviewed within a framework of required conditions for successful standardisation: that global market segments exist; that global economies of scale exist; and that a distribution infrastructure is available to realise these potential economies of scale world wide.

Factors such as international consumer homogeneity and the creation of regional trading blocs play a central role, since companies may derive economies from research and development, sourcing, design, manufacturing, distribution and many aspects of marketing, both within and across trading blocs. It is important therefore, for managers to begin to identify their potential positioning within the developing international marketplace.

INTRODUCTION

Global marketing of standardised products to global consumers is a concept that has generated a great deal of interest in recent years. The creation of trading blocs across the world adds a further dimension to the

---

* An earlier version of this paper was published in *The Journal of Global Marketing* (1992), Vol 5, No 3

globalisation debate, representing additional opportunities for companies to trade on a world-wide basis. The arguments in favour of global standardisation, as initially stated by Levitt (1983), contain three assumptions:

1. That consumers' needs and interests are becoming increasingly homogeneous world wide
2. That people around the world are willing to sacrifice preferences for such things as product features, functions, and design, for high quality at low prices
3. That substantial economies of scale in production and marketing can be achieved through supplying global markets.

There are however, a number of problems associated with these propositions. First, there is a lack of evidence of homogenisation; it has been argued by managers and academics alike that the differences both within and across countries are far greater than any similarities that may exist. Secondly there has been a growth of intra-country fragmentation, leading to increased segmentation of domestic markets. Thirdly, developments in factory automation allowing flexible, lower-cost, lower-volume, high-variety operations are challenging the standard assumptions of scale economy benefits by yielding variety at low cost.

Therefore, attempts to implement global standardisation are only likely to prove successful in international markets under the following conditions:

- *Global market segments* – ie the presence of groups of consumers across diverse international markets with similar tastes and preferences
- *Potential economies from standardisation* – ie the ability to reduce costs by designing, manufacturing, distributing and marketing products across a number of national markets in a similar fashion
- *A world-wide distribution infrastructure* which would enable a company to deliver its offerings to internationally targeted consumer segments within competitive cost and time scales.

The rest of this chapter will review to what extent these conditions for successful standardisation exist. The general discussion will be illustrated by reference to some international strategies in the retail sector, since the internationalisation of retailing has been relatively recent and remains highly contentious.

THE GLOBALISATION/ADAPTATION DEBATE

The desirability of product standardisation for broadly defined international market segments has centred around the notion that there is increasing similarity between certain groups of consumers across national market boundaries. These groups thus represent actual or potential global market segments, whose consumer needs may be met in similar ways, with similar goods and services. Obvious examples of such segments might be teenage pop culture or the business traveller.

International consumer segments

This belief in consumer homogeneity is controversial. Much debate has taken place in the marketing literature over the opportunities for, and the barriers to, such standardisation (Levitt 1983, Kotler 1985, Quelch and Hoff 1986, Douglas and Wind 1987, Onkvisit and Shaw 1989, Mueller 1991). However, for those companies which subscribe to it, it conditions their view of how best to address international markets. The controversy is derived from the geographical locations of similar consumer segments, the degree to which similarities in taste occur across the world, and whether fragmentation rather than homogenisation may describe more appropriately international consumer trends.

In the fiercely competitive trading environment which most domestic firms face, particularly in developed economies, redefining target market segments as global segments can provide a route out of concentrated, mature markets and provide fresh opportunities for growth. For example, the problems of concentration and market saturation within the retail sector of developed economies, such as the USA, the UK and Germany, have been instrumental in propelling some companies to move into international markets (Akehurst 1983, Nielsen 1987, Salmon and Tordjman 1989). This is in turn leading them towards more regional (eg Aldi of Germany) and in some cases, global (eg Toys 'R' Us of the USA or IKEA of Sweden), operations.

Several changes have occurred within the competitive arena that have had far-reaching implications for both consumers and producers of goods and services. The effect of technology upon such areas as transparency of electronic information, global media and communications have been instrumental in increasing the similarities between consumer tastes across geographical boundaries. In addition, a variety of internal developments in the economic and social environment have contributed to the reshaping of consumer demand. These include demographic change such as falling birth-rates and ageing populations, smaller households including more single-person units, better education, increased disposable incomes, and a widespread concern for health, energy and environmental issues. Greater choice and control have emerged as important consumer aspirations, both in terms of the products and services available and the time spent in consumption. A movement towards what has been called 'open citizenship' (Nelson 1989), observable across all the international trading regions, has indicated an understanding of the value of, and necessity for, economic integration in modern trading environments. Individuals sharing these values hold shared loyalties in that they have feelings of belonging to both their own country and culture, whilst simultaneously consuming and being influenced by world-wide products and trends. Such influences often include art, films, clothing, ethnic foods and popular music. Indeed, Ohmae (1989) has stated that it no longer makes sense for a company to assume that all its customers will be of one nationality or that domestic companies can best supply their home markets. He argues that although consumer tastes will differ within the Triad of developed economies (Asia-Pacific, Europe and North America), there may well be market segments of different sizes in each part of the Triad that share many of the same preferences.

In addition to such developments within the OECD (Organisation for Economic Cooperation and Development) countries, Jain (1989) believes there are pockets of consumers within less developed countries (LDCs) and newly industrialising countries (NICs) that have the same patterns of consumption. He argues that rather than targeting markets in terms of rich or poor nations, it is better to look for similar and heterogeneous segments across this divide; that is, in both developed and developing countries. In India, for example, the market for consumer durables, once confined to a very small number of wealthy families, has grown at an unprecedented rate, reflecting the rise of the middle class. Demand for international brands in India now makes it an attractive further market for companies which already trade on a global basis. Also, the relaxation of many of India's barriers to foreign trade and investment under Prime Minister Rao since 1992, has created a rapid expansion of multinational activity in the subcontinent (*The Economist* 1992).

These types of developments have been taking place at varying rates across the world. The growing commonality of individuals within and across differing geographical locations qualifies them as members of global segments which has, in turn, provided the platform for the introduction of more innovative ways of integrating rather than differentiating markets. Furthermore this has been the force behind the emergence of cross-market segments and lifestyles that have challenged many sectors and provided opportunities for more integrated international strategies (Thorelli and Becker 1980, Levitt 1983, Jain 1989, Ohmae 1989, Perlmutter 1991). Lifestyle marketing is based upon the process of identifying the patterns in which people live and spend time and money (Engel and Blackwell 1982). Its success indicates similarities between such patterns across international consumer segments, allowing for more standardised marketing and distribution strategies of products and services that companies as diverse as Sony and Matsushita in consumer electronics, or Burger King and Kentucky Fried Chicken in fast food, or Benetton and IKEA in retailing, provide. Their products and services have proved, over time, to have universal appeal across global markets.

The advantages of global operations

One of the most significant advantages of global trading is associated with size of operations. Economies of scope and scale allow for greater efficiency in current operations (Ghoshal 1987, Chandler 1990). Economies of scale provide not just lower unit costs, but also potentially greater bargaining power over all elements in the company's value chain. An obvious example of such bargaining power in action can be seen in the shift in the balance of bargaining power from manufacturers to retailers with the growth of retailer concentration into supermarket chains in many advanced economies (Segal-Horn and McGee 1989). Economies of scope can allow for the sharing of investments (both tangible such as buildings, technology or salesforces, or intangible such as expert knowledge) and costs, across products, markets and businesses. Indeed, branding is a useful illustration of economies of scope. The global brand name of Mars for, example, has been successfully transferred from chocolate bars to icecream bars, or that of Benetton has allowed that company to diversify into new product areas such as a range of toiletries and perfume, which they distribute across their existing branch network.

Some of the most vehement rebuttals of the standardisation approach occurs with regard to international marketing activities. This is largely because the requirement for in-depth information about consumer tastes and preferences is considered a basic marketing function, and one which must, by definition, take place as close to the markets as possible. However, much of this function can now be performed by retailers' electronic point-of-sale (EPOS) data-capture technology. In fact, considerable standardisation of international marketing has occurred for some time, as the data in Table 2.1 indicate.

Table 2.1 Degree of marketing standardisation among selected US and European multinationals

Elements of Marketing	Degree of standardisation (%)		
Programme	High	Medium	Low
1. Product characteristics	81	4	15
2. Brand name	93		7
3. Packaging	75	5	20
4. Retail price	56	14	30
5. Basic advertising	71	6	20
6. Creative expression	62	4	34
7. Sales promotion	56	11	33
8. Media allocation	43	10	47
9. Role of salesforce	74	10	15
10. Management of salesforce	72	10	17
11. Role of middleperson/intermediaries	80	7	13
12. Type of retail outlet	59	7	34

Source: Sorenson and Weichmann 1975

Standardisation is particularly evident with respect to brand name, product characteristics, role of intermediaries, packaging, role and management of salesforce and the basic advertising message. These are all still considered controversial areas for standardisation, yet Takeuchi and Porter (1986) confirm the earlier work. They examined some of the most common activities within the marketing function, based on ease or difficulty of international coordination. Their results, as given in Table 2.2 were an attempt to combine the organisational costs of coordination, with the extent to which national differences made standardisation impossible or inappropriate.

These arguments imply a real possibility for the availability of cost savings in marketing overheads, as well as the identification of consumer tastes sufficiently homogeneous to justify such marketing approaches. International companies such as Benetton, the Body Shop and McDonald's have such large international operating chains that they are viewed by the consumer as global brands and their original home base is not discernible to the general public (Treadgold 1989). Their ability to create and sustain a successful international brand image and the goodwill attached to it, is one of the most important corporate assets of these companies. It is worth noting that many successful international

Table 2.2 Ease/difficulty of standardising marketing activities across countries

Easier	More difficult
Brand name	Distribution
Product positioning	Personal selling
Service standards	Salesperson training
Warranties	Pricing
Advertising themes	Media selection

Source: Takeuchi and Porter 1986

brands are for services; for example, Sheraton hotels, American Express financial and travel-related services. This advantage of international branding eases the transfer of the service concept to different geographical locations around the world.

Spreading operations across a number of different national markets can provide the opportunity to standardise the way in which the product or service is marketed to the consumer. Substantial cost savings may be available, for example in advertising. Pepsi-Cola's savings from not producing a separate promotional film for individual national markets has been estimated at $10 million per year. This figure is increased when indirect costs are added; for instance, the speed of implementing a campaign, fewer overseas marketing staff, and the management time which can be utilised elsewhere (Link 1988). Visa International, whilst considering global TV advertisements to be inappropriate for all their local markets world wide, does utilise some 'regional' advertisements in the EMEA (Europe, Middle East and Africa) region. This consists of a basic 25 second commercial to which a Visa member company (such as a local bank) adds on a 5 second ending which promotes the individual bank within the overall Visa brand.

The restructuring of transportation and distribution, although proceeding at quite different speeds in different regions of the world, creates further opportunities for streamlining international operations, even though within regions, rates and levels of convergence differ markedly. For example, levels of retailer concentration in Europe vary from an 80 per cent market share for the top three chains in Belgium, to a 22 per cent market share for the top five chains in Spain. Retailer concentration is itself a trigger for distributor concentration since it foreshadows a shift from manufacturers' own transport to the use of specialist contract distribution companies and common user systems. The use of centralised distribution and specialist distribution contractors grows in tandem with the increase in retail concentration. As the highly concentrated UK retail chains have entered continental Europe, they have taken with them their distribution practices and expertise (eg Marks & Spencer into France). This restructuring of transportation and distribution provides opportunities for all competing companies in a sector, whether internal or external to a region. European restructuring will benefit non-European just as much as European producers. North American and Asian companies, previously marketing separately to highly individual countries, are able to import products through centrally placed Holland or Belgium and then transport them throughout Europe. Companies may additionally wish to locate centralised production plants in the same way, just as Pillsbury (a large UK-owned American food manufacturer) opened its first European factory for its Haagen-Dazs icecream brand at Arras in Belgium in 1992.

Cost reductions, shorter journey times and dramatic technological developments in transportation have together created new international markets for products which previously had no shelf-life beyond local consumption. Container systems which use computer-controlled temperature, humidity and atmosphere levels have extended the geographic scope for such products as fresh fruit or flowers, just as surely as international information systems have created transparent 24 hour trading in financial products.

Increasingly globalisation is utilised by practitioners at whatever points in their value chain advantages can be derived, although often falling short of global operations across all functions. In other words, there is a wide range of possible benefits available from globalisation. These may include any or all of the following: design, purchasing, manufacturing operations, packaging, distribution, marketing, advertising, customer service measures or software development. These make possible standardised facilities, methodologies and procedures across locations. Indeed, companies may be able to benefit even if they are able to reconfigure in only one or two of these potential areas. Such a contingent approach has long been recommended for product and market standardisation, to allow flexibility between the two extremes of full global standardisation and complete local market responsiveness (Quelch and Hoff 1986, Douglas and Wind 1987). Such opportunities for world-wide coordination can provide measurable benefits such as clarifying brand identities, within the domestic as well as foreign markets, when a consistent international brand strategy is being planned or in streamlining the launch of new offerings, such as the Ford Motor Company's Mondeo car in 1993, designed and positioned as a 'world' (ie global) car.

There are thus a number of opportunities across and within world markets for standardisation and global marketing, as well as adaptation and local marketing. It is not a question of commitment to one or the other, as both approaches may be used simultaneously. The strategic objective is to achieve the major advantages to be had from global structuring of part of the product/service offering, whilst, at the same time, adapting or fine-tuning to develop other parts of the same offering to closely match the needs of a particular local market. This process of combining the advantages of both global and local operations has become known as 'glocalisation'. The experience of Kentucky Fried Chicken (KFC), an American international fast food chain, may illustrate the point. After its initial entry into the Japanese market KFC rapidly realised that it was necessary to make three specific changes to its international strategy. First, the product was of the wrong shape and size, since the Japanese prefer morsel-sized food. Second, the locations of the outlets had to be moved into crowded city eating areas and away from independent sites. Third, contracts for the supply of appropriate quality chickens had to be negotiated locally, although KFC provided all technical advice and standards. After these adaptations to the product and the site, KFC has been successful in Japan.

A global marketing strategy therefore is more about looking for opportunities for integration of associated activities across geographic locations, where appropriate, rather than exact replication of the concept in all locations. Whilst disregarding traditional market boundaries, it needs awareness of, and responsiveness to, shifts between globally homogeneous and locally differentiated markets. Such a strategy will derive maximum benefit from the exploitation of similarities between international segments where they exist or can be created, while such trends as the growth of middle-income groups and suburbanisation continue.

THE CREATION OF REGIONAL TRADING BLOCS

The momentum of economic and political deregulation of both internal and international markets has accelerated over the last decade. China, India, the majority of the countries of Central and Eastern Europe emerging from the old Soviet (USSR) command economy, together with most of South America, are all engaged in shifts towards more open market economies. These moves towards the liberalisation of international trade go hand in hand with restructuring into larger and larger regional trading blocs. There are several advantages accruing from international trading agreements, in terms of overall growth in international trade, healthier balance of payments, international goodwill and political stability. Such movements are providing communication and distribution infrastructures which are enabling companies to offer their goods and services to consumers on a world-wide basis, as well as rising levels of household income to stimulate consumer demand and provide purchasing power for these products.

At the same time, this build-up of the three main Triad regions of North America, Asia-Pacific and Europe has changed historic patterns of world trading relationships. For example, Australia, New Zealand and Malaysia are now firmly part of the Asia-Pacific trading bloc, with most future growth in trade expected to come from Asia-Pacific trading partners, rather than from 'old' trading partners such as the UK and other former Commonwealth countries. This example merely serves to illustrate one of the most powerful outcomes arising from the consolidation of these international trading blocs: the realignment that it represents both of international trade and also of international investment.

Foreign investment is extremely important in international trade because of its links to trade, financial flows and technology transfer. A growing share of internal foreign direct investment (FDI) is concentrated in the Triad itself. Recipients of FDI tend to be dominated by a Triad member in the same region, for example, Latin America by the USA, Eastern Europe by the European Community (EC), Asia by Japan (UNCTC 1991). Developing countries are therefore increasingly under pressure to strengthen links with a Triad member and participate in regional integration or risk losing their place in the investment pecking order. Both international trade and international investment are thus exhibiting faster intra-regional than inter-regional growth.

The structure and membership of the trading blocs themselves appear all to be growing, although each is at very different stages of development and has widely different degrees of formal institutional framework. The EC, currently with twelve member states, has a queue of additional nations applying for membership. These include the countries of the European Free Trade Area (EFTA) such as Sweden, Austria, Norway and Switzerland, as well as many from Eastern Europe such as Poland, Hungary and the Czech and Slovak Republics. A free market in services in New Zealand and Australia is already in place, as is the Canadian/USA Free Trade Agreement (FTA), which provides for the total elimination of tariffs by 1999. Mexico has received ratification by the United States to join an enlarged North America Free Trade Agreement (NAFTA). NAFTA may well gradually extend to include much of Central and South America over time. Already there are many bilateral and trilateral agreements in place in South America, such as the Andean pact between Venezuela, Colombia and Bolivia, or the Mercosur FTA between Brazil, Argentina, Uruguay and Paraguay. Finally in the North American region, there is Caricom, a customs union created in 1991 between the English-speaking Caribbean countries. These do not have the scope or structure of the EC, but all have ambitious long-term agendas, not least eventual full participation in NAFTA. Since 1987, the USA has signed sixteen 'framework' agreements with Latin American countries. The groundwork exists for a pan-American trading bloc embracing all the Americas.

Evidence is mixed for the existence of a 'yen' bloc in Asia, centred around Japan (Emmott 1988, Connell 1990, Frankel 1991). The yen is increasingly used as a regional currency, despite deeply rooted historical animosity between Japan and many of its neighbours. Asian central banks' holdings of yen as a proportion of their foreign exchange reserves rose from 13.9 per cent in 1980 to 17.5 per cent in 1989, while the proportion of Asian countries' international debt denominated in yen rather than dollars nearly doubled between 1980 and 1989 to 40 per cent. Japan's direct investment in the Asian region rose from $2 billion in 1985 to $8.2 billion in 1988. However, it invested heavily in the EC and North America as well. Intra-regional trade between Japan, Hong Kong, South Korea, the five ASEAN (the Association of South East Asian Nations) countries (Singapore, Malaysia, Indonesia, Philippines and Thailand), Australia and New Zealand, has grown from 33 per cent of the region's total exports and imports to 37 per cent between 1980 and 1989. Yet much of this growth is seen simply as a natural reflection of Asia's increased importance in world trade. The faster economic growth in this region than elsewhere in the world has in itself provided greater trading opportunities. However, none of this is governed by a legal and institutional framework like the EC or, to a lesser extent, NAFTA. The only regional grouping in the area is ASEAN. However, Connell (1990) has argued that: '...it is no longer a case of Japan against the other two blocs, rather the whole region's interests are increasingly interlinked'.

The ongoing reduction of structural and fiscal barriers to trade, including the ambitious and growing agenda to the General Agreement on Tariffs and Trade (GATT) negotiations, means that these geographical regions can begin to represent major forces in world markets. Within Europe, the reduction and harmonisation of both tariff and non-tariff regulatory barriers has created new customer groupings of a potential size sufficient to encourage companies from both within and outside the EC to introduce new products or services, or to rationalise existing product ranges for these changed market structures. The creation of trading blocs also improves the potential for extending successful concepts from one country to another. The implications for brand strategies include global brands, umbrella concepts, line extensions and the test conversion of key national brands.

The food industry is a particularly interesting vehicle for illustrating trends in globalisation since it faces the most culture-specific notions of 'taste' and preferences in eating habits. As a result, it faces the greatest problems of acceptability of standard products and formats across cultures and domestic market boundaries. Yet, even here, evidence for some consumer convergence exists. There is increasing acceptance of multilingual packaging and a questioning of assumptions that a proliferation of products is necessary to meet market needs. When Philip Morris, a US multinational with predominantly food and tobacco interests, reduced its five different European recipes for the same food product to just one, no discernible effect on demand occurred (Collins et al 1989). Similarly, at that time in 1988, a study by the UK Ministry of Agriculture, Fisheries and Food found that long-established regional food preferences were disappearing as a result of the big supermarket chains making similar products available in all regions of the UK – an example of demand-creation under changed market conditions.

New products are the least culture bound and therefore often easier to market internationally than existing products (Quelch and Hoff 1986). However, given the high failure rate of new products, Capara (1989) recommended that existing brands should be looked at first. Jacob Suchard, a Swiss international food company now owned by Philip Morris, used this approach to build an existing brand, Milka chocolate, into an international brand. Milka was sold only in tablet form until 1985, then was extended into a countline (a small chocolate bar), praline and seasonal. Product extension was accompanied by successful geographic market expansion, from an initial four countries in 1985 (Austria, Germany, Switzerland and France), to an additional ten countries by 1989 (Spain, Argentina, Hong Kong, Japan, US, Canada, UK, Belgium, Italy and Holland). Further geographic expansion has continued.

THE RETAIL SECTOR AND THE GLOBALISATION DEBATE

The retail sector has historically been a domestic market industry. Its primary activities of marketing, sales and service were seen as best carried out downstream, as close to the customer as possible. This type of industry with a predominance of local activity, has been understandably viewed as difficult to globalise and possibly fundamentally unsuitable for globalisation (Porter 1985). In addition, low entry and exit barriers resulted in domestic retail sectors made up of large numbers of small independents. However despite this, the retail sector has exhibited significant internationalisation and globalisation over the last decade. The characteristics which kept it a locally based industry have, in many respects, changed fundamentally. The late 1980s saw an increasing number of mergers, acquisitions and international expansion (Dawson and Burt 1989, Treadgold 1989). Furthermore, most retailers now buy from suppliers outside their country of origin and most retail organisations face marketing, financial and operational impact from foreign competitors entering, and being successful in, their national markets.

Of the many factors that have contributed to this change, of particular importance is the trend towards concentration, with fewer but larger store chains controlling greater and greater proportions of market share in each national market. While there is great disparity between the proportions of market share dominated by the largest five or the largest ten store chains, both within different national markets and across the international trading blocs, the trend towards greater levels of concentration is a universal one. Large retailers are gaining market share from independent stores. This is also a trend observable in other service industries such as professional service firms of accountants, management consultants or lawyers, or advertising agencies. Both nationally and internationally, organisations of considerable size have emerged. Market share is becoming concentrated in far fewer hands.

Although there will always be a proportion of the retail market served by small independent units and thus a natural limit to the absorption of independents by multiples, the proportion of retail sales accounted for by large chains has steadily increased. Even the independents have formed buying groups to gain advantages of economies of scale in purchasing (eg international 'symbol' groups such as Spar). Indeed, one of the biggest recent concepts in retailing, the convenience store, is formulated to look like a small independent but is most often part of the portfolio of formats of a larger parent chain. The most dramatic example of this trend may be taken from the rapid development of 'forecourt retailing' by the oil companies at their petrol (oil and gas) filling stations. Oil giants such as Shell and Exxon have expanded rapidly into the retail end of the business, making the petrol station forecourt the retail outlet rival to the corner shop in the 1990s and the epitome of modern convenience shopping. The time is long past when all that was offered at a visit to the petrol station was petrol.

The retail sector has always been regarded as highly labour intensive, whereas it has actually become much more capital intensive. This has resulted partly from increasing use of information technology (eg EPOS systems) and the cost of large, well-situated sites. Further potential change arises from the political and economic restructuring that is taking place across the world. The formation of trading blocs and declining barriers to trade have been instrumental in transforming the traditional cost structure of the retail industry, particularly in terms of the ability to source world wide and to utilise trans-regional distribution systems. As a result of these factors, upstream retail activities such as purchasing, sourcing, logistics, distribution and warehousing have become increasingly large scale. As illustrated in Figure 2.1, this shift has provided the opportunity for greater standardisation in management practices both to improve efficiency and to bring lower costs, and in the possibilities for extending retail offerings across borders.

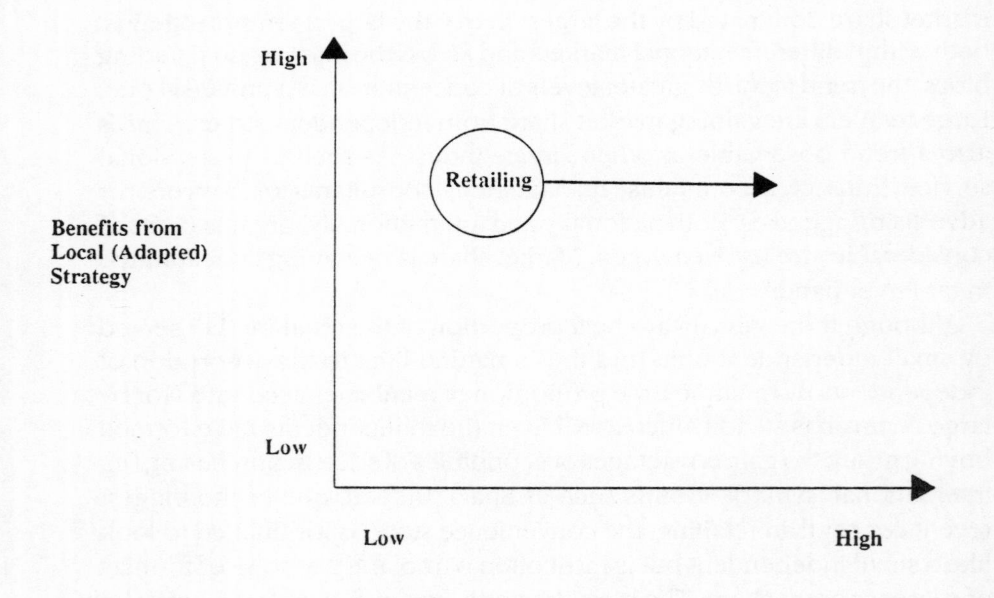

Source: Adapted from Prahalad and Doz 1987

Figure 2.1 Benefits from standardised or adapted strategies: direction for the 1990s in retailing

The transfer of retail concepts

Both historically and currently, there is a strong view of received wisdom in the retail industry, expressed both by practitioners and analysts, that retail concepts do not travel. For that reason, company share prices have often suffered significant slumps following announcements of planned international expansions or acquisitions by retail chains. Despite this entrenched 'local' ethos, and in response to the challenges and opportunities described above, some major companies are transferring their existing retail offering, or developing new concepts and moving into new foreign markets, or alternatively creating alliances such as consortia with other retailers.

Although transfers of existing concepts or techniques are thought to be more acceptable in countries that have similar social and cultural environments, and are at comparable stages of economic development (Kacker 1988), the increasing similarity of these factors across many economies can be seen in the swift endorsement of new retailing concepts and modes of operation across the world. In Japan for example, supermarkets and fast food restaurants gained acceptance after the economy had undergone significant structural changes, women had entered the workforce, and some elements of a more Western lifestyle had been adopted. This in turn, makes successive introductions of non-Japanese trading concepts and retail formulas easier. For example, the American retail chain Toys 'R' Us opened its first store in Japan, north of Tokyo in December 1991, and plans about 100 outlets in Japan within the decade. In recreating its discount superstore format in Japan, it benefited from Japan's recent modifications to its Large Retail Store Law, which reduced the time local retailers could block the opening of rival stores in their neighbourhood from ten years to eighteen months. This change was itself due to pressure in international trade negotiations. In addition, the McDonald's hamburger chain has a 20 per cent stake in the Japanese operation of Toys 'R' Us, which makes available to them twenty years' experience of making American retail concepts acceptable to Japanese consumers. Since the Japanese spent $4.7 billion on toys in 1991, the prize for getting it right is significant.

For developing and less developed countries (LDCs), attention has been drawn to the difficulties in adapting elements of an existing retail mix to prevailing local conditions. Adequate levels of demand and local market stability have to be assessed against specific problems common to LDC economies. Piercy (1982) cited such things as lack of physical distribution systems, currency problems, lack of agents, and wide gaps in the market between the rich and poor, urban and rural groupings, in the population. In fact, research on retailing in the LDCs (see for example many contributions in Kaynak 1988), supports the general conclusion that its successful progression is related to the level of a country's economic development, as in the case of the rapid development of supermarkets in Hong Kong (Lau and Lee 1988), mirrored by an equally rapid recent spread in Malaysia.

Similarly, McDonald's took fourteen years to extend its chain to Russia, not only because negotiations with the Soviet authorities at the time were very slow and fundamentals, like legal ownership of outlets, difficult to establish, but also because no sourcing or supply chain existed for a steady provision of the raw materials for making hamburgers and 'french fries'. The company had to go to extraordinary lengths to create a reliable supply chain of appropriate quality ingredients for its product. These included not only agreements with farm cooperatives to grow the right strain of potato needed, but even importing American bull sperm to ensure that Russian beef herds yielded the correct beef quality expected in the hamburgers. Even on opening, aspects of the offering were almost incomprehensible to the local customers, such as the menu itself, since the notions of choice and availability were not familiar to the Russian consumer.

Marketing is also an unfamiliar concept in China, since goods and services can be unobtainable for long periods of time and demand usually exceeds supply, or at least supply of reasonable quality. That being said, the introduction and ease of transfer experienced by a number of retailing companies, demonstrates a growing acceptance of, and in some cases demand for, innovative and different retail offerings by international consumers within these very different national markets. This is evident in a growing number of trading formats such as self-service, supermarkets, hypermarkets, discount warehouses, retail parks and convenience stores. The hypermarket format, which originated in France, spread to Spain, Italy, Brazil and the UK in the 1970s and is now establishing itself in the North American market. The formula evolved by the US toy retailer Toys 'R' Us blends the concepts of self-service and discounting with speciality retailing, as does Ikea the Swedish international furniture retailer. Both companies have been able to infiltrate the whole spectrum of overseas markets, and their global success is due in part to the acceptance of this mode of operation by consumers across the world.

Problems do frequently occur in the process of transference. Inadequate understanding of the Canadian and French markets by Marks & Spencer led to several years of poor trading, as was also the case for the rapid start-up and closure of the 'Money Shops' started up in the UK in the 1970s by Citibank of the US. The concept was not comprehensible to the UK consumer at that time, although by the 1990s it had been widely copied. More recently in 1990, the collapse of the UK speciality retailer Sock Shop, due to inappropriate locations and massive debt incurred in funding a rapid expansion in the US, showed the dangers of attempting to rework a successful domestic concept internationally. However, evolution of retailing appears to be following similar patterns in the developed economies. Lusch (1987), Segal-Horn (1987) and Dawson (1989) reviewed developments in the retail sectors of the US, the UK and Japan respectively. Their findings show similarities in broad patterns of structural responses to consumer change, particularly to demographic and economic trends, market structure, technology, locations, retailer buying power and distribution. This suggests that a context for the export of retail concepts exists, but that great attention to the detail of implementation market by market is required.

Organisations involved in international operations expect to undergo a learning curve. For retailers, many valuable lessons have been learned about market research, site selection, and redefinition of offers, as well as the logistics problems of setting up and managing international supply chains. Indeed one of the most important things that has been learnt by retailers who operate internationally is that formats, merchandising, store design and store location often have to be customised to local conditions to achieve success. But it should be noted that such 'tweaking' of the core concept or merchandising mix, while representing modification, does not remove regional or global operating benefits. Benetton may sell different colour and range combinations in its Asia-Pacific stores from its European ones, but this does not reduce the scale benefits the company gains in purchasing, design, manufacturing, marketing, distribution and branding. The US fast food chain Pizza Hut protects the core elements of its brand by copyrighting its individual product brand names, for example Perfect Pizza. It also ensures standardisation across markets by operating a strict specification of product ingredients. However, the concept is adapted to suit local needs; for example some elements of the menu (such as desserts) will vary, as will store design and even the way in which products are served to the customer. In the same way McDonald's hamburger chain began to provide tea on the menu of its outlets in the UK, to respond to a specific demand of that national market. None of these adaptations interferes with the core concept or alters the basis of the operational efficiency of these organisations; but it does enable them to maximise their responsiveness to local market conditions and customer preferences.

Modes of international market expansion

All organisations wishing to expand into international markets are faced with a variety of methods of entry, from organic growth as a start-up in the new market, to acquisition, franchising or licensing.

Any acquisition strategy is regarded as a faster route to expansion and new product or market development than organic growth. For retail companies, acquisition of a controlling interest in a foreign company provides immediate market share, sites, location, concept and distribution. It may also provide a route to diversification of activities. However, acquisition as a strategy is always problematic in whatever industry it occurs, since potential synergies are often unrealised as organisational cultures fail to blend or information systems remain incompatible. It nevertheless remains a viable and popular path to international market expansion. The 1993 merger of the UK chain Kingfisher (formerly Woolworth) with the French leading electrical retailer Darty, was based on compatibility with Kingfisher's successful UK electrical subsidiary Comet. The two groups were felt to have similar trading policies and formats and an ability to benefit from increased scale in sourcing, joint development of in-store and management information systems, shared capital expenditure on computer hardware and EPOS terminals, and extension of their format into other European markets.

Organic growth as a strategy for developing overseas operations has been used by retailers such as The Gap of the US, Carrefour, a French supermarket group, or IKEA of Sweden. It is also the option used by the global petrol retailing chains such as Exxon. Organic growth ensures that financial and management control is retained by the parent company of the overseas operations. When the company is presenting a uniform image, brand name, or product with little variation, such quality control factors are extremely important. Such considerations are particularly relevant for companies retailing luxury goods and services. For example, the Louis Vuitton network of stores (part of the French luxury goods group LVMH) across Japan, the Far East and North America, sells a range of luxury travel goods and accessories to a closely defined target market, which expects a very high-quality but standardised product. Table 2.3 gives some examples of the breadth of coverage across the major trading blocs that luxury companies of this type have established. These speciality retailers are characterised by particularly high levels of vertical integration and typically manufacture their own products.

Table 2.3 Indicative Triad coverage – speciality retailers

Retailer	Trading bloc presence North America	Europe	Asia-Pacific
Dunhill (UK)	*	*	*
Gucci (Italy)	*	*	*
Joseph (UK)	*	*	*
Louis Vuitton (France)	*	*	*
Mappin & Webb (UK)	*	*	*
Ralph Lauren (US)	*	*	*
Wedgwood (Ireland)	*	*	*

Source: Company reports

Cooperative agreements such as franchising, joint ventures and licensing provide further alternatives for overseas market entry. Franchising has been a particularly popular means of international expansion for a variety of reasons. It is financially a low-cost means of achieving very rapid growth. That is because one of the major costs of expansion, the outlets, is borne by the franchisee. This same factor also means that it is possible to carry out a very high degree of expansion very quickly. Without very tight management control systems however, franchise operations may lack adequate standards of quality and consistency in all outlets, thus gradually diluting the brand franchise. Another benefit provided by franchising may also be the access to local market knowledge from franchisees, although the quality of that benefit would depend on the quality of the recruitment and selection of franchisees and agents. Franchising has been the expansion route taken by the Body Shop (UK), Benetton (Italy), Stefanel (Italy), PreMaman (France).

Joint ventures have been particularly favoured in countries such as Japan and India which were difficult to penetrate. In Japan there have been a number of agreements between Seibu Saison and US and UK companies such as McDonald's (US), Mulberry (UK fashion) and Paul Smith (UK fashion). The ventures work mainly on a concession, shop-within-a-shop basis, although stand-alone sites are being established bearing the foreign retailer's name, but run by companies created by the two participants in the joint venture.

Another type of cooperative agreement has emerged in the form of buying associations or consortia. One European grocery retail consortium involves retail chains from seven European countries. Retail consortia are not just for bulk purchasing of goods for sale in the stores, Increasingly, more sophisticated procurement benefits are sought, such as the joint purchase of vehicles, computers, shared development costs for specialised retail software and possibly even the eventual international transfer of trading formats. With strong potential benefits from collaboration, different types of joint venture are likely to grow in popularity, despite the difficulties of managing such collaborations effectively over the long term, especially with multiple participants. Indeed, with the financial cost of entry and the managerial risk associated with acquisition, and the additional market knowledge risks attached to organic growth, joint venture and cooperative agreements may become the preferred route into international markets.

CONCLUSIONS

This chapter explored the extent to which consumers in different parts of the world are becoming increasingly influenced by similar social, economic and technological trends across the world. Homogeneity of tastes and preferences, creating genuine international market segments, provides an opportunity that must affect the strategic thinking of any company whatever their industry or sector. It should affect thinking about every stage of the design and delivery of a product or service. The removal of barriers to trade within and between countries, together with the gradual consolidation of trading blocs across groups of countries and whole regions, is accelerating these developments. Previously enduring characteristics such as national barriers, which have governed perceptions of segmentation and existing trading conventions, are becoming more transparent. Of course traditional national and local differences will still exist, but they will exist alongside cross-border customer groupings.

The discussion has been placed in the context of the debate on the relative merits of global standardisation strategies compared with local adaptation strategies as the most effective way of trading across borders and succeeding in a range of different national marketplaces. It has considered the contribution that the continuing evolution of trading blocs makes to this debate. The retail sector, a sector where international strategies are increasingly popular yet remain controversial, has been used to explore some of the issues raised and some of the corporate strategies adopted. The discussion has reviewed these issues in the light of the three key conditions set out in the introduction: that a global standardisation strategy can only be successful if evidence can be found for the existence of global market segments, of global economies of scale, and the availability of a distribution infrastructure to realise these potential economies world wide. Under all three categories there does appear to be an *a priori* case for international trends in patterns of demand, both within regional clusters and across them, to encourage each firm to look again at its existing and potential markets.

LESSONS FOR MANAGERS

Many companies arrive at the point where they have little choice but to think seriously about international expansion as a way out of saturated domestic markets, but are unclear what cross-border opportunities exist for them. Some key points to think about in this regard arising from issues discussed in this chapter are as follows.

- Two seemingly contradictory market trends have emerged: fragmentation (ie a proliferation of segments) *within* national markets and consolidation (ie international concentration of segments) *across* national boundaries. This may be helpful to companies facing a shrinking segment in their domestic market. Markets which are not viable, in terms of domestic market size, may become viable if expanded across a number of country markets.
- Even the different stages of development of many national markets, especially within the same trading bloc, represent an opportunity for product or market expansion. If Spain has a low level of concentration of multiple retail chains and the UK is very highly concentrated, this represents an opportunity for transfer of the concept from the more to the less developed market. This is a process often seen at work in world markets. A typical example in the 1990s is the decline in the market for tobacco products in North America and the Northern European states, while demand is taking off in China and Eastern Europe.
- Companies should assess the impact of the emergence of international market segments on their existing strategies and the opportunities created for supplying these segments more efficiently. In the retail sector for example, while not all aspects of a retail format or merchandising mix are (or should be) adopted within or across trading blocs, underlying economies are derivable and being actively pursued, from sourcing, distribution and many aspects of marketing. A contingent approach to international markets therefore makes sense, with continuous review and adjustment to developing demand

conditions and the efficiency-seeking possibilities to which they give rise.

- A presence in international markets creates antennae for gathering market intelligence, mentioned by many international companies as one of the most important benefits of being international and a factor which is leading other companies to rethink single-site operations. Many successful product or service innovations have been a result of ideas observed elsewhere.
- Greater transparency of information will create an increasing requirement for uniformity and consistency in quality, delivery and marketing of products and services across borders. Although this raises additional problems for managers since it will necessitate the restructuring of channels and the tighter management of quality across wider and wider boundaries, it also offers openings for early distinctiveness and success.

REFERENCES

Akehurst, G (1983) 'Concentration in Retail Distribution: Measurement and Significance', *Service Industries Journal*, 3, (2), 161–79

Capara, F (1989) 'Trading With Our European Partners', *The EEC's Food Industries: Completion of the Internal Market*, Paper No 3, Dept of Agricultural Economics and Management, University of Reading

Chandler, A D (1990) *Scale & Scope: The Dynamics of Industrial Capitalism*, Harvard University Press, Cambridge, Mass

Collins, R, Schmenner, R and Whybark, D (1989) 'Pan-European Manufacturing: The Road to 1992', *European Business Journal*, 1, (4), 43–51

Connell, P J (1990) 'Asia Pacific: The Next Regional Trading Bloc?', *The International Executive*, May–Jun, 31, (6), 37–40

Dawson, J (1989) 'Japanese Distribution: Effectual Yes, But is it Efficient?', *The Japanese Market – A Guide to Distribution*, Anglo-Japanese Economic Institute, London, 4–6

Dawson, J and Burt, S (1989) *The Internationalisation of British Retailing*, Institute of Retail Studies, Stirling University

Douglas, S and Wind, Y (1987) 'The Myth of Globalisation', *The Columbia Journal of World Business*, winter, XXII, (4), 19–29

Economist, The (1992) 'Freeing India's Economy', 23 May, 23–5

Emmott, W (1988) 'Limits to Japanese Power', *Amex Bank Review*, Oct, 16, 5–24

Engel, J and Blackwell, R (1982) *Consumer Behaviour*, CBS College Publishing, New York

Frankel, J (1991) 'Is a Yen Bloc Forming in Pacific Asia?', *Amex Bank Review*, Nov

Ghoshal, S (1987) 'Global Strategy: An Organising Framework', *Strategic Management Journal*, Sep–Oct, 8, (5), 425–40

Jain, S (1989) 'Standardization of International Marketing Strategy: Some Research Hypotheses', *Journal of Marketing*, Jan, 53, (1), 70–9

Kacker, M (1988) 'International Flow of Retailing Know-How: Bridging the Technology Gap in Distribution', *Journal of Retailing*, spring, 64, (1), 41–67

Kaynak, E (1988) *Transnational Retailing*, Walter de Gruyter, New York

Kotler, P (1985) *Global Standardisation – Courting Danger*, Panel Discussion, 23rd American Marketing Association Conference, Washington DC

Lau, H-F and Lee, K-H (1988) 'Development of Supermarkets in Hong Kong: Current Status and Future Trends', in Kaynak, E (ed) *Transnational Retailing*, Walter de Gruyter, New York, 321–9

Levitt, T (1983) 'The Globalisation of Markets', *Harvard Business Review*, May–Jun, 61, (3), 92–102

Link, G (1988) 'Global Advertising: An Update', *The Journal of Consumer Marketing*, spring, 5, (2), 69–74

Lusch, R (1987) 'A Commentary on the US Retail Environment', in Johnson, G (ed) *Business Strategy and Retailing* Wiley, Chichester, 35–41

Mueller, B (1991) 'Multinational Advertising: Factors Influencing the Standardized v. Specialized Approach', *International Marketing Review*, Vol 8, No 1, 7–18

Nelson, E (1989) 'Marketing in 1992 and Beyond', *Royal Society of Arts Journal*, Apr 292–304

Nielsen Marketing Research (1987) *International Food and Drug Store Trends*, Annual Marketing Review, A C Nielsen Co, USA

Ohmae, K (1989) 'Managing in a Borderless World', *Harvard Business Review*, May–Jun, 67, (3), 152–61

Onkvisit, S and Shaw, J (1989) 'Standardised International Advertising: A Review and Critical Evaluation of the Theoretical and Empirical Evidence', *The Columbia Journal of World Business*, fall, XXII, (3), 43–55

Perlmutter, H V (1991) 'On the Rocky Road to the First Global Civilization', *Human Relations*, Vol 44, No 9, 897–920

Piercy, N (1982) *Export Strategy: Markets and Competition*, George Allen & Unwin, London

Porter, M (1985) *Competitive Advantage*, The Free Press, New York

Prahalad, C K and Doz, Y (1987), *The Multinational Mission: Balancing Local Demands and Global Vision*, The Free Press, New York

Quelch, J and Hoff, E (1986) 'Customizing Global Marketing', *Harvard Business Review*, May–Jun, 64, (3), 59–68

Salmon, W and Tordjman, A (1989) 'The Internationalisation of Retailing', *International Journal of Retailing*, 4, (2), 3–16

Segal-Horn, S (1987) 'The Retail Environment in the UK', in Johnson, G (ed) *Business Strategy and Retailing*, Wiley, Chichester, 13–33

Segal-Horn, S and McGee, J (1989) 'Strategies to Cope with Retailer Buying Power', in Pellegrini, L and Reddy, S K (eds) *Retail and Marketing Channels*, Routledge, London

Sorenson, R and Weichmann, U (1975) 'How Multinationals View Marketing Standardisation', *Harvard Business Review*, May–Jun, 53, (3), 39

Takeuchi, H and Porter, M (1986) 'Three Roles of International Marketing in Global Strategy', in Porter, M (ed) *Competition in Global Industries*, Harvard Business School Press, Boston, Mass, 111–46

Thorelli, H and Becker, H (1980) 'The Information Seekers: Multinational Strategy Target', *Californian Management Review*, fall, XXIII, (1), 46–52

Treadgold, A (1989) '1992: The Retail Response to a Changing Europe', *Marketing Research Today*, Aug, 17, 3, 161–6.

United Nations Centre on Transnational Corporations (UNCTC) (1991) *World Investment Report 1991; The Triad in Foreign Direct Investment*, New York

PART TWO

CHALLENGES INVOLVING PEOPLE: CULTURE, LEARNING AND TRANSFERABILITY

3

National Culture and International Business: The Idea of Cultural Fluency

Sally Butler and Collin Randlesome, Cranfield University School of Management

INTRODUCTION

The management of financial, technical and productive resources across national boundaries has developed further and faster than international approaches to human resource management (Adler 1991). This is creating increasing dilemmas for both organisations as a whole and for individual managers. Managing change at the technical and economic level is no longer sufficient. All multinational managers, not just expatriates, must be aware of, and cope with, cultural differences, often on a day-to-day basis (Brewster, 1991).

The fact that business is conducted according to different sets of rules in different areas of the world is no secret to international businesspeople. Pioneering American and European multinational corporations during the post-war periods realised that, in order to be able to make any sort of profit in the developing economies outside their own jurisdiction and understanding, they had to accommodate local business customs or work on becoming an integral part of the local culture themselves.

The impact of differing national cultures may, paradoxically, be less of a problem when the artefacts of the cultures, such as the language, food and clothing are visibly very different. In the latter case there is more of an expectation that there may have to be some compromises, and a realisation of the need for caution. What many multinationals are now having to grapple with is the fact that even seemingly similar cultures can actually think and behave in fundamentally different ways. The well-known saying describing the UK and the USA as two nations 'divided by a common language', clearly contains some truth.

There are two basic and extremely difficult problems facing those interested in culture. The first is the delicate issue of cultural stereotyping whereby the characteristics of whole nations may be overgeneralised to the point of caricature. The second is the wealth of contradictory and somewhat confusing literature on the concept of culture itself, which has tended to be treated in a descriptive and situation-specific fashion.

The consequence is that there exists a dearth of tools available to practising managers that reach merely beyond the interesting or the amusing. This chapter presents a manager's guide to understanding the concept of national business culture, its impact on the way that business is conducted, and a framework for understanding how one might be a more effective manager across cultures.

WHAT IS CULTURE?

The concept of culture has been very difficult to define – its academic and popularist uses range from specific cognitive processing to covering widespread nationally created art forms such as music and clothing. Cultural studies originated in the field of anthropology and there are three characteristics of culture which appear to be generally held:

- It is shared by all or almost all the members of a group
- It is passed on from the older to the younger members
- It shapes behaviour and perceptions of the world.

One of the leading current management researchers in the field, Geert Hofstede, defines culture as 'the collective programming of the mind which distinguishes the members of one human group from another'. In other words, people are from different cultures if their ways of doing things differ as a group.

The culture of a society is expressed through the interaction of the beliefs, attitudes and values displayed by its members. It is also of course manifested in artefacts such as food, clothing and language. Anyone familiar with traditional French cuisine will relate to the culturally influenced attitude of 'living to eat' rather than 'eating to live'. The often complex and time-consuming recipes are testament to the value placed on the preparation and eating of food. This attitude contrasts quite starkly with the US-influenced concept of fast food.

In this chapter, our focus will be on national business culture, which we define as the commonly held beliefs and values of the people in a country which shape and define the way that business is conducted in that country. The word culture should be reserved for these conscious, and often subconscious, framers of the perceptual mindset which are learned during socialisation. Quite commonly, the prevailing values are taught in the home, reinforced by the education system and continued in the workplace. Whether we like it or not, we are all living examples of our culture.

Hofstede (1991) illustrates culture as the intermediate layer of mental programming in a pyramid of programming making up the individual mindset (Figure 3.1). At the base of the pyramid is human nature – the fundamental programming that is common to all humans and is entirely inherited. This consists of our basic physiological and psychological functioning, such as the ability to feel fear and love. The way in which we express these emotions is, however, determined by our culture.

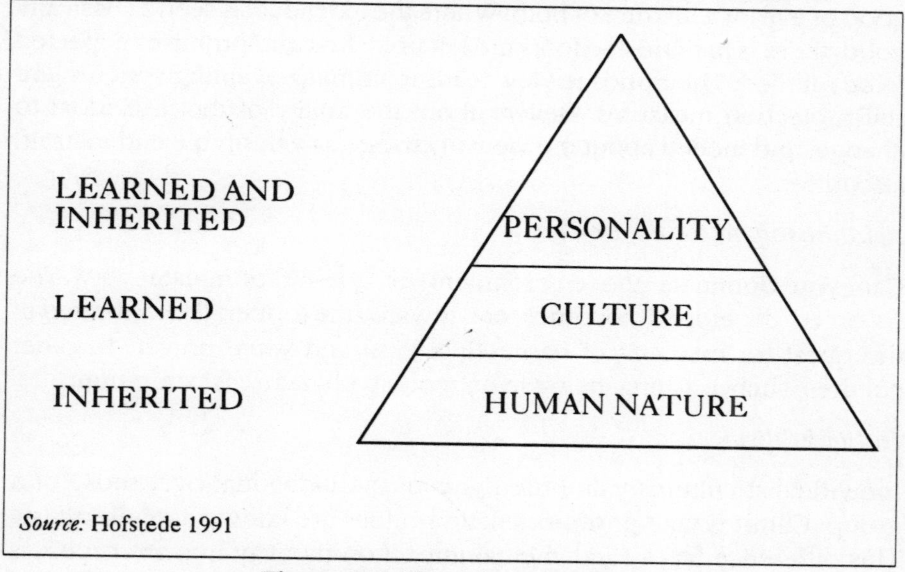

Figure 3.1 The cultural pyramid

At the tip of the pyramid sit the learned and inherited behaviours that are peculiar to the individual. So why is it then that, having been part of a very similar social system, we are not all exactly the same in terms of our core beliefs, attitudes, and values? The answer is two-fold: first, we each have different actual life experiences. Our parents may have influenced us in different ways; our education and circle of friends may be very different; our job function and organisational experience may range enormously. Second, culture impacts only our learned behaviours. The different and interesting aspect of culture is that it is something that we share in common, the 'group mindset' that unites us.

Cultural differences

Cultures vary in a variety of significant ways. Quite how much and in precisely what ways, we are often not aware until faced with something that differs substantially from our own. Yet there are some very clear differences which have been explored by researchers in this field, every one of which has clear implications for managing people according to their different perspectives.

Perception of the individual

This relates to our perception of whether the individual is fundamentally good or evil, or a mixture of both. Where the individual is seen as basically good, there is high trust – doors are left unlocked and promises expected to be fulfilled. The opposite view leads to crime-preventing systems and self-protection measures. Beliefs about the ability of the individual to change, and indeed about the view of change as a desirable end in itself, also differ.

Relationship to the environment

Can you dominate the environment or does it dominate you? The so-called 'developed' countries tend towards the former, demonstrated in the quest for methods of harnessing wind and wave power. In other cultures, such as China, being in harmony with nature is paramount.

Individualism

Individualist cultures value the rights of the individual over those of a group. Cultures with group-orientated values are known as 'collectivist'. This difference has a fundamental impact on the way human resources are managed – appraisal, remuneration, motivation and so on.

Activity orientation

Cultures tend towards action (doing), or being, which relates to a more passive, present-oriented tendency. Western cultures tend to value and stress action and change. This contrasts with other cultures where the process of experiencing and enjoying life is more important.

Time

The time orientation is often one of the most visible cultural differences. The US view of time is very much as a commodity, to be earned, spent, wasted and managed. This can seriously clash with other cultural views where the concept of deadlines and leadtimes is not meaningful.

Space

How we treat physical space is culturally determined. What is considered 'close' differs greatly between the Arab and British cultures, for example. Office layouts and house designs are also good reflections of the division that cultures make between public and personal space.

THE ORIGINS OF BUSINESS CULTURE

The business culture of any one nation is shaped by, and in turn shapes, the business environment in which it operates. The culture grows up in the initial stages from the environment of a country – particularly from the geographical, technical, economic and political factors prevailing. Once established, the relationship between the culture and the environment becomes essentially dynamic, each influencing and affecting the other (Figure 3.2).

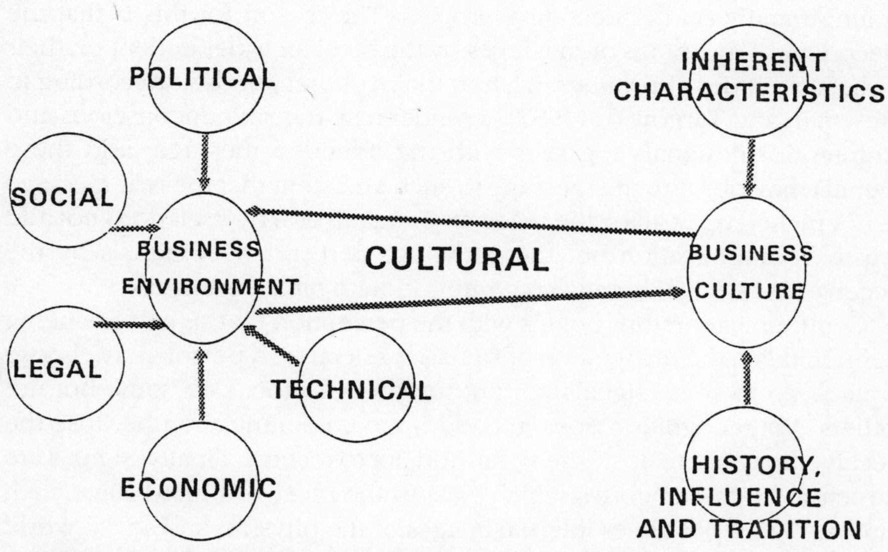

Figure 3.2 The relationship between business environment and business culture

Just as people study foreign languages in order to achieve linguistic fluency, and thus to communicate better, business practitioners acquaint themselves with national cultures other than their own. In this process, linguistic fluency in the target culture is indubitably useful, but by itself it does not inevitably lead to cultural fluency. Linguistic skill is not always accompanied by cultural competence. Conversely, a lack of linguistic

competence in the target culture is not necessarily a barrier to cultural fluency: it is at most an inhibitor which could serve to slow down the process.

WHAT IS CULTURAL FLUENCY?

Cultural fluency has been described as the facility to decode and encode meanings in so-called 'matches' which tally with the meanings originating from the communicator's repository or database (Beamer 1992). The process by which cultural fluency is achieved is not, however, generally appreciated. Having no clear idea about what cultural fluency is, and the process by which this end is achieved, business practitioners often flounder. The wrong messages are received; the wrong messages are sent. At best confusion and at worst ruined business relationships can be the end result.

The most promising way of understanding cultural fluency is concentrating mainly on the decoding process. The reason for this is that the decoding of meanings or messages by the receiver is dependent on their beliefs, attitudes and values, in short their cultural mindset. According to Bowman and Targowski (1987), a sender may transmit unconscious and unintentional signals together with the intended message, and these signals may obscure the message to such an extent that the real message is not picked up at all by the receiver. Transmission by itself does not add up to communication but the conscious perception of signals by the receiver is essential for any communication to have occurred.

Communication thus begins with the perception that signals are being sent. Initially, the recognition of signals is selective. A person may choose to face up to some signals but not to others, to focus on some but not others. Yet recognition does not add up to communication because the receiver may opt to 'lose' the signal and not to retain it. Finally, signals are structured into categories which exist in the receiver's mind since each human being possesses internal images of the physical and social world (Samovar et al 1981, Gudykunst and Kim 1984). Culture itself conditions the categories, so the signal is structured as dictated by culture.

Understanding what happens when intercultural communication occurs enables us to consider how to bring about cultural fluency. In order to communicate across cultures, the encoding or conscious directing of signals to a receiver must take into account the factors which shape the structuring categories of the receiver's repository. But these are in themselves cultural factors: beliefs, attitudes, values and forms of behaviour (Beamer 1992).

HOW IS CULTURAL FLUENCY ACHIEVED?

The learning process by which people become fluent in a culture other than their own is the subject of a wide variety of research. A review of some of the models of intercultural appreciation indicates that not only is the process itself often misunderstood but that learning for the specific purpose of international business has not received the attention which it deserves.

Many writers agree that the process of becoming interculturally fluent is developmental (Brislin et al 1983), and suggest six seemingly incremental antecedents to describe how intercultural behaviour takes place. Gudykunst and Hammer (1983) propose a three-stage approach to learning cultural fluency, but this model concentrates on so-called 'sojourners', rather than practitioners who do not necessarily reside for any length of time in the target culture. Albert (1983) posits an informal model of cultural learning as a spiral in which new intelligence once learned cognitively leads to experiential and behavioural phases which prepare the individual for further learning.

Finally, Beamer (1992) proposes an intercultural communication model. The principles underlying her model are

- Culture is learnable (Terpstra and David 1991)
- Cultures are whole and coherent
- All cultures are equally valid in the way in which they organise and explain human experience
- The interculturally competent communicator acknowledges that cultural bias always exists.

This model postulates five levels of learning which are represented by a circle or disc. The discs are stacked like records in an old jukebox. The five levels as proposed by Beamer are:

1. Acknowledging diversity
2. Organising information according to stereotypes
3. Asking questions to challenge the stereotypes
4. Analysing communications episodes
5. Generating 'other culture' messages.

Beamer maintains that the aim of the learning process is 'to decode effectively signs that come from members of other cultures within a business context, and to encode messages using signs that carry the encoder's meaning to members of other cultures'.

The model itself is extremely useful for showing the stages of intercultural communication, but it needs to be adapted for our present purpose of showing the steps towards achieving cultural fluency, which is not quite the same. The model should be modified because it follows too closely Hall's dictum that 'culture is communication' and 'communication is culture' (1959), which has been challenged in the meantime by Goodenough's principle that 'culture governs communication behaviour' (as cited in Baxter 1983). Finally, Beamer's examples need to be enhanced to satisfy the demands of international business practitioners rather than focusing perhaps too narrowly on students in the classroom.

FIVE LEVELS OF CULTURAL FLUENCY

The five levels are better represented as five permeable layers rather than discs in an old jukebox which, if memory serves correct, tend not be permeable and to fall down on to one another once their playing-time is exhausted. Figure 3.3 better expresses the process for business purposes.

Level 1: acknowledging diversity

The initial level on the ascent to cultural fluency is the realisation that cultural differences exist. The business practitioner gradually becomes aware that unknown and unrecognised signals are being sent. Indeed, people who have grown up in homogeneous, high-context cultures such as the North American or Japanese ones might be puzzled when they first encounter this phenomenon. The realisation gradually begins to dawn that, say, not all businesspeople act and react like a North American businessperson. Other ways of communicating, other ways of doing things actually do exist. What is more, they might just possess equal validity to those in the practitioner's own culture.

Level 2: stereotypic organisation of information

The second level of cultural fluency is reached when the practitioner begins to identify certain characteristics which distinguish a particular culture. The temptation here is to plunge immediately into stereotypic categories and to perceive, for example: all Swedes as wishing to discuss a business problem at interminable length; all German businesspeople reluctant to clinch a deal before consulting their lawyers; all Latin Americans being disinclined to do business with people who fail to evidence interest in their family affairs.

These stereotypic categories are not without their uses; they help the

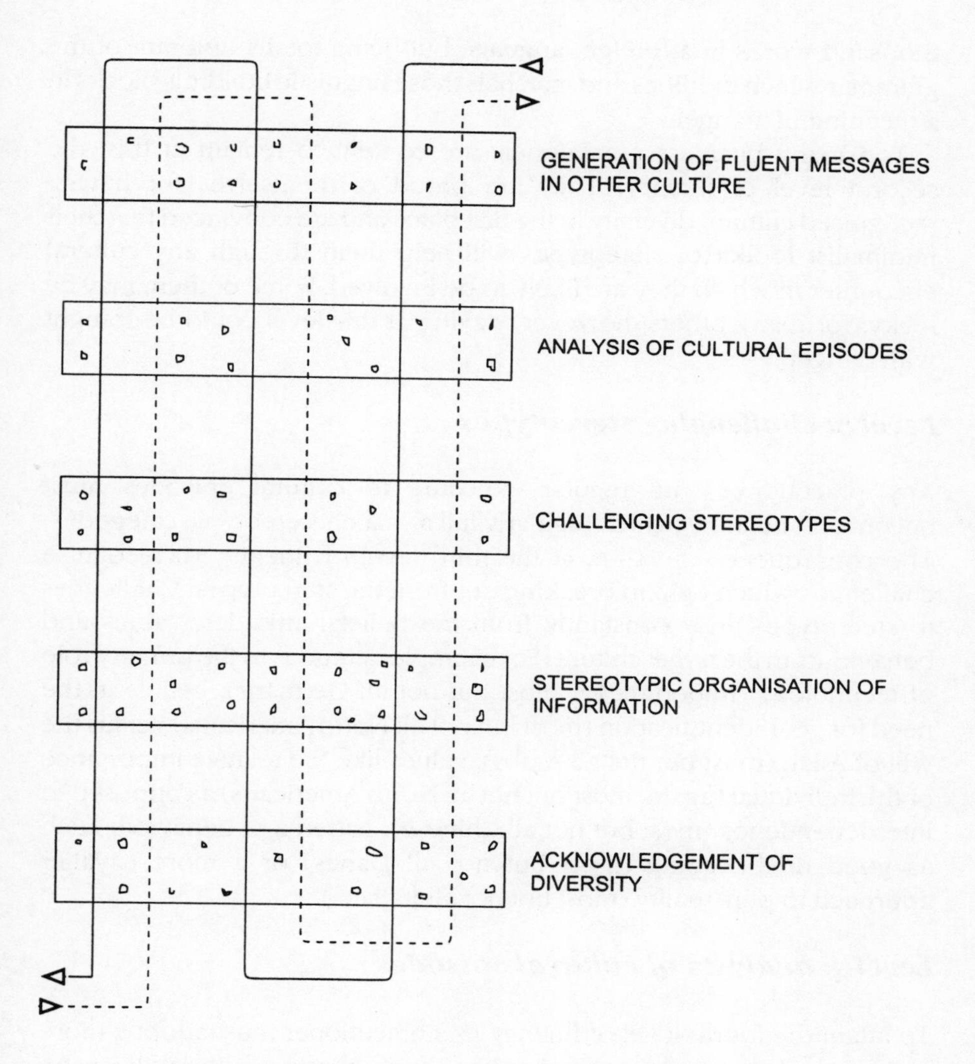

Source: Adapted from Beamer, 1992

Figure 3.3 A model of cultural fluency on five levels

practitioner initially to render the target culture comprehensible to himself or herself. Indeed, they may be accurate to a cèrtain degree, but they are restrictive. Even ten, twenty, thirty stereotypic categories relating to a particular culture do not add up to anything like cultural fluency. They indicate at best a superficial level of insight, rather like knowing one thousand words in a foreign language but being totally ignorant of the grammar which modifies and marshals those linguistic building-blocks in a meaningful manner.

Too many business practitioners are content to remain at this, the second level of fluency. They are proud of themselves for having recognised cultural diversity in the first place and are convinced that their minimalist toolkit of stereotypes will help them through any cultural encounter in which they are likely to be involved. Some of them may be lucky; for many others, however, staying at this level could be fraught with danger.

Level 3: challenging stereotypes

Any practitioner with regular exposure to cultural episodes must encounter situations which regularly fail to match stereotypic categories. The consequence must be, at the third level of fluency, to recognise challenges which help in breaking out from the stereotypes. Challenges to stereotypes arise constantly from the beliefs, attitudes, values and behaviours in the target culture. For example: attitudes to the primary role of technology (important for most but not all Germans); beliefs in the need for goal-identification (most but not all North Americans) versus the will of Allah (most but not all Arabs); values like the relative importance of the individual (again, most but not all North Americans) as opposed to interdependence (most but not all Chinese); patterns of behaviour such as good time-keeping (most but not all Danes) or a more cavalier approach to punctuality (most but not all Italians).

Level 4: analysis of cultural episodes

To attain the fourth level of fluency, the practitioner must adopt a more active role. Hitherto, he or she has been fairly passive; cultural diversity, stereotypes and challenges to stereotypes have presented themselves to the learner. The mental effort needed at the first three levels of fluency has been restricted to awareness of diversity, compartmentalisation of the stereotypes, and alertness in recognising the challenges to stereotypes. Now a step-change in mental activity is required. The time has come for the practitioner to reflect in some depth and analyse the cultural episodes through which he or she has passed. This activity increases competence in decoding, and beginning to encode, cultural messages. Again, the analogy with linguistic competence offers itself; the learner is moving from passive understanding to active mastery of the foreign tongue.

Level 5: generation of fluent messages in the other culture

The practitioner becomes fluent when messages from the other culture can be decoded successfully and appropriate responses can be encoded as if from within the target culture itself. A standard of fluency has been achieved which is akin to that proposed by Brislin et al (1983) and described as the facility 'to walk in the other's moccasins'. Once practitioners have reached this level of cultural fluency, they have virtually 'become the other' (p 5). Now they are constantly evaluating messages, judging messages against the store of signals which they have accumulated in their own mental databases. Moreover, they possess the flexibility of response either to alter the database or to match incoming messages with those already recognised. Indeed, Hofstede (1991) refers to culture itself as 'the software of the mind'.

Fluency in one target culture often produces the ability and confidence required to move on to master fluency in another. This second target culture and any others which are encountered should, however, be approached with the same rigour as applied to the first. Otherwise, the danger is ever present that appreciation of these other cultures will stall at the second level, that of the stereotypic organisation of messages.

HOW BUSINESS CULTURE IMPACTS INTERNATIONAL BUSINESS

Sadly, a substantial weight of examples relating to the impact of business culture refer to mistakes or businesses which foundered on the rocks of cultural misunderstanding. The travelling business executive has to come to terms with these differences and learn to step outside his or her own cultural parameters if he or she is to be successful. A particularly good example of this in action is recounted in Adler (1991).

A Scottish executive on his first visit to Japan was keen to sample the local food and to stay in a traditional Japanese hotel. On one memorable evening, when they had finished dinner, he was astonished to be asked, 'Can I sleep with you?' in a very embarrassed way by his Japanese host. Fearing the consequences of putting the business at risk, but with trepidation, he agreed. The host had his mattress fetched from his room and laid it down next to that of the Scot. The night passed without incident. He later learned that for the traditional Japanese, one of the greatest compliments you can be paid is for the host to ask to sleep with you. This dates back to feudal times when the invitation implied trust that you would not be killed during your sleep. Henceforth you are by implication 'true friends'.

Another obvious area of influence of different national cultures is the buying habits and advertising standards which affect the sorts of products that can be successfully marketed. What makes a product sell fantastically in one country does not necessarily transfer to another.

Diversity within the European brewing industry is a case in point. Recent research into the area concluded that the markets varied significantly from country to country. In Denmark, 74 per cent of beer is drunk at home, whilst in Ireland the figure is only 6 per cent. Tastes also differ significantly according to national or even regional variations. Germany, for instance, has a tradition for very localised consumption with the vast majority of production being sold within a small radius of the individual brewery. Even products which may be considered as 'essentials' in one country, can have a totally different cultural connotation in another. Toothpaste, for example, is considered as a therapeutic product in the UK and Holland, whereas in Spain and Greece it is viewed as a cosmetic. This has obvious implications for the product's advertising, so that in the latter two countries commercials are much more glamorous. Mismatching assumptions about such products could be potentially very harmful to an organisation's sales success and image overall.

Beyond these two externally focused areas there are fundamental questions that need to be addressed within the organisation if the best use of local resources is to be made. Recruitment and selection policies should be checked for cultural bias. Attitudes towards employing women and members of the same family may be different. Pay and reward systems may be related to group rather than individual performance.

These influences cannot be ignored by the organisation wishing to operate successfully across boundaries. Failure to take account of them in the past has led to spectacular mistakes by major corporations.

LESSONS FOR MANAGERS

- All business cultures are relative, and not absolute. What is regarded as a virtue in one culture may be regarded as a vice in another. For example, the high value which North Americans place on time can cause them to act in ways which other cultures interpret as offensive. Or, the Far East's polite behaviour of avoiding eye contact with strangers can be perceived as shiftiness, insecurity, or lack of courtesy.
- What is seen is easier to handle than what remains unseen. The most

obvious cultural differences, such as name customs or greetings rituals, can be assimilated with most ease. The more covert, intangible differences, such as power and leadership assumptions, response styles, non-verbal signals of agreement and disagreement are very difficult to master.

- All people react emotionally, not just rationally, to cultural differences. For example, even if we are perfectly aware that another culture prefers a short conversation distance, it is difficult not to back away when one's personal space is being invaded. It is all too easy to offend and feel offence without realising it.

- The international business manager should be flexible. Most cultural differences can be bridged if other people are carefully observed and sufficient thought is given to the process. The international manager must always be aware that all cultures have their own validity and that his or her culture is not inherently better or more worthy than any other.

The international manager is no fool. He or she would not be allowed by their company to operate across borders or overseas if they lacked intelligence, drive, and a high degree of sensibility. And it is this latter quality of sensibility, or the facility to react with sensitivity to other people's ways of doing things, that is the key to success in other business cultures. As businesspeople drive across frontiers or step out of aircraft on to foreign soil, it is this sixth sense of sensibility that should be at its sharpest and most receptive. Only then can most of the pitfalls, which illuminate the ever-burgeoning literature on national business cultures, be avoided.

REFERENCES

Adler, N J (1991) 'International Dimensions of Organisational Behaviour', 2nd Ed, *Kent International Business Series*, Kent Publishing Company, Boston, Massachusetts

Albert, R D (1983) 'The Intercultural Sensitizer or Culture Assimilator: A Cognitive Approach', in Brislin, R W and Landis, D (eds) *Handbook of Intercultural Training*, Vol 2, Pergamon, Toronto

Baxter, J (1983) 'English for Intercultural Competence: An Approach to Intercultural Communication Training', in Brislin, R W and Landis, D (eds), *Handbook of Intercultural Training*, Vol 2, Pergamon, Toronto

Beamer, L (1992) 'Learning Intercultural Communication Competence', *The Journal of Business Communication*, Vol 29, No 3

Bowman, J P and Targowski, A S (1987) 'Modelling the Communication Process: The Map is not the Territory', *The Journal of Business Communication*, Vol 24, No 4

Brewster, C (1991) 'Culture: The International Dimensions', *Cranfield Working Paper*, 5, Cranfield University

Brislin, R W, Landis, D and Brandt, M E (1983) 'Conceptualizations of Intercultural Behaviour and Training', in Brislin, R and Landis, D (eds), *Handbook of Intercultural Training*, Vol 2, Pergamon, Toronto

Gudykunst, W B and Kim, Y Y (1984) *Communicating with Strangers*, Random House, New York

Gudykunst, W B and Hammer, M R (1983) 'Basic Training Design: Approaches to Intercultural Training', in Brislin, R and Landis, D (eds), *Handbook of Intercultural Training*, Vol 1, Pergamon, New York

Guido, G (1991) 'Implementing a Pan European Marketing Strategy', *Long Range Planning*, Vol 24, No 5

Hall, E T (1959) *The Silent Language*, Anchor, Garden City, New York

Hofstede, G (1991) *Culture and Organisations: Software of the Mind*, McGraw-Hill, London

Randlesome, C and Butler, S (1992) 'Business Environment and Business Culture', *Business Studies*, Vol 5, No 1

Samovar, L A, Porter, R E and Jain, N N (1981) *Understanding Intercultural Communication*, Wadsworth Publishing Company, Belmont, California

Terpstra, V and David, K (1991) *The Cultural Environment of International Business*, South-Western Publishing Company, Cincinatti

RESULTS

Frequencies, means and standard deviations of the variables characterising expatriates, spouses and their expatriate environments are displayed in Table 4.1. Correlations between these variables are displayed in Table 4.3.

The relationship between the influence of the expatriate environment and the extent of social activities with host nationals is displayed in Table 4.2.

Correlations between these characterising variables and the respondents' perceptions of the programme are shown in Table 4.4 for expatriates and in Table 4.5 for spouses.

Correlations between the spouses' perceptions of the programme and the degree of difficulty they encountered in adjusting to aspects of the expatriate environment appear in Table 4.6.

The results in terms of the hypotheses we established are interesting. Firstly (H1), expatriates and their partners are very positive about the value of this kind of preparation prior to the assignment. Murray and Murray (1986) suggest that information briefings make little difference to subsequent performance on the assignment. Whilst our study did not address performance specifically, it is clear that the expatriates themselves believe firmly that such briefings have helped them in their assignments.

Expatriates and their partners (H2) tended to be almost equally positive about the programme although there was some variation with regard to certain of its elements. For example, women were more critical of the 'living in the host community' elements of the programme.

Expatriates were divided into three age groups: under 30, 30–39, over 39. There were no significant differences between the responses of these age groups (H3).

Expatriates were asked whether (a) this was their first expatriate assignment or (b) they had previous expatriate experience. They were also asked to list their most recent six expatriate assignment destinations and durations. 'Previous expatriate experience' was restricted to those respondents who reported at least six months sojourn in a single destination. There were no significant differences in response between those with and those without previous expatriate experience (H4).

The point of data capture (H5) made little difference: those on assignment appeared to be a little less positive than those yet to depart, and those who had returned from the assignment were less positive still. Responses were not significantly modified by time elapsed since

Table 4.1 Personal and environmental variables

	Frequency	Percentage		
Age of the expatriate ('AGE')				
Up to 29 years	37	15	Cases	254
30 to 39 years	112	44	Mean	38.6
40 years and over	105	41	Std Dev	8.83
Previous expatriate experience ('EXP')				
1 First assignment	111	44	Cases	254
2 Previous experience	143	56	Mean	1.56
			Std Dev	0.5
Expatriate status ('CAPTURE')				
1 Pre-departure	15	6	Cases	252
2 On assignment	161	64	Mean	2.24
3 Returned	76	30	Std Dev	0.55
Type of sponsoring organisation ('EMP')				
1 Commercial	193	82	Cases	236
2 Mission	36	15	Mean	1.18
3 Teaching culture	7	3	Std Dev	0.39
Expected length of expatriate assignment (measured in months) ('LENGTH')				
12 months	9	4	Cases	232
24 months	74	32	Mean	33.5
36 months	98	42	Std Dev	12.08
48 months	40	17		
60 months	11	5		
Time on current assignment (measured in months) ('PART')				
Up to 2 months	6	4	Cases	160
3 to 11 months	16	10	Mean	28.55
12 to 23 months	36	22	Std Dev	14.26
24 to 35 months	60	37		
36 to 47 months	32	20		
48 months or more	11	7		
Influence of the expatriate community ('COMM')				
1 Small	23	14	Cases	165
2 Medium	41	25	Mean	2.47
3 Large	101	61	Std Dev	0.73
Extent of socialisation with host nationals ('SOCAT')				
1 Almost none	68	42	Cases	162
2 25%	44	27	Mean	2.1
3 50%	24	15	Std Dev	1.21
4 75%	18	11		
5 Almost all	8	5		

Table 4.2 Relationship between size of the expatriate community and interaction with host nationals

Expatriate community	Almost none	25%	50% or more	
Small	2	2	19	Cases
	9.7	6.2	7.1	Expected Value
	8.7	8.7	82.6	Row %
	2.9	4.5	38.0	Column %
Medium	12	14	14	Cases
	16.8	10.9	12.3	Expected Value
	30.0	35.0	35.0	Row %
	17.6	31.8	28.0	Column %
Large	54	28	17	Cases
	41.6	26.9	30.6	Expected Value
	54.5	28.3	17.2	Row %
	79.4	63.6	34.0	Column %

*Chi-Square Statistic:*41.2 *Significance:* 0.0000

assignment, however, which implies that 'point of data capture' is a step function, and that the psychological effects caused by arrival in the assigned country take place comparatively rapidly.

Destination (H6) was a significant variable, but in an unexpected way. Responses were broadly similar for all destinations across the world, with the exception of North America and Europe. The numbers for these destinations are comparatively small, so that this finding has to be treated with caution. Three related reasons can be advanced for it. First, the Centre for International Briefing has only recently begun to offer courses in these two areas: it is possible, therefore, that this lack of experience means that the programmes are not so well presented. Second, there is evidence (Hofstede 1980, Laurent 1983) that these areas are culturally similar to the United Kingdom, so that the traditional Centre programmes are less relevant and the expatriate and their families require less preparation. Third, these are areas which tend anyway to be much more familiar to the mainly British expatriates and their partners who attend the Centre: their knowledge of these areas is much higher, through all forms of media and often via personal visits or holidays, so they start from a higher base and are more critical of the programmes.

The type of organisation that the expatriate worked for (H7) made little difference to responses.

For both expatriate and spouse, the variable which most affected their perceptions of the programme was 'influence of the expatriate community' (H8). This variable significantly modified 7 of the 15

Table 4.3 Correlations between personal and environmental variables

VARIABLES		AGE	EXP	CAPTURE	EMP	LENGTH	PART	COMM
EXP	Previous expatriate experience	0.28 ***						
CAPTURE	Point of data capture	–0.08	–0.13 *					
EMP	Type of sponsor	0.11	0.13 *	–0.06				
LENGTH	Expected length of assignment	0.17 **	0.15 *	–0.22 ***	–0.03			
PART	Time on assignment	0.00	–0.09	–0.06	–0.14	0.26 **		
COMM	Influence of expat community	0.01	0.07	–0.02	–0.02	0.07	0.24 **	
SOCACT	Socialisation with host nationals	0.02	–0.06	0.13	0.17 *	–0.16	–0.03	–0.54 ***

Two-tailed significance
* 0.050
** 0.010
*** 0.001

Table 4.4 Expatriate variables, standard deviations and correlations

VARIABLES		MEAN	STD DEV	AGE	CAPTURE	PREV EXP	LENGTH	TIME OUT	EMPLOY	XPA COMM	SOCACT
FRECOMM	Recommend the programme	1.08	0.26	−0.08	0.10	−0.02	−0.04	−0.15	0.05	−0.24 **	0.08
FAIMS	Programme met its aims	2.56	1.04	−0.12	1.17 **	−0.10	−0.02	−0.10	−0.12	−0.17 *	−0.12
	Help with:										
FHELP1	Interacting with host nationals at work	1.94	0.61	0.18 **	−0.04	0.13	0.03	0.03	0.03	0.06	0.02
FHELP2	Interacting with host nationals day to day	1.94	0.56	0.19 **	0.02	0.12	−0.03	0.03	0.07	0.08	0.01
FHELP3	Everyday customs	2.01	0.56	0.05	−0.04	0.04	0.00	−0.07	0.00	0.19 *	0.07
FHELP4	General living conditions	2.02	0.61	0.07	0.01	0.04	−0.13 *	−0.01	0.19 **	0.10	−0.03
FHELP5	How host nationals view expatriates	1.72	0.66	0.11	−0.08	0.10	0.02	−0.07	0.05	−0.03	−0.13
FHELP6	How host nationals view women	1.96	0.63	0.02	−0.13	0.13	0.04	−0.11	0.01	0.20 *	0.03
FHELP7	Socialising with host nationals	1.79	0.64	0.08	0.08	0.06	0.10	0.05	0.01	0.17 *	0.07
FHELP8	Interaction with the expat community	1.82	0.62	0.02	0.02	−0.03	−0.02	−0.05	0.04	0.17 *	0.12
FHELP9	Climate	2.20	0.61	0.08	0.08	−0.02	0.00	0.14	0.07	0.20 *	0.10
FHELP10	Shopping	1.85	0.66	0.09	0.09	−0.01	0.00	0.01	0.12	0.05	−0.09
FHELP11	Transport	1.72	0.53	−0.07	−0.07	−0.03	−0.09	−0.02	0.06	0.07	−0.03
FHELP12	Home help	1.78	0.67	−0.02	−0.02	0.05	0.01	0.15	0.08	0.15	0.14
RFHELP13	Medical facilities	1.96	0.64	0.12	0.04	0.07	−0.13	−0.10	0.18 *	0.04	−0.07

Two-tailed significance
* 0.050
** 0.010
*** 0.001

Table 4.5 Spouse variables: means, standard deviations and correlations

VARIABLES		MEAN	STD DEV	AGE	CAPTURE	PREV EXP	LENGTH	TIME OUT	EMPLOY	XPA COMM	SOCACT
SRECOMM	Recommend the programme	1.05	0.22	–0.08	0.04	–0.03	–0.05	0.00	–0.02	–0.23 **	–0.15
SAIMS	Programme met its aims	2.46	1.07	0.20 **	0.20 *	–0.07	0.03	0.12	–0.17 *	–0.30 **	–0.19 *
	Help with:										
SHELP1	Interacting with host nationals day to day	1.82	0.58	0.17 *	–0.12	0.02	0.00	–0.02	0.14	0.33 **	0.14
SHELP2	Everyday customs	1.88	0.55	0.08	–0.09	0.02	0.09	0.01	0.09	0.26 **	0.17 *
SHELP3	General living conditions	1.90	0.64	0.20 *	–0.10	0.13	–0.01	0.03	0.19 *	0.18 *	0.12
SHELP4	How host nationals view expatriates	1.70	0.58	0.20 *	–0.05	0.09	–0.13	–0.04	0.11	0.01	–0.06
SHELP5	How host nationals view women	1.67	0.64	0.17	–0.01	0.04	0.11	–0.12	0.03	0.13	0.05
SHELP6	Socialising with host nationals	1.71	0.58	0.16	–0.08	0.00	0.15	–0.02	–0.01	0.09	–0.03
SHELP7	Interaction with the expat community	1.86	0.59	–0.03	–0.13	0.06	0.03	–0.06	0.02	0.31 **	0.25 **
SHELP8	Climate	1.99	0.59	–0.06	–0.04	–0.03	0.04	0.13	0.10	0.22 **	0.25 **
SHELP9	Shopping	1.78	0.58	–0.06	0.12	–0.02	–0.02	0.15	0.17 *	0.35 **	0.26 ***
SHELP10	Transport	1.63	0.59	0.09	0.07	–0.01	–0.12	0.09	0.12	0.26 **	0.24 **
SHELP11	Home help	1.75	0.63	0.08	–0.11	–0.03	–0.04	–0.02	–0.04	0.25 **	0.21 *
SHELP12	Medical facilities	1.92	0.66	–0.02 *	0.02	0.05	0.03	0.07	0.03	0.25 **	0.12
SEASY1	Ease of adjustment to:	2.64	1.18	–0.12	–0.03	0.02	0.05	0.01	–0.23 **	–0.04	–0.25 **
SEASY2	Interacting with host nationals day to day	2.39	0.85	–0.57	–0.12	0.14	–0.08	–0.10	–0.18 *	–0.08	–0.20 **
SEASY3	Everyday customs	2.23	0.97	0.03	0.00	0.00	–0.12	–0.13	–0.07	–0.16 *	–0.04
SEASY4	General living conditions	1.69	1.02	–0.13	0.05	0.05	0.02	0.00	–0.17 *	0.07	–0.16 *
SEASY5	How host nationals view expatriates	2.98	1.21	–0.11	–0.02	0.10	0.07	0.07	–0.11	0.05	–0.18 *
SEASY6	How host nationals view women	2.88	1.21	–0.19 *	–0.14	0.12	0.23 **	–0.07	–0.17 *	0.10	–0.35 ***
SEASY7	Socialising with host nationals	1.87	1.00	0.00	–0.06	–0.06	–0.04	0.05	–0.03	–0.30 **	0.29 ***
SEASY8	Interaction with the expat community	2.44	1.01	0.13	0.09	0.09	0.06	0.01	0.03	–0.13	0.11
SEASY9	Climate	2.54	1.10	–0.02	0.07	0.07	–0.06	–0.12	0.10	–0.22 **	–0.04
SEASY10	Shopping	2.73	1.25	0.07	0.04	–0.05	0.01	–0.05	–0.08	–0.11	–0.01
SEASY11	Transport	2.12	1.07	0.08	–0.05	–0.06	–0.05	0.03	–0.05	–0.18 *	0.07
SEASY12	Home help	2.59	1.23	–0.14	0.02	0.03	–0.12	–0.08	–0.01	–0.32 **	0.15
	Medical facilities										

Two-tailed significance
* 0.050
** 0.010
*** 0.001

Table 4.6 Correlations between ease of adjustment and perception of training programme

VARIABLES	SPOUSE	SHELP1	SHELP2	SHELP3	SHELP4	SHELP5	SHELP6	SHELP7	SHELP8	SHELP9	SHELP10	SHELP11	SHELP12
	Ease of adjustment to:												
SEASY1	Interacting with host nationals day to day	–0.15	0.07	–0.13	–0.16	–0.05	–0.21 *	–0.06	0.07	–0.11	0.01	–0.19 *	–0.09
SEASY2	Everyday customs	–0.13	–0.08	–0.04	–0.08	–0.02	–0.13	–0.03	–0.02	–0.13	–0.10	–0.14	–0.06
SEASY3	General living	–0.13	–0.08	–0.18 *	–0.05	0.01	–0.13	–0.06	0.09	–0.19 *	–0.11	–0.17	–0.06
SEASY4	How host nationals view expatriates	–0.10	–0.05	–0.04	–0.16	–0.04	–0.07	–0.07	0.07	0.01	0.11	–0.06	–0.02
SEASY5	How host nationals view women	–0.08	0.03	–0.02	–0.10	–0.07	–0.11	–0.07	0.11	–0.08	0.00	–0.03	0.02
SEASY6	Socialising with host nationals	–0.08	0.03	–0.07	–0.21 **	–0.05	–0.33 **	–0.02	0.15	0.06	0.04	–0.13	–0.03
SEASY7	Interaction with the expat community	–0.20 *	–0.20 *	–0.09	–0.15	–0.08	–0.21 *	–0.02	0.15	0.06	0.04	–0.13	–0.03
SEASY8	Climate	–0.17 *	–0.03	–0.07	–0.08	–0.10	–0.14	–0.03	–0.04	–0.14	–0.07	–0.03	–0.03
SEASY9	Shopping	–0.24 **	–0.18 *	–0.29 **	–0.12	–0.14	–0.19 *	–0.14	–0.06	–0.40 **	–0.31 ***	–0.16	–0.23 **
SEASY10	Transport	–0.16	0.03	–0.16 *	–0.04	–0.07	–0.14	–0.09	0.14	–0.15	–0.18 *	–0.05	–0.14
SEASY11	Home help	–0.30 **	–0.09	–0.22 **	–0.21 *	–0.17	–0.29 **	–0.23 **	–0.09	–0.17 *	–0.13	–0.35 ***	–0.17
SEASY12	Medical facilities	–0.29 **	–0.16	–0.35 **	–0.17 *	–0.30 ***	–0.24 **	–0.34 **	–0.12	–0.34 **	–0.25 **	–0.14	–0.33 ***

Two-tailed significance
* 0.050
** 0.010
*** 0.001

expatriate responses, and 11 of the 14 spouse responses. Both expatriates and spouses in locations with influential expatriate communities were more likely to recommend the programme, more likely to consider that it had met its aim, and more likely to find the programme helpful with adjustment to the environment.

The influence of the variable 'extent of social activity with host nationals' (H9) significantly modified responses for the spouse, but not for the expatriate: this despite its high (negative) correlation with 'influence of the expatriate community'.

Spouses with higher levels of social interaction with host nationals found the programme to have been more helpful in adjusting to 6 of the 12 environmental aspects: these same 6 environmental aspects were also modified by the variable 'influence of the expatriate community'.

By contrast, 'influence of the expatriate community' modified spouse responses to 4 of the 12 questions relating to ease or difficulty of adjusting to the environment, while 'extent of social activity with host nationals' modified spouse responses to 6 of the same 12 questions: the 2 variables, however, tended to influence different responses so that, between them, 9 of the 12 responses were modified by these 2 variables.

The interaction of these 2 variables, then, appears to be as follows: larger expatriate communities lead to lower levels of interaction with host nationals and easier adjustment to the environment, yet higher levels of interaction with host nationals also lead to easier adjustment to the environment.

After considering the implications of this interaction, therefore, we propose a model of the adjustment process which appears in Figure 4.1. This model applies particularly to the spouse, and may be somewhat less valid for the expatriate.

We propose that:

- Large expatriate communities provide considerable levels of support to the newly arrived spouse, and can act to isolate the spouse from the host environment. This support and isolation allows the spouse to 'adjust' relatively easily, (though this 'adjustment' may be more to the local expatriate community than to the host country environment itself). Therefore, spouses will be more likely to find the training to have been 'very helpful' or 'helpful.'

- In some locations having an influential expatriate community, a minority of spouses will seek out and/or accept social activity with, and support from, host nationals, in addition to accepting the mutual support available from the expatriate community. Having the best of

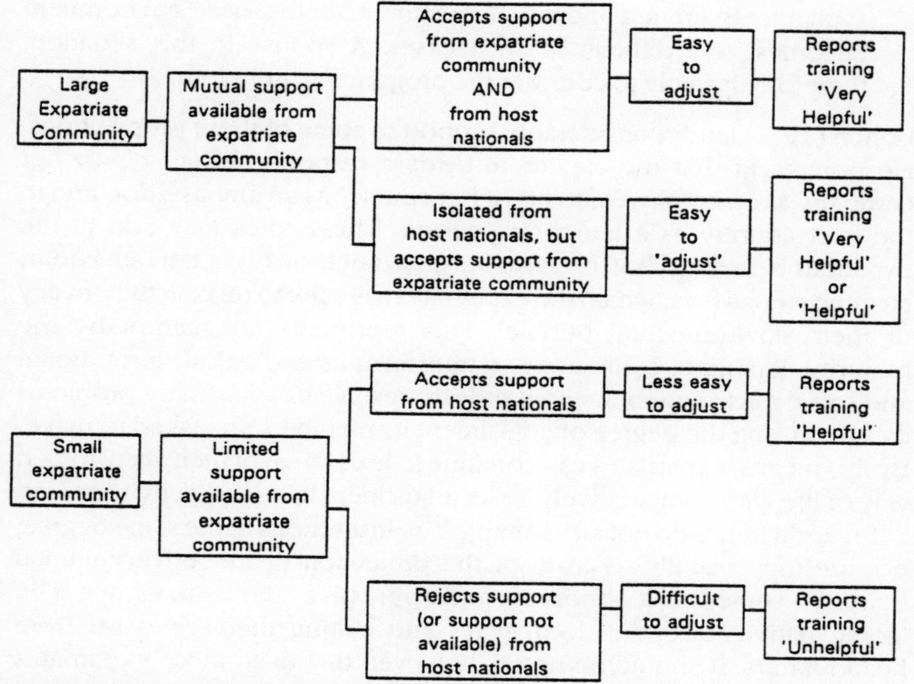

Figure 4.1 Proposed model of the influence of the expatriate community upon adjustment and perception of training

both worlds, as it were, these spouses find it comparatively easy to adjust to the host environment. This easy adjustment also leads them to determine the programme to have been 'very helpful' or 'helpful'.

- Small expatriate communities will be less able to provide support to the newly arrived spouse, and will have less scope for isolating the spouse from the host environment. If social interaction with host nationals is possible and is accepted by the spouse, then this interaction may provide a significant measure of support and assistance in adjusting to the new environment. The process of adjustment is, however, likely to be more difficult than it would have been in a location having a significant expatriate community. A spouse in this situation, therefore, may have some difficulty in adjusting to the host environment. This will be reflected back in their attitude to the training, which they will judge as having been less successful in helping them to adjust.
- In a location having a small expatriate community and where social interaction is seen as difficult or is rejected by the spouse, the support

available is limited indeed. Adjustment to the host environment becomes very difficult in such cases. A spouse in this situation, therefore, is likely to consider the programme 'unhelpful'.

Cohen (1977) lends considerable support to some of these propositions. He points out that the expatriate bears a responsibility to his or her company as an employee, to his or her country as an ambassador, and to the host country as a temporary citizen. These roles may add to the expatriate's prestige, but they also put constraints on his or her behaviour, creating strains from which the expatriate may seek to relax in the privacy of their 'environmental bubble'. This represents an attempt by the minority expatriate community to transform its ecological, institutional and social microenvironment in order to resolve its adjustment problems by minimising the degree of adjustment its members are asked to make. By this means, expatriates can continue to lead much of their accustomed way of life with comparatively lesser adjustment to the host environment.

But individuals do not all use expatriate institutions to the same degree, nor are they equally desirous of the protection of the 'environmental bubble' – some find it obnoxious and oppressive, and try to escape it by 'going native', adopting local ways and cutting themselves off from headquarters. It should be noted, however, that even those expatriates tend to avail themselves occasionally of both its institutions and its social support.

Female spouses experience more severe adjustment problems than male expatriates. Firstly because the expatriate community is male centred: it is usually the husband's job which is the *raison d'être* for the family's stay abroad. His associates and companions in the sponsoring organisation define the context within which social relationships and friendship circles are established. Secondly, while the husband's role is continuous, it is the wife who must transfer family life to the new surroundings, build new friendships, and deal with issues about health and schools. Furthermore, the role of the wife is likely to change: working women may be unable to continue working, and the accustomed housewife's role may be changed through different household arrangements and by the availability of cheap household help.

That wives face severe and particular adjustment problems becomes important when laid against research indicating that spouse adjustment is a major factor in the success or failure of expatriates (Harvey 1985, Tung 1981). Much of this work relied upon the opinions of US human resource managers. Nevertheless, empirical research (Black 1988, Black and Stephens 1989) has found a significant and positive relationship between spouse and expatriate adjustments.

or the personal dilemmas faced by local managers working for multinational corporations operating in their home country.

Existing research in this area has concentrated on how, for example, Japanese multinationals localised their management staff in the US or Europe (Sigiura 1990, Negandhi and Serapio 1991) and the implications for the company of replacing expatriate managers (Yoshihara 1987, Kobrin 1989). In general such research has looked at the implications of localisation from the multinational or head office perspective, rather than from the perspective of the localised manager. As a result, contemporary research into the role of multinational managers is arguably too reliant on the perspective of expatriate managers, and rooted in the experience of the industrialised world. Researchers have rarely concerned themselves with the dynamics of localisation, the pressures to localise, the operational and financial implications, the difficulties of localising management in developing countries, or the potential conflict of interest or cross-cultural dilemmas faced by such local managers, nor the process of selecting and training local managers (Buckley and Brooke 1992).

These are crucial issues for local managers working in cultures that are very different from the home country or dominant culture of the multinational involved. Thus, for local managers of US multinationals operating in Europe such issues are seen as a hassle, rather than a matter of major concern. But for a local manager employed by the same company in, for example, a developing country with a distinct cultural identity, social structure or economic base such issues are a matter of serious concern. For too long these issues have been overlooked by researchers. Whether this reflects a lack of commercial sponsorship, academic recognition or merely ethnocentric bias is debatable; but obviously as more firms operate in the diverse cultures and expanding markets of the developing world, the issues raised by the use of local managers appointed to positions of trust and responsibility deserve further exploration.

In many developing countries the post-independence pressure to localise and remove expatriate managers from high-profile positions (particularly the older generation of experienced, but somewhat intractable, 'colonial expats') has had to be balanced with the need to employ local executives who could be trusted, who understood company procedures, and who could manage effectively in the contemporary international business environment (Negandhi 1983). The development of local managers with the knowledge, expertise and experience required to mobilise resources in a timely and cost-effective manner is crucial to long-term profitability.

This process can also be seen as part of the wider development process, and in many cases the immediate costs of indigenisation have to be seen as a tradeoff between short-term sacrifice and longer-term developmental goals. As Potter (1989) commented, 'the key problem facing many multinationals and local organizations in Third World countries is how to balance the two goals of high quality and a nationalised work-force'. He identified the major obstacles to effective localisation as: inappropriate job specifications, irrelevant training, cultural attitudes to the value of training, impatience and ambition, an underestimation of the skills and experience required, and the attitude of expatriates and their attempts to maintain local dependence on themselves.

Unfortunately because of these obstacles, and the associated costs, it has not always been possible to maintain momentum to develop and promote local managerial talent. This may partly explain both the failure to retain the staff that have been trained, and the failure to develop a second generation of local managers. Such staff are all too often tempted away by high-paying positions in international agencies, the local business community, consultancies or politics. In the resulting managerial vacuum a variety of third country nationals, return-expats or consultants (disguised expats) have had to be employed at great expense.

The issue of failed retention was explored by Cohen in his review of the role of expatriates in Kenya. He examines why it is that a disproportionately high number of local staff who have been trained to take over positions previously held by expatriates do not actually fill these posts; or if they do, they are transferred or resign in a relatively short space of time. He suggests that this phenomenon can be partly explained by the fact that the training provided is of limited practical relevance, and that the selection and promotion procedures are often inappropriate or biased; but, most importantly, because the post-training terms and conditions offered to such ambitious highly trained young managers or civil servants are so poor that they offer little incentive for such high flyers to take such positions, particularly as there are plenty of other employers ready to poach such talent (Cohen 1991).

The failure to maintain the localisation momentum of promoting and training second generation managers can be partly explained by the lack of investment in management training, but also possibly by an unwillingness of first generation managers to invest in a new managerial elite that might jeopardise the status quo or threaten their position. There is sufficient evidence in hindsight to suggest that this first generation managerial elite used their positions to further their own personal, business, or political ambitions. Many therefore either relaxed, resigned, or milked their position for their own political or entrepreneurial gain.

Moreover, as many of the first generation of local managers were promoted to relatively senior positions at an early age, a career log-jam at the top of the organisation developed, which limited the promotion chances of younger managers. Furthermore, many of this first generation of local managers felt threatened by these younger, ambitious, often better educated, management trainees. This state of affairs did little to add to the morale of younger, second generation, managers who could see little future in the company. This failure to develop or motivate a second generation management cadre, meant that many left or failed to fulfil their potential. The consequent managerial vacuum means that many companies face the 1990s with a young and inexperienced team of third generation managers, who have had limited training or international exposure, and are ill equipped to assume senior positions. In some cases this has resulted in companies having to employ return-expats or consultants in executive positions. This not only reflects the cyclical nature of the expatriation process, but also highlights the problems associated with the ongoing process of localisation.

EXPATRIATION AND LOCALISATION

It is obviously hard to estimate the total numbers of expatriates that are employed in both the public and private sectors internationally; but the evidence suggests that, while their public profile and importance is less apparent than it was a generation ago, the number of expatriates has increased in real terms. The most obvious growth internationally has been in the numbers of aid-funded expatriates and itinerant consultants working in both the public and private sectors.

It is difficult to gauge the number of expatriate managers employed by established multinationals and their subsidiaries, let alone by the growing number of smaller companies who are expanding internationally. But it appears that their numbers are still rising because of the number of new joint-venture operations, strategic alliances, the expansion of the service sector (particularly commerce, tourism, and transport), and new investments in mining, energy and export manufacturing in Economic Free Zones. Recent research by Scullion (1992) in the United Kingdom suggests that 50 per cent of companies operating overseas had increased the number of expatriates they employed during the 1980s, while only 20 per cent had reduced the number. Research by Brewster (1991) indicates that multinationals continue to employ expatriates because of the need for shareholder control and coordination with local partners, their technical expertise and managerial capability, or their understanding of corporate procedures, international markets, banks and financial systems.

Researchers cite contrary evidence as to the numbers of expatriates working overseas. Some point to the reduction in the number of expatriate executives employed by Japanese, Swedish and US multinationals, and the corresponding increase in the number of local managers employed (Kobrin 1989), whereas others suggest that there has been an expansion in the relative number of expatriates working, for example, within the European Community countries because of legislation that removes cross-border employment restrictions (Brewster 1991, Scullion 1992). However, all the indicators from the developing world point to an increasing use of expatriates despite the efforts to localise key positions. Recent figures suggest that there are well over 200,000 advisers, consultants and seconded experts currently working in the Third World; and more specifically in the late 1980s in the 40 sub-Saharan Africa countries the World Bank estimated that there were at least 100,000 resident foreign advisers employed at cost of $4 billion annually (World Bank 1989).

This continued role of expatriates in many developing countries reflects the recognition of the need for such external expertise to help tackle some of the intractable problems associated with development. This perception is reflected in the context of Africa by the observation that:

> If you look at the handful of African countries that have combined economic progress with political stability since Independence . . . they all use a large number of Europeans in the private and public sectors. By moving cautiously in the 'Africanization' of their economies, the countries maintained levels of expertise in key positions and were less apt to be run on a trial-and-error basis by untrained Africans. (Lamb, 1982)

Notwithstanding this perception many multinationals faced strong pressure to localise key management positions that was hard to resist. This pressure came from three distinct forces: first, the local government and politicians; second, local managers; and third, corporate headquarters.

Pressure from local government

The localisation of high profile senior management positions held by expatriates was seen as an essential part of the post-independence process of nation building. The role of expatriates and multinationals operating in the economy became a political issue, as many local politicians reacted to the perceived economic power of such corporations, encouraged by accusations of transfer pricing, exploitation of local labour or raw materials, and excessive profits. Legislation was therefore introduced to restrict the number of expatriates or ensure a certain proportion of local shareholding. In this way government could be seen to be doing something with high profile popular appeal, which had few immediate repercussions locally. They also used such legislation to quell opposition critics; particularly as accusations of collaborating with multinationals and expatriate managers was a popular weapon used by opposition politicians and trade unionists to criticise the government. Thus in many countries in the years immediately after independence expatriate quotas were established, work permits were restricted, and financial or fiscal controls on expatriate salaries were introduced.

Pressure from local managers

As investment increased and multinational operations expanded in the relatively buoyant economic climate of the developing world in the 1950s and 1960s, multinationals recruited a growing cadre of supervisory and middle management. In time this group became increasingly frustrated at the way their careers were blocked by expatriates holding senior executive positions, some of whom were relatively young or inexperienced, and relied heavily on the experience and contacts of local staff. This frustration was fuelled by their resentment at the perks and fringe benefits enjoyed by expatriate staff, as well as the lack of recognition of their role in the company's success. Consequently trade unions and management associations began to aggressively pressurise companies to reduce the number of expatriates and promote local managers to positions of responsibility.

Pressure from corporate headquarters

Faced with these pressures companies came to see expatriates not only as a public relations liability, but a major block to staff morale or improved productivity. Expatriates became increasingly redundant as a cadre of experienced, well-educated local managers was recruited or developed. Furthermore, because of the growing costs involved in recruiting and maintaining expatriates, they came to be seen as a drain on profits.

Questions were also being asked in corporate headquarters about the quality and capabilities of many career expatriates who had by the early 1970s become increasingly isolated from the changing international business environment, or who were unable to adapt to the cultural and economic challenges facing many newly independent nations. This was also a time when companies found it increasingly difficult to persuade ambitious management recruits to take up what were seen as 'dead-end' expatriate postings with an uncertain future. Moreover, with improved telecommunications and airline links it became much easier for head office executives to maintain regular contacts with overseas subsidiaries from a distance.

Thus a number of inter-related factors coalesced in such a way that multinationals were motivated to localise senior positions. These factors were part political, part financial, but also partly as a result of the internal pressure from within the company itself. In many developing countries the immediate post-independence years were marked by a resurgence of nationalism and visions of self-sufficiency and economic independence. But the pressure to localise came not just from local politicians, but also from the management of multinationals operating in the developing world. As a result many multinational companies reduced their shareholdings in local subsidiaries and began to localise senior management positions.

A key element in the localisation process was increased investment in an accelerated programme of management training for a new generation of indigenous managers. Unfortunately the evidence suggests that there was little ongoing investment in the next, or second, generation of local managers. Consequently a managerial vacuum has appeared that expatriates are again being asked to fill. Expatriates and consultants (who could be classified as disguised-expats) therefore continue to play a significant role in both the public and private sectors of many developing countries. Furthermore experienced expatriates are increasingly requested to return to previous careers; such return-expats commonly play a key managerial role as consultants or counterpart advisers. The following case study explores these issues in the context of Guinness Nigeria Limited, and assesses their long-term implications.

GUINNESS NIGERIA: A CASE STUDY

This analysis of the localisation process undertaken by Guinness Nigeria over the last twenty years reveals the complex dynamics of the localisation process, and highlights some of the limitations of the post-independence localisation process. This case study raises serious questions about the continued role of expatriates and the cyclical nature of the expatriation/localisation process. It is arguable that if international companies are to break this cycle and operate profitably in the burgeoning markets of the developing world the role of expatriate managers should be redefined and greater investment should be made in training appropriate to the needs of a new generation of indigenous managers.

Guinness Nigeria Limited (GNL), a drinks distribution and brewing operation, was established as an equal joint-venture between the United Africa Company (Unilever's West African subsidiary) and the brewers Guinness. GNL established breweries in a number of different regions, developed a national marketing policy, and nation-wide distribution system. As with many similar British-owned subsidiaries most key posts were initially held by a cadre of expatriate managers and technical staff. The pressure to promote local staff and encourage local ownership grew inexorably through the 1960s and '70s, so that by the early 1980s the process of localisation was all but complete.

GNL's localisation process involved three distinct issues:

1. An increase in the level of local shareholding
2. The appointment of Nigerian directors, and
3. A reduction in the number of expatriate managers.

The pressure to localise, as has already been suggested, came from three sources – government, local staff, and corporate head office. This case study attempts to describe briefly the operation of these three different pressure groups, to analyse the dynamics of the localisation process, and to explain the recent reappointment of one of the original cadre of expatriates to a senior executive position.*

Local shareholders

The process of increasing the level of local ownership of GNL began in 1964 when, in line with government policy, the two overseas shareholders (Guinness and Unilever) sold 10 per cent of their holding to the Western Nigeria Development Corporation. Within a year the

* This case study is based on interviews with, and the research of, Dr John Brown who was managing director of Guinness Nigeria Ltd (1976–9), and returned recently to Nigeria as managing director of Jos International Brewery, a Guinness Brewing International joint venture.

company had sold a further 10 per cent to nearly 1,400 local shareholders, and throughout the 1970s the level of shareholding increased substantially. This was partly as a result of legislation enacted in 1972 which required that 40 per cent of company equity be owned by Nigerian interests, and partly because of the Nigerian Enterprises Promotion Decrees of 1977 which increased this figure to 60 per cent. As a result by the end of 1978 over 50,000 Nigerian shareholders owned nearly two-thirds of the company. Yet in reality effective control remained in the hands of the two overseas partners, because the largest individual Nigerian shareholding was only 8.5 per cent and the remaining 40 per cent was controlled by the two overseas shareholders.

Local directors

As pressure to localise grew in the 1970s, the board of directors was not only localised, but began to reflect the ethnic and regional diversity of the country. This was in line with government policy to reflect the 'federal character of the nation'. By 1982 eight out of fourteen board members were Nigerians, and most of them had well-established contacts in both government and the local business community. But despite these moves to localise the board the two overseas parent companies maintained a powerful influence over board decisions through their advisory board and its successor, the liaison committee. Both these comprised company executives with considerable seniority and experience. Thus the advisory board, for example, exerted considerable influence over policy, operational issues, and the appointment of directors and senior managers. As a result the overseas shareholders (Guinness and Unilever) maintained *de facto* control over the operations of the company, and the appointment of local directors to the board did not reflect any real shift in power.

Local managers and executives

It was the localisation or 'Nigerianisation' of the executive directors that signalled a real move towards the localisation of senior management and transfer of power. In 1975 the first Nigerian executive director was appointed, and this process continued so that by 1982 over two-thirds of the executive directors were Nigerian, and the first local managing director was appointed. The decline in the influence of expatriates working for GNL is reflected in Table 5.1, and a change from the position in 1965 when 60 per cent of the company's managers were expatriates, to a situation twenty years later in 1985 when 96 per cent of the management cadre were Nigerians.

Table 5.1 Nigerianisation in GNL for selected years

Year	Expat Mgrs	Nigrn Mgrs	Total Mgrs	% Nigrn	Sales 000s Hl*
1961	7	1	8	12.5	152
1965	22	15	37	40.5	180
1970	17	46	63	73.0	397
1975	21	133	154	86.4	1,068
1980	14	275	289	95.1	1,578
1985	10	300	310	96.7	2,131

* Hl = Hectolitres

Source: GNL records

The pressure to localise

It is worth looking in more detail at the process of Nigerianisation of senior management to see the impact of pressure from both local managers and local politicians, as well as the decision-makers in corporate head office.

Internal pressure from local staff

In the early 1970s the first internal moves towards Nigerianisation were initiated when the authority of the expatriate directors and managers was challenged by local managers in the guise of the Association of Managers of Guinness Nigeria Limited (MSA). The emergence of this informal association took the company by surprise, particularly as most expatriates had prided themselves on their ability to get along with their local colleagues, a feeling not necessarily shared by local managers. In 1971 the first MSA 'Bulletin' pointedly referred to the expatriate management as '15 privileged overlords who assume power of life and death over the 900 Nigerians engaged in the Company'. The Bulletin went on to suggest that these 'overlords' were 'power drunk', and so made the company 'hell on earth' for its employees, who 'live only from hand to mouth thus wallowing in perpetual misery'.

At first the company refused to recognise the MSA officially, thinking incorrectly that the association's concerns reflected the views of only 'four or five' local disaffected managers who had stirred up the affair for their own ends and intimidated the rest. In reality the establishment of the MSA reflected the local management's growing frustrations at their lack of involvement in running the business or in the decision-making process; as well as the lack of recognition of their contribution to the company's success, and a general resentment at the benefits enjoyed by the expatriate managers.

This latter issue was the most tangible in that expatriate staff enjoyed such benefits as an 'intercontinental' allowance of 30 per cent of basic salary, fully furnished accommodation, subsidised electricity, free medical attention, company car and driver, heavily subsidised education, and exclusive use of a beach chalet. As a result the cost of employing an expatriate manager was more than double that of employing a Nigerian manager. This was justified by the company on the grounds that it helped the majority shareholders to maintain effective control over the business, and because they believed that expatriates contributed substantially to the efficiency of the business, an argument which only managed to further antagonise the local management staff.

Other complaints raised by the MSA included concerns at the calibre of recently recruited expatriates vis à vis the capabilities or experience of local staff, and the general attitude of many of the expatriates to Nigerian staff. For example, the fifth MSA Bulletin noted that GNL expatriates had 'nothing else to offer Nigeria than arrogance, intolerance and insensitiveness'.

The feelings generated and the comments articulated in the MSA Bulletins reflected a spontaneous reaction to the rapid changes in post-independence Nigeria, and the position of both the company and expatriates within it. Expatriate complacency was shaken, and the lack of any meaningful dialogue between expatriate managers and local staff was exposed. But once the initial tensions had subsided and consultations commenced, a more open and consultative style of management emerged that was more appropriate to the changing environment of Nigeria in the mid-1970s, and a number of local managers began to be promoted to senior positions.

The frustrations that led to the creation of the MSA was indicative of the tensions that had been developing in Nigeria since independence. There were the understandable frustrations at limited career opportunities within the company because of the dominant position of expatriate managers, and resentment at the privileges they enjoyed. These tensions were fuelled by burgeoning nationalism, a vicious civil war, the oil boom and rapid economic growth, and the resulting political and social instability.

Pressure from the Nigerian government

As with many other newly-independent countries in the 1960s and '70s the various governments introduced policies and legislation designed to ensure that international companies operating in Nigeria began to localise both ownership, boards of directors and management positions. Politicians articulated their concern at the lack of local directors and executives employed by multinationals operating within Nigeria, and threatened punitive legislation. In fact, as has already been noted, legislation was passed in 1972 to ensure that local shareholders controlled at least 40 per cent of multinational subsidiaries operating in the country, and later in 1978 a decree was issued which raised this proportion to 60 per cent local shareholding.

The government attempted to reduce the number of expatriates employed by companies like GNL by limiting the number of work permits available for expatriates. Quotas on the number of expatriates a company could employ existed unofficially even prior to independence. The colonial government had tried to limit not just the number of expatriates, but also to prescribe the jobs they could perform and define their responsibilities to train local counterparts. Immediately after independence in 1960 the government took a relatively liberal view towards the number of expatriates employed in the country as they were seen as essential for Nigeria's push towards industrialisation. But by the early 1970s the quota system began to be operated more rigorously, with work permits only being granted to those with sufficient experience and suitable qualifications. Moreover companies had to submit a succession plan with each application for an expatriate work permit. This plan was expected to include the name of the Nigerian who had been nominated to take over from the expatriate, normally within a three- to five-year period.

Pressure from corporate headquarters

The policy of the major shareholders to reduce the number of expatriates they employed came partly as a result of changing management attitudes and political pressure to localise senior positions, but also partly as a result of the cost of employing expatriates. Such expatriates not only cost double their local counterparts in terms of salary package and fringe benefits provided, but needed (and demanded) an expensive management and personnel support system. Moreover, the cost of employing GNL expatriates became an increasing drain on overall corporate profitability. In most countries, multinationals expected to pay expatriates out of locally generated profits, but in Nigeria foreign exchange restrictions forced overseas shareholders to underwrite expatriate remittances in hard currency. These additional costs became increasingly hard to justify, and pressure was put on GNL to cut costs by reducing the number of expatriates employed in Nigeria.

There was also an added cost in terms of low morale of local staff frustrated because of the presence of expatriates in key positions they felt they could perform equally well, and the consequent impact on productivity and quality. Furthermore the board of directors and the liaison committee recognised that it was hard to justify the continued use of expatriates in all but a few positions because of the time it took for expatriates to adapt to the managerial and cross-cultural demands of post-independence Nigeria, and the availability of increasingly capable and experienced local staff.

Between the early 1970s and the mid-1980s, a great deal appeared to have changed. By 1985 expatriates no longer held executive positions, and despite earlier concerns that productivity and profits would suffer, the evidence suggests otherwise and during the Nigerianisation years (1970–1985) turnover and productivity per manager increased (see Table 5.2). Thus from the perspective of the overseas shareholders the process of localising the GNL management was, for all intents and purposes, completed by 1985, when 96 per cent of the management staff were Nigerian, or 300 out of the 310 managers employed by the company. The 10 remaining expatriates mainly filled key technical and advisory positions, or acted as shareholder representatives.

Table 5.2 GNL's sales and turnover per manager for selected years

Year	Managers*	Turnover N† 000s	Total sales 000s Hl	Sales per manager 000s Hl	Turnover per manager N 000s
1965	37 (22)	10,308	180	4.86	278.6
1970	63 (17)	25,482	397	6.30	404.5
1975	154 (21)	64,550	1,068	6.93	419.1
1980	289 (14)	151,896	1,578	5.46	525.6
1985	310 (10)	258,214	2,131	6.87	833.9

* = Expatriate managers in brackets
† = Naira (Nigerian currency)

Source: GNL records

THE CURRENT POSITION

In general terms the localisation process at GNL has been sufficiently successful for nearly two-thirds of the respondents of a recent survey to agree that GNL was a Nigerian company with foreign shareholders, rather than a foreign company with Nigerian shareholders. The impetus to localise management positions and reduce the number of expatriates employed by GNL can be explained by:

1. Pressure from government that reflected the changing political and economic climate in post-independence Nigeria, a climate which encouraged self-sufficiency and the Nigerianisation of senior positions in all organisations and businesses throughout the country
2. Internal pressure from senior local managers who were frustrated at their role and status within the company, and resentful at the terms and conditions enjoyed by expatriate managers
3. Pressure from overseas shareholders to reduce the number of expatriates employed, partly as a result of changing attitudes and political pressure, and partly because of the rapidly increasing costs, in both financial and operational terms, of employing large numbers of expatriates, as well as a recognition of the skills and experience of local managers.

Although GNL invested heavily, in both time and money, in its efforts to localise senior positions, there is some concern that, along with many other Nigerian companies and multinational subsidiaries, they face the 1990s with a young, often inexperienced, team of third generation managers. The task of these managers is all the more difficult because of economic uncertainty, rising inflation, reduced consumer spending, competitive markets, uncertain profitability, little reinvestment in new plant or training, and growing political interference in the operation of many companies. This situation has been further exacerbated by the recent devaluation of the local currency, and the impact of World Bank imposed Structural Adjustment Programmes.

The GNL case study has described in some detail the pressure to create a first generation of post-independence managers; yet the need for ongoing expatriate support in key executive positions suggests that the management development programmes introduced to prepare a second or third generation of indigenous managers have not been entirely successful. This 'oversight' is not limited to GNL alone, and in many ways GNL was a model employer with considerable investment in training and staff development.

Thus, despite all the pressure to develop a cadre of local managers and localise key positions, the continuing need to hire return-expats and employ overseas consultants (disguised expats) suggests that the localisation process has not been entirely successful. This contradiction maybe partly explained by the growth in the demand for specialist skills and the flexible contract culture of the 1980s, but it is more likely to be the result of the failure of the localisation process to create a new generation of skilled local staff to take over key positions.

In many developing countries there appears to be little ongoing investment in human resource development generally, and management training in particular, that is appropriate to the needs of local managers. The first generation of local managers who inherited positions previously held by expatriates often benefited from some degree of support and training. But as the first generation of local managers either retired or moved on to a career as entrepreneurs, consultants or politicians, a managerial vacuum was created which second generation local managers have not always been able to fill.

Possible explanations for this state of affairs include the self-interest of the first generation of local managers protecting their position from the ambitions of a new generation of younger managers, or that the downturn in economic conditions and declining profits precluded any additional investment in management training. However, other issues to be considered include the extent to which the parent company failed to sanction ongoing investment in staff development in order to discredit the localisation process generally, a strategy that in time would ensure they could justify the re-employment of expatriate managers in positions of authority and control.

It is also necessary to question whether the momentum to localise was ever really embedded in the management values or the culture of the local company, because pressure to localise was driven by external forces (for example, legislative pressure and political imperatives), rather than recognised need within the corporation. This lack of commitment may explain why much of the training provided was inappropriate and ineffective. The research of Cohen (1991) and Brewster (1991) would suggest that the training provided was predominantly technical in nature, rather than being geared to behavioural or attitudinal change. The latter approach would possibly have been more effective in embedding corporate values and building trust between employees. This would have been more appropriate in the long term for local managers employed to run local operations in times of change and uncertainty.

In conclusion, it is argued that more strategic thinking and research is needed into the problems faced by local managers employed by multinationals, the dynamics of the localisation process, the strategic role of expatriates in this process, and the efficacy of efforts to develop a new generation of local executives. Moreover, the continued employment and influence of expatriates and return-expats appears not only to reflect the cyclical nature of the expatriation process, but also the limitations of the post-independence initiatives to localise management, and the need for further resources to be invested in ongoing training to develop indigenous managers who can operate effectively in both local and international markets.

LESSONS FOR MANAGERS

The following lessons can be drawn from this analysis of the localisation process.

- Managers must recognise that the pressure to localise comes from a wide range of stakeholders, including local politicians, local employees and corporate headquarters.
- Companies must be fully committed to localising senior management positions, and consequently must be prepared to invest sufficient resources in a comprehensive localisation policy. If not, they will find themselves with a managerial vacuum which they will have to fill with expensive expatriates and consultants who commonly apply short-term solutions and have little understanding of local markets or business conditions.
- If return-expatriates are employed to fill a managerial vacuum they are only effective when they have a well-established local track-record and reputation, and have the public support of the local board, and their bankers.
- Human resource strategists must recognise that effective localisation takes time and resources, and must be embedded in the company's overall human resource policy. This should include a package of long-term career planning, international transfers, and investment in a comprehensive programme of management development courses rather than merely technical skills training.
- Multinational managers should be prepared to handle the repercussions of such common operational problems as: the failure to design appropriate job specifications for local managers; or the underestimation of the skills and experience required for them to perform

effectively; as well as the impact of different cultural perspectives on appropriate management styles; and the negative perceptions of local managers to expatriate staff.

- Multinational companies must accept that there is no universal formula for localising senior management positions. They should therefore invest in research that will benchmark localisation strategies, and assist them in their understanding of the dynamics of the localisation process. This will help them assess what localisation strategies are appropriate to their own needs as a company, and those of the countries in which they operate.

REFERENCES

Brewster, C (1991) *The Management of Expatriates*, Kogan Page, London

Brown, J (1990) *British Capitalism and the Development of Nigeria*, PhD Thesis, University of Sussex

Buckley, P and Brooke, M (1992) *International Business Studies: An Overview*, Blackwell, Oxford

Cohen, J (1991) *Expatriate Advisers in the Government of Kenya*, Harvard IID, Cambridge, Mass

Kobrin, S (1989) 'Expatriate Reduction in American Multinationals', *ILR Report*, fall, 27, 1

Lamb, D (1982) *The Africans*, Random House, New York

Negandhi, A (1983) 'Management in the Third World', *Asia Pacific Journal of Management*, Sep

—and Serapio, M (1991) 'Management Strategies and Policies of Japanese Multinationals', *Management Japan*, Spring 24, 1

Potter, C (1989) 'Effective Localisation of the Work-force', *Journal of European Industrial Training*, 13, 6

Scullion, H (Sep 1992) 'Staffing Policies and Practices in British Multinationals', Paper to EIASM Conference, Cranfield School of Management, Cranfield

Sigiura, H (1990) 'How Honda Localises its Global Strategy', *Sloan Management Review*, fall, 32, 1

World Bank, (1989) *Sub-Saharan Africa: From Crisis to Sustainable Growth*, IBRD, Washington

Yoshihari, H (1987) 'Internationalization at the Top', *Management Japan*, autumn 20, 2

6

The International Transfer of Learning: The Key to Successful Strategic Alliances

David Faulkner, Cranfield University School of Management

INTRODUCTION

International strategic alliances are currently a very fast-growing cross-border organisational form due in the main to a number of underlying forces in the current global business environment. This chapter explores the transfer of learning as a key feature in alliance success with reference to one of the best-known British/Japanese alliances, that between the car groups Rover and Honda.

It is likely that the next decade will see an economic world of larger trading blocs, lower tariff levels, and dramatically shortened transmission times both of product and of information. In addition there is developing an increasing globalisation of market arenas in an ever-widening band of industries (Ohmae 1985), coupled with the development of global technologies and a consequent ever-increasing demand for investment resources to cope with this changing environment. In these circumstances cooperative strategy becomes at least as important as competitive strategy in achieving competitive advantage, and a major form of cooperative strategy is the international strategic alliance. Strategic alliances may be defined as:

> A particular mode of inter-organisational relationship in which the partners make substantial investments in developing a long-term collaborative effort, and common orientation... (Mattsson 1988)

Cooperative strategy

Throughout the 1980s and into the 1990s, cooperative forms of doing business have grown rapidly, and continue to increase as firms of all sizes and nationalities in an increasing number of industries and countries perceive value in them. Collective or cooperative strategies and competitive strategies may now be thought of as being in a position of rough equivalence:

> Whether competitive or collective strategies prevail at any one point in time appears largely irrelevant for obtaining viability and long-term stability. What is relevant is the ability to react to instabilities by switching from more collective forms of scrutinizing to more competitive ones and vice-versa. (Bresser and Harl 1986)

Strategic alliances, joint ventures, dynamic networks, constellations, cooperative agreements, collective strategies, all make an appearance and develop significance. In tune with the growth of cooperative managerial forms, the reputation of cooperation, in the views of the commentators, is enjoying a notable revival, to set against the hitherto unassailable theoretical strength of the competitive model as the paradigm of resource allocation efficiency.

Globalisation of markets is currently probably the strongest force leading to this development. Stopford and Turner (1985) reinforce the argument for globalisation by adding the technology dimension, pointing out that all of what they describe as the meta-technologies, namely microelectronics, genetic engineering, and advanced material sciences, are subject to truly global competition. They suggest that the major forces leading to globalisation are:

1. Technology, principally through the microelectronics revolution
2. Cultural evolution, ie the homogenisation of tastes through the media and other forces
3. The breaking down of barriers, eg deregulation and economic integration.

A major factor behind the growing globalisation of markets then has been the development of global technologies, which both dramatically reduce communication times thus 'shrinking' the world in Vernon's phrase (1979), and facilitate the design and manufacture of products with truly global appeal. Failure to appreciate this in the USA may well have been a major factor leading to the growing predominance of Japan in international markets. US companies cooperate with Japanese ones, and export their technological knowhow. The Japanese carry out the production function, whilst the US firms accept functional substitution, instead of engaging in organisational learning. The Japanese then improve the technology, quality and costs, and successfully attack the US market.

> The Japanese have become internationally competitive by a sustained emphasis on refining the products and processes invented in the West. (Zimmerman 1985)

Technology has also been a key factor behind the dramatic growth of cooperative agreements in the 1980s. Osborn and Baughn's research (1987) showed that there were 189 cooperative agreements registered between Japanese and US companies between October 1984 and October 1986. Of these 20 per cent involved cooperative R & D and 50 per cent crossed industry boundaries but still had a strong technological content. Friar and Horwitch (1985) also emphasise the growth of technology strategy as a key element in determining a firm's level of competitive advantage, and illustrate how this is frequently leading to interfirm technology cooperation. An international alliance may be an effective way of spreading technology.

The federated enterprise

Organisational form has also been dramatically influenced by the globalisation of markets and technologies, through a decline in the automatic choice of the integrated multinational corporation as the only instrument appropriate for international business development. The movement away from the traditional concept of the firm is accentuated by the growth of 'federated organisations' (Handy 1992) of which perhaps the largest recent convert is IBM, one of the most powerful MNCs in the world. It decided in 1991, after experiencing a significant decline in performance, and suspecting a loss of competitive advantage, radically to restructure its operations from that of an integrated world-wide firm with a strong single culture, to that of a federation of 14 potentially competitive companies. The culture shock was so great, and the immediate results so mixed that the chief executive has recently resigned, and his successor has come from outside the computer industry. The IBM of the future is likely to be a federated enterprise, although the company has clearly not yet successfully adapted to such a radically changed paradigm.

The concurrent growth of alliances approaches the flexible transnational structure from the other end; that is, the amalgamation of previously independent resources and competencies in contrast to the federation of previously hierarchically controlled resources and competencies. (See Figure 6.1.)

Christelow's research (1987) indicates the growing importance of international joint ventures to US companies wishing to internationalise their operations. The INSEAD research (Morris and Hergert 1987)

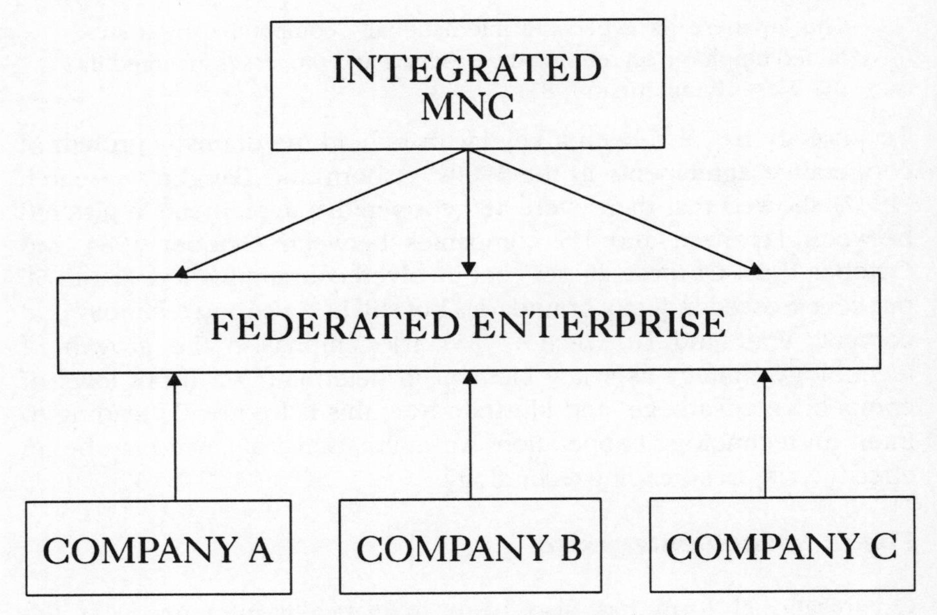

Figure 6.1 The federated enterprise

confirms the accelerating growth of all form of strategic alliance, as does recent UK research (Glaister and Buckley 1992) which suggests that Europe is the area of fastest growth in recent years. It is noticeable that the prime motor for growth since 1986 appears to have been amongst firms within the EC. Contractor and Lorange (1988) also highlight the importance of joint ventures by pointing out that there were approximately 10,000 foreign wholly owned affiliates of US firms, but approximately 12,000 joint ventures in which US companies had between a 10 and 50 per cent ownership.

The learning organisation

This chapter suggests that strategic alliances are most frequently formed from resource dependency motives (Pfeffer and Salancik 1978), and that the ability of the partners to achieve and sustain competitive advantage in their chosen market is strongly influenced by the degree to which they place corporate learning as a high priority on their alliance agenda, and seek to cause the alliance to be:

> ... used for the transfer of organisationally embedded knowledge that

> cannot be easily blueprinted or packaged through licensing or market transactions. (Kogut 1988)

Thus a firm will diagnose its resource and skill deficiencies in relation to a particular external challenge, and through the process of deliberate and planned corporate learning set about remedying these deficiencies.

True strategic alliances should be competence driven (Roos and von Krogh 1992); that is, explicitly adding to either the task or the knowledge system or to the organisational memory of each partner. The idea of the organisation as a residuary for learning is a popular one. Decision theory emphasises the importance of the search for information to enable organisations to make informed choices. Hamel (1991) stresses the role of learning as a source of competitive advantage, through the development of unique competencies. Senge (1992) describes learning organisations as the survivors of the future. Corporate learning may be regarded as having two fundamental dimensions: individual learning and organisational learning.

Individual learning may be rational (how to work a computer), or intuitional (learnt unconsciously, like riding a bicycle). Howsoever achieved, individual learning adds to the competencies of the organisation, but is in theory easily appropriated, as the individual with the developed competence is attracted into leaving the firm. Organisational learning develops at a level beyond that of the individual, and becomes embedded in the rituals, routines and systems of a firm, in its culture. As such, it is more deeply rooted in its core competencies, and may therefore survive the tenure of individuals. Corporate organisational learning may be construed as consisting of both types described above.

THE FORMATION OF INTERNATIONAL ALLIANCES

Strategic alliances are formed for a wide variety of reasons. First, there is generally an external stimulus. In the 1980s and '90s this has been most commonly the globalisation or regionalisation of markets. Companies which had been equipped quite adequately to prosper in national markets suddenly found themselves having to cope in their home market with major global competitors. In many industries the same products were to be found in department stores simultaneously in New York, Tokyo and London (Ohmae 1989).

Other external driving factors were: the development of global technologies and ever-shortening product life cycles. This led to the need for larger investment commitments as firms had to face the need to develop new products almost as soon as they had launched the last product. Few firms were adequately equipped to do this.

A further factor was the growing need to have a sufficiently large volume of sales to be able to take advantage of economies of scale and of scope that were available through modern automated manufacturing processes, in order to secure the low unit costs necessary to achieve competitive advantage. Additionally the world economy had, since the oil shocks of the 1970s, become an increasingly turbulent and uncertain place, and only corporations of large financial strength had the flexibility to cope with such uncertainty. If they additionally felt the urgent need to get new products on the market to take advantage of major opportunities that might not remain long enough for their R & D department to develop the products internally, and if they felt the need to economise with their finances and seek a partner to spread the risk, then they were strongly motivated towards seeking an alliance with an appropriate partner. Most companies, even the very large, faced these external forces with concern. Strategic alliances became an important item on their agenda, if they felt themselves to be deficient in global terms of resources, skills or what Prahalad and Hamel (1990) call 'core competencies'.

The partner selected would of course need to be one with complementary assets and capabilities, with identifiable synergies, with a compatible culture and with whom the firm believed it could achieve sustainable competitive advantage, that it could not achieve alone. In short the partners would perceive their relationship as having a good strategic fit.

The nature of alliances

Strategic alliances come in many different forms and have been classified in the literature (Faulkner 1992a) in a variety of ways. However, a classification by:

1. nature,
2. structure and
3. membership

provides clear and simple categories of alliances. Thus under 'nature' the alliance can be classified as either:

- focused, or
- complex.

A focused alliance is specific in its objectives, and may well involve only one activity from each partner's value chain (Porter 1985). A complex alliance has more diffuse objectives, and may involve complete value chains, and lead to their reconsideration. Under 'structure' the alliance is either a joint venture with a separate legal existence or a collaboration without one. Under 'membership' the classification is as a two-partner alliance or a consortium. Thus a given alliance may be a focused two-partner joint venture, or a complex two-partner collaboration, or a focused consortium joint venture, and so forth. Clearly the three axes of the taxonomy give a possible eight alliance forms, as shown in Figure 6.2.

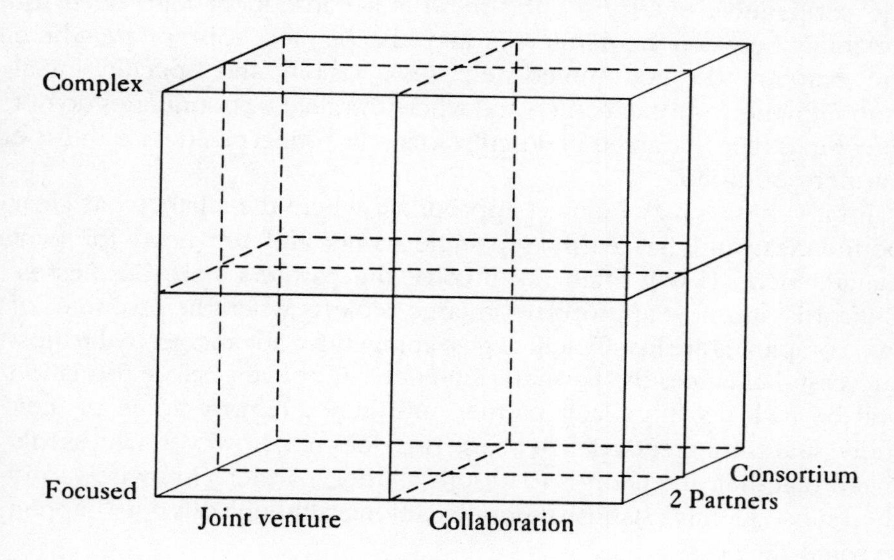

8 types of strategic alliance

1. Focused/complex
2. Joint venture or collaboration
3. Two partners or consortium

Figure 6.2 The strategic alliance options

An analysis of 228 alliances (Faulkner 1992a) showed two-partner joint ventures to account for 45 per cent of the sample, consortium ventures 22.5 per cent and two-partner collaborations 22.5 per cent.

The life history of an alliance can be divided into three parts:

1. Formation
2. Management
3. Evolution.

Stages 2 and 3 will overlap as stage 3 emerges from stage 2. For an alliance to demonstrate the primary characteristics of success, it needs to evolve from the initial pact, and the process of evolution needs to be strongly influenced by positive attitudes on the part of the partners towards corporate learning.

The selection of alliance form is also important, as different situations favour different forms. The collaboration form (ie the form chosen for the Rover/Honda alliance) may be most appropriate for situations where there is high uncertainty at the outset as to what tasks will be involved in the cooperative enterprise, and there is a consequent high need for flexibility between the partners. It may also be most appropriate where the partners do not immediately seek visible and specific initial commitments from each other, and where the alliance boundaries do not encompass specific assets or describe a clearly distinct business within the partners' portfolio.

Joint ventures may be most appropriate where the alliance has clear boundaries, and has easily separable assets and the need for joint management. It will often not involve the partners' core businesses. Consortia are most appropriate in large projects when the resources of two companies are insufficient to give competitive advantage. In the most successful alliances the partners' intentions at or even before formation will be to learn from their partner, and hence remove some of their individual competence deficiencies. This does not, however, necessarily mean that their intention is to absorb all their partner's knowhow, and then subsequently establish themselves alone, although this does happen in some alliances.

SOME BASIC PRINCIPLES IN THE MANAGEMENT OF INTERNATIONAL ALLIANCES

A genuine strategic alliance is formed for the long term: 'Strategic alliances are not tools of convenience. They are critical instruments in fulfilling corporate strategic objectives' as Roland Bertodo, strategic planning director of Rover and the key architect of the Rover/Honda alliance, states. As such, the management system for running them needs to be established with as much care as that devoted to the choice of alliance form.

Important principles in this area involve agreeing good dispute resolution mechanisms, and if possible a divorce procedure to cater for the possibility that the alliance may cease to meet the needs of the parties. It is also important that the long-term goals of the partners should not be in conflict, although this does not mean that they need be identical.

Most importantly, attitudes need to be positive and flexible. For example, it is highly unlikely that the partners' company or national cultures will be similar. If they are, of course, this may smooth the way for a harmonious working relationship. However, most strategic alliances are formed precisely because the partners are different, and valued the more for their difference. The cultural atmosphere in the partner company is therefore unlikely to be similar. A sensitive attitude to cultural differences is therefore necessary if the alliance is to prosper, since the cultural differences in ways of operating will inevitably lead to confusion in the partner company. If attitudes are positive, sensitive and flexible this need not have a negative impact on the alliance, and may lead to the partners absorbing what is best in each other's culture to their mutual benefit. Once more, learning from the partner is the key to success.

Two further attitudes are vital to success, namely commitment and trust. Commitment is the degree to which partners dedicate time and other resources to alliance matters, and are not discouraged by problems that arise. Trust is a more difficult area. Trust normally has to be earned in relationships and this takes time. In alliances, however, it is suggested that an attitude which says 'I trust my partner, unless and until I have reason not to' is more likely to lead to positive results than the attitude which says 'I don't know my partner well. It will have to earn my trust over time'.

A further important area is the establishment of systems to disseminate information throughout the company. In the absence of such systems the risk is high that the vital information, especially 'knowhow', will remain with the partner, and be merely used but not absorbed, or that it will go no further than the executives directly interfacing with their alliance partners, and not become embedded in the partner companies' tacit knowledge fabric. Both Hamel (1991) and Grant (1991) stress the need for companies to appropriate the value they create, if they are to benefit from alliances in the future, and particularly if they are to maintain or increase their bargaining power in relation to their partner.

Thus we have the paradox that to gain from an alliance, a partner needs to establish the ability to appropriate a substantial proportion of the value created by the alliance in the form of the successful internalisation of new core competencies learnt from the partner. However, the more successful the firm is in doing this, the less it appears to need its partner, and hence the weaker the bonds of the alliance become. Fortunately for the inherent value of alliances, like all good paradoxes this is only an apparent contradiction and it arises from too static a view of an alliance. It assumes a finite set of competencies and skills, and that appropriation of value by one partner diminishes the pool available for the future.

ALLIANCE EVOLUTION

An important factor in the life of an alliance seems to be that, if it ceases to evolve, it starts to decay (Thorelli 1986). Entropy is present in all networking, and needs to be actively combated on a continuous basis. Despite the continuance of the original agreement, management may start to lose interest in the liaison if nothing new comes from it. The trading view however, underlies a static 'fixed set of goods' philosophy. Yet the reality of a successful alliance is that it not only trades competencies but also realises synergies. In fact, the successful evolution of that alliance depends upon the realisation of synergies between the companies, and the establishment of a durable competitive advantage for the partners, that each could not realise alone.

Evolution is about continuous value creation which will, in a successful collaborative alliance, be appropriated by the partners in a balanced fashion. Figure 6.3 illustrates the stages by which this process may develop. Some value will emerge in terms of increased profits for shareholders, or for future investment, and some will emerge in the form of increased core competencies. But a third part will remain intrinsically dependent upon the continuance of the alliance and will form a strong bonding factor. For example, economies of scale and, to some extent, of scope would be difficult to realise by the partners separately, however adept their competence internalisation. There may be joint patents and designs, and frequently joint development of assets of a tangible or intangible nature, which live naturally within the alliance, and are not subject to individual appropriation. Plus over time, and with evolution, the alliance as an entity will begin to develop a life of its own, even more so in the joint venture form of an alliance.

Alliance theory proposes that conditions for evolution include:

- Perception of balanced benefits from the alliance by both partners
- The development of strong bonding factors
- The regular development of new projects and responsibilities between the partners
- The adoption of a philosophy of constant learning by the partners.

THE ROVER/HONDA ALLIANCE

In the Rover/Honda alliance a high level of strategic fit with mutual resource dependency existed at the outset, and continues to do so. When the alliance was formed in 1979, Rover produced cars with a reputation for variable quality, had a management system based on confrontation

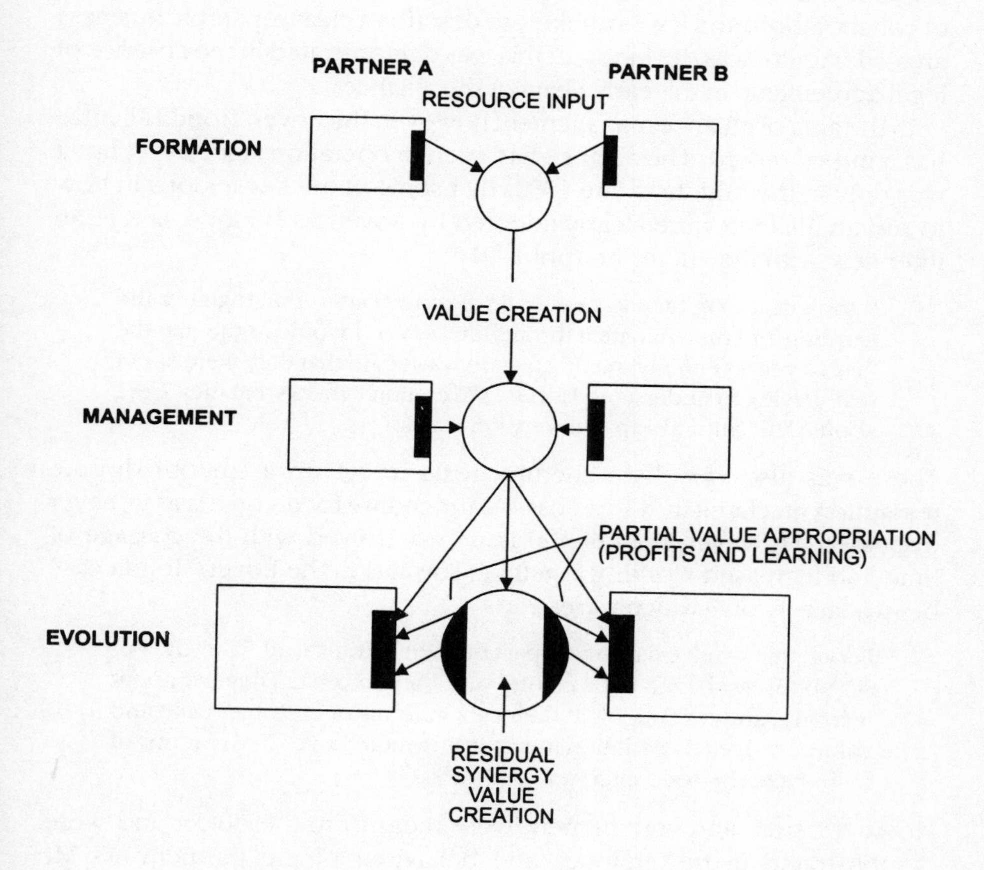

Figure 6.3 Evolution through value creation and appropriation

and a poor labour relations record. It badly needed a new model for its mid-range, and to learn quality management processes from the Japanese company. Honda, for its part, looked to obtain low-cost, speedy and low-risk entry into Europe, access to Rover's surplus manufacturing capacity, an understanding of European taste and styling, and introduction to a well-developed network of suppliers. All this was not on offer at the outset, or even appreciated by the partners, but it grew through the deepening relationship.

The collaboration alliance form met the needs of the partners very closely as only this form provided total flexibility for development. At the outset it was uncertain what the alliance would involve in terms of areas of collaboration, and it was unlikely to describe a clear separable business area. Flexibility was the key, and this was demonstrated in the absence of legal agreements in the early years of the alliance.

In the area of alliance management however, the Rover/Honda alliance has a mixed record. The alliance has been in operation since 1978, but it was only in the middle to late 1980s that some of the key lessons in how to run an alliance were clearly adopted by Rover, as Bertodo said in an interview with the author in April 1991:

> It took us a long time to get our lines sorted out to pull together the learning and disseminate it throughout Rover. I would argue that the first 10 years certainly the first 6 were wasted, in that they were spent really trying to understand Honda. We couldn't grasp what they were about. The cultural gap was very very wide.

There was also very little attempt made to set up a smooth dispute resolution mechanism, and a possible procedure for divorce was not ever discussed. However, the cultural issue was solved with the passage of time and increased working together. This has in the Rover/Honda case been a largely one-way progress:

> I don't think we've had any impact on their culture at all. They did not set about to change their culture and they haven't. They set about learning, and if you look at their cars in terms of customer taste and values, with each evolution they became more Rover-like in terms of ambience. (Bertodo interview, April 1991)

However, trust and commitment were there from the outset and were demonstrated in the attitudes and behaviour of the partners. As Mr Hayashi, managing director of Honda (UK) puts it:

> Both companies have a policy of strong commitment. If we broke apart we would be in competition with the same technology and the same products and suppliers – a duplicate of each other. This would not be sensible. (Hayashi interview with the author, June 1991)

However, collaboration is limited to production processes, design, supplier sourcing and technology. In the sphere of marketing and sales, the companies compete and are very careful to avoid informal information transfer.

A key question is whether the two companies have now learnt all they needed to from each other, and the argument would run as follows. As a result of the alliance, Rover have now learnt how to produce very high-quality cars, to manage production processes more effectively, to adopt a more open attitude to learning, to increase its productivity and to reduce its model lifecycle from ten to four years.

Honda has effected a successful entry into Europe, has developed a high-quality network of European suppliers and has internalised its understanding of European taste and styling requirements. So why not say thank you and henceforth pursue separate developments? Certainly the temptation may be there. However, this brings us to a key aspect of successful alliances, continual evolution.

Bertodo of Rover is keenly aware of this and is conscious of the need to maintain a balance between the two companies' relative need for each other. He sees it as trading 'packages' of competencies on a regular basis.

> As guardian of the company strategy...I have got to have something ready to trade if the company decides it needs to trade, which will depend on how fast it is learning. I think we don't learn fast enough, but I would say that wouldn't I.

There have so far been five basic 'trades' over the life of the alliance, all leading to continuous evolution. Balanced benefits have been achieved in the view of the partners. As Bertodo puts it:

> Buttressed by the ability to achieve better scale through joint manufacture and a spread of fixed overhead recovery over greater production volumes, manufacturing productivity has risen sharply over the period of the collaboration. Defect rates have shown a threefold reduction; the whole organisation has moved away from a conventional hierarchical structure and self contained functions towards an environment of personal interaction and fluid integration. Multi functional, multi skilled teams led by entrepreneur specialists became the rule, the payback has been a 10 per cent reduction in administration burden and a halving of the human resource needed to achieve a given workload.

And for Honda, its establishment as a force to be reckoned with in the UK and Europe, and a growth of understanding of European tastes and style, leading to the decline of the traditional Honda box-style car, have resulted from the alliance. In addition a £500 million inter-trading account between the two companies has developed. Bonding factors have been evident externally, in the exchange of 20 per cent of shares between the two companies, and internally by the establishment of close relationships at working team level in production, and design and development functions between senior executives. An exchange of personnel between Honda and Rover has helped to cement this. Honda personnel have been seconded to Rover, and, for language reasons, Rover executives have been seconded not to Japan but to Honda USA.

A steady stream of new projects has then been evident over the life of the alliance and with it a growth of closeness and cooperation between the two companies. What began as an arm's-length 'knock-down' kits licence for the Triumph Acclaim in 1979 has progressed to real cooperative design development, and production of the Rover 200/400 and the Honda Concerto, which includes cross-sourcing of components.

Finally, and most importantly, the philosophy of constant learning, which was already deeply embedded in the Honda culture, has been embraced wholeheartedly by Rover at least in the last five years. In the early days of the alliance Rover adopted an attitude towards an alliance which essentially saw Honda as being able to supply the deficient resources and capabilities that Rover needed:

> I think Michael Edwardes saw it as a temporary alliance to plug a gap and to share costs so as to give us breathing space. (Bertodo interview 1991)

On this basis Honda would still have been valuable to Rover. It would be able to provide Rover with a product which could be rebadged as Rover or Triumph (eg the Acclaim). This would economise greatly on Rover's stretched R & D finances and enable 'new' models to be brought to the market at least two years earlier than could have been done using Rover's internal resources. In addition Honda would be able to take up some of Rover's excess manufacturing capacity and thus spread overheads.

However, an alliance on this basis would be doomed to long-run failure since Rover would have become dependent upon Honda, and would have failed to learn and internalise any of the competitively advantageous skills that Honda had to teach. The transformation of Rover would not have taken place and the alliance would have done no more for Rover than temporarily and marginally improve its profit and loss account.

As the alliance continued, however, attitudes within Rover began to change, and an appreciation that alliances provide unique opportunities to learn and to improve skills and capabilities began to take over. By the time of the signing of the Statement of Understanding in 1985, the nature of the relationship had deepened:

> We had perceived the possibility of learning from Honda as they had perceived the possibility of learning from Rover, and joint development of a car was seen as bringing these common desires together and consummating the relationship. (Bertodo interview 1991)

From this point Rover has not looked back. In fact, learning has become the touchstone of their new company culture, symbolised perhaps in the internal subsidiary, The Rover Learning Business, which is responsible for a wide range of training and for stimulating the living of the Rover Success Through Learning policy. The Rover Learning Business is now extending its remit to the Rover dealer network, reminiscent of the Japanese Keiretsu attitude to suppliers and distributors as all part of the team.

Rover's learning and application has been dramatic in recent years, especially in view of the painful and difficult need to 'unlearn' previous practices. As evidence of its transformation, Rover now includes: just-in-time (JIT) inventory management, through an intermediary third party buffer company, BRS, which maintains a constant flow of parts to the assembly line; six end-of-the-line cold-test stations with electronic function test (in line with practice at Honda, Nissan and Toyota); multifunctional teams; single source suppliers; and the flattening of the management hierarchy from ten layers down to four. Managers up to director level are even donning uniforms with the Rover logo on them in characteristic Japanese fashion. The traditional Western attitude of managers as teacher has been replaced enthusiastically by that of managers as student.

However, this is not to imply that there is total transparency of knowledge between the partners. Marketing and sales are areas of competition, and whilst Rover and Honda have learnt to be good colleagues in R & D, design and production, they remain strong competitors once the marque badges have been fixed. This requires a strong self-discipline, more natural to the Oriental than the Western behavioural pattern. It is, however, vital to alliance success to retain separate identities and separate aspirational dreams, whilst sharing a common bed, in Bertodo's picturesque phrase.

Beyond that the two companies recognise that alliances only continue to evolve if this is valuable to the partners: 'There is no specific strategy between the companies in relation to the development of the alliance. We both look to an on-going relationship to our mutual advantage', as John Bacchus, Rover's director of Honda Collaboration stresses (in an interview with the author, June 1992). 'If we can grow together to our mutual advantage while maintaining our independence it will be a wonderful thing,' said Mr Kume, current president of Honda, to Sir Graham Day in 1991.

LEARNING IN INTERNATIONAL ALLIANCES

Even faced with this evident success story of Rover/Honda, of the evolution of an alliance through mutual learning leading to competitive advantage, a perceptive analyst might still harbour nagging doubts about the role of value appropriation in the form of learning by the partners, and of the consequent stability of the alliance. Many commentators will in fact declare the alliance to be an unstable and transitory arrangement, and undoubtedly, if opportunistic attitudes are adopted by the partners, it can be.

Further explanation of what is meant by learning and stability is probably merited. Perhaps due to the influence of the concept of 'equilibrium' from the economists, stability is felt to be a state after which all wise organisations hanker. It is felt to be a 'good' thing. But what do we mean by stability in a world that is constantly changing? Professor Teramoto of Japan puts it this way:

> It is often said that alliances are unstable. This is based on a failure to understand business life. Stability is in instability, and instability in stability. All are based on change, and this is the norm. Alliances are therefore no more unstable or stable than any other organisational form. All react by changing as they adapt to a constantly changing environment. (Teramoto interview with the author, June 1992)

The often cited comparison of an alliance with a marriage is pertinent here. Marriages could be regarded as unstable as they currently have a high failure rate. In fact they have many of the qualities of strategic alliances. The partners retain separate identities but collaborate over a whole range of activities. Stability is threatened if one partner becomes excessively dependent on the other, or if the benefits are perceived to be all one way. But, nonetheless, successful marriages are stable, and for the same reason as successful alliances. They depend upon trust, commitment, mutual learning, flexibility and a feeling by both partners that they are stronger together than apart. Many businesses point to the need to negotiate decisions in alliances as a weakness, in contrast to companies, where hierarchies make decisions. This is to confuse stability with clarity of decision-making, and would lead to the suggestion that dictatorships are more stable then democracies.

In this analogy, it is commitment to the belief that the alliance represents the best available arrangement that is the foundation of its stability. The need for resolution of the inevitable tensions in such an arrangement can as easily be presented as a strength, rather than as an inherent problem. It leads to the need to debate, see and evaluate contrasting viewpoints.

How then is the learning issue resolved and does it influence alliance evolution? In terms of the possibilities presented by an alliance, there are a number of different types of learning each with different implications:

1. *Technological learning*; this is a mixture of the technology describable in blueprints plus the knowhow involved in using them
2. *Process learning*; this is more deeply embedded in the culture of the partner, and therefore more difficult to transplant
3. *Opportunity learning*; this involves practical matters like: Who are the best suppliers? What is the best way of getting skilled labour? Who are the best agents?
4. *A learning philosophy*; this is an attitude very difficult to translate but the most crucial to ultimate alliance success and the most guaranteed to transform the company

		TECHNOLOGY TRANSFER	PROCESS LEARNING	OPPORTUNITY LEARNING	LEARNING PHILOSOPHY
CONDITION OF LEARNING RECIPIENT	INTENT	✓✓✓	✓✓	✓	✓✓✓
	RECEPTIVITY	✓✓✓	✓✓	✓	✓ → ✓✓✓
NATURE OF KNOWLEDGE	TRANSFERABILITY OF KNOWLEDGE	✓✓	✓	✓✓✓	✓
	TRANSPARENCY OF KNOWLEDGE	✓✓	✓✓	✓✓✓	✓✓✓

Figure 6.4 Rover's knowledge absorption

The ease with which learning takes place within an alliance depends upon, firstly, the type of learning and, secondly, the relationship between the nature of the learning and the condition of the would-be receptor. Figure 6.4 attempts to show the differences and strengths in Rover's condition, the learning opportunity presented to it, and the four types of learning. The figure represents the situation by 1990, and will clearly be different, and with fewer ticks, in the early days of the alliance. It uses the following concepts (Faulkner 1992b).

- *Intent* represents the strength of the firm's determination to learn. Without that, there would be little advantage in terms of growth of core competencies, and the alliance would be limited largely to resource substitution from Rover's viewpoint.
- *Receptivity* represents the condition in the company with regard to its level of sophistication and hence capacity to learn. A low-tech company can only learn from a high-tech one, for example, after substantial education.
- *Transferability* shows the ease with which the type of learning can be transferred, ie tacit knowledge is difficult, overt product knowledge easier.
- *Transparency* is the willingness of a partner to release information and to explain difficulties.

The figure suggests the following therefore.

Technical learning has been relatively easy for Rover, particularly in the later stage of the alliance, as Rover has been receptive and keen to learn. The nature of technology transfer has been clear, and Honda has been willing to provide the information in joint learning working teams.

Process learning has been more difficult, since by its nature it involves a lot of tacit knowledge and cultural aspects related to Japanese paradigms. This has been less easily transferred and less transparent but, as Rover's intent and receptivity has grown, it has been one of the success stories of the alliance from the Rover viewpoint, and processes have been transplanted and 'Roverised' (cf JIT).

Opportunity learning has not been a key area for Rover, but has been mainly Honda's concern, ie identifying European opportunities and quality suppliers. Inherently, its transferability and transparency are high, but perhaps less durable than the other learning forms.

The learning philosophy is arguably the most important learning type of all, since it underlies the whole way in which a company is run. It meshes closely with the Honda philosophy of 'continuous improvement'. It is difficult to transfer, in the case of Honda being part of its essential cultural paradigm. However, there seems to have been little difficulty in transparency and, once Rover's intent and receptivity had increased dramatically after 1985, the whole nature of Rover's attitude to itself, its personnel and its way of working became transformed, so that a learning philosophy came to underlie it.

LESSONS FOR MANAGERS

Many collaborative activities between companies are set up for short-term gains in order to deal with temporary situations. These obscure the nature of the true strategic alliance, in which the intent is a learning one, in the pursuit of joint sustainable competitive advantage, and the extension of individual and joint core competencies.

From the evidence of the development of the Rover/Honda alliance a number of key points emerge of perhaps general value to managers wishing to set up and run international strategic alliances.

- The key to continued success is not skill (or product) substitution, but the ability and determination to develop by learning from one's partners the competencies in which one is deficient.
- Sensitivity to cultural differences is vital to this process, but this is a different thing from the requirement for cultural similarity when selecting a partner. This latter characteristic may not be an advantage, since dissimilarities provide learning opportunities.
- To achieve genuine learning transparency is necessary, and this can only be brought about through positive inter-partner attitudes. In this regard, commitment, trust and flexibility are the attitudes most necessary for success in an alliance. If some personal bonding can be achieved between the partners, this also aids successful alliance development.
- Finally, it is obviously important to choose a partner with complementary assets and abilities, but after that point the alliance will only succeed through the mutually supportive behaviour of the partners, and a willingness by them both to learn and to teach each other in the areas where they feel they need to learn.

Given appropriate attitudes, and good strategic fit of the partners, the author's research has indicated that strategic alliances can, through mutual learning, evolve into powerful global enterprises able to challenge the multinationals on their own terms and sometimes win.

REFERENCES:

Bresser, R K and Harl, J E (1986) 'Collective Strategy: Vice or Virtue?', *Academy of Management Review*, 11, (2), 408–27

Christelow, D B (1987) 'International Joint Ventures', *Columbia Journal of World Business*, summer

Contractor, F J and Lorange, P (eds) (1988) 'Why Should Firms be Cooperative?:

The Strategy and Economic Basis for Cooperative Ventures', in *Cooperative Strategies in International Business*, Lexington Books, Boston, Mass

Faulkner, D O (1992a) 'Cooperating for Competition: A Taxonomy of Strategic Alliances', Conference of British Academy of Management, Bradford

—(1992b) 'Strategic Alliance Evolution through Learning: The Rover/Honda Alliance', Conference of Strategic Management Society, London

—(1993) 'International Strategic Alliances: Key Conditions for their Effective Development', Cranfield University School of Management

Friar, J and Horwitch, M (1985) 'The Emergence of Technology Strategy', *Technology in Society*, 7, 143–78

Glaister, K W and Buckley, P J (1992) 'UK International Joint Venture: An Analysis of Patterns of Activity and Distribution', Working Paper

Grant, R M (1991) 'The Resource-based Theory of Competitive Advantage: Implications for Strategy Formulation', *California Management Review*, spring, 114–35

Hamel, G (1991) 'Competition for Competence and Inter-partner Learning within International Strategic Alliances', *Strategic Management Journal*, 12, 83–103

Handy, C (1992) 'Balancing Corporate Power: A New Federalist Paper', *Harvard Business Review*, Nov/Dec, 59–72

Kogut, B (1988) 'Joint Ventures: Theoretical and Empirical Perspectives', *Strategic Management Journal*, 9, 319–32

Mattsson, L G (1988) *Interaction Strategies: A Network Approach*, Working Paper, Stockholm

Morris, D and Hergert, M (1987) 'Trends in International Collaborative Agreements' (INSEAD research), *Columbia Journal of World Business*, summer

Ohmae, K (1985) *Triad Power: The Coming Shape of Global Competition*, The Free Press, New York

—(1989) 'The Global Logic of Strategic Alliances', *Harvard Business Review*, Mar/Apr, 143–54

Osborn, R N and Baughn, C C (1987) 'New Patterns in the Formation of US/Japanese Cooperative Ventures: The Role of Technology', *Columbia Journal of World Business, summer, 57–64*

Pfeffer, J and Salancik, G (1978) *The External Control of Organisations: A Resource Dependency Perspective*, Harper, New York

Porter, M E (1985) *Competitive Advantage*, The Free Press, New York

Prahalad, C K and Hamel, G (1990) 'The Core Competence of the Corporation', *Harvard Business Review*, Vol 90, 79–91

Roos, J and von Krogh, G (1992) 'Figuring Out Your Competence Configuration', *European Management Journal*, Vol 10, No 4 Dec, 422–7

Senge, P M (1992) *The 5th Discipline: The Art and Practice of the Learning Organization*, Century Business, London

Stopford, J M and Turner, L (1985) *Britain and Multinationals*, Wiley, Chichester

Thorelli, H B (1986) 'Networks: between Markets and Hierarchies', *Strategic Management Journal*, 7, 37–51

Vernon, R (1979) 'The product life – cycle hypothesis in a new international environment', *Oxford Bulletin of Economics and Statistics*, Nov, 255–67

Zimmerman, M (1985) How to do Business with the Japanese, Random House, New York

PART THREE

CHALLENGES INVOLVING ASSET UTILISATION: FINANCE, INVESTMENT AND THE SUPPLY CHAIN

7

International Investments may confer Options: Evaluate them as Such

Adrian Buckley, Cranfield University School of Management

The financial analysis of international investment decisions is complex. The basic methodology which homes in on incremental cash flows needs to be refined in order to focus upon cash flows which are remittable to the parent company, for it is only these that would logically add shareholder value. Build in the complications of two lots of tax and changing exchange rates and the equation looks anything but simple. But there's another complexity too which renders the traditional discounting methodology less than wholly appropriate. And this applies not just to international investment but to any situation where capital is committed with an option to expand or curtail embedded in it. This is not to say that the typical model cannot be adapted to meet the situation. It can and it's not too difficult.

THE STANDARD APPROACH

In the usual discounted cash flow (DCF) calculations which are familiar to virtually all company executives, the project's anticipated cash flows are viewed as one of the early ports of call in terms of developing a capital investment appraisal's data set. To be sure, sensitivity analysis is available to sophisticate the appraisal – this might involve looking at out-turns with lower sales projections or higher cost levels or different timing of sales penetration and so on. Notwithstanding this approach, the angle that is so often taken in investment appraisal is a static one – static in the sense that operating decisions are viewed as being fixed in advance and, as such, giving rise to the base case set of incremental cash flows. It is this feature that is at the heart of why the pure discounted cash flow techniques, as used by so many companies, may be less than perfect in simulating the business world. This is the source of tension between finance and strategy referred to by Barwise, Marsh and Wensley (1989).

In reality, good managers are frequently good because they pursue policies that maintain flexibility on as many fronts as possible and they maintain options that promise upside potential. In respect of investment decision-making, this means keeping open the opportunity to make decisions contingent upon information to become available in the future. For example, dependent upon actual levels of demand, or of competition or of cost, the rate of output of a new product may be accelerated, existing facilities may be extended or, should out-turns be less attractive than expected, they may be closed temporarily or even abandoned altogether.

Research and development is an obvious case in point. Testing out a new market via a pilot plant is clearly another. Oil exploration obviously falls into this category, levels of exploration and investment being highly contingent upon oil prices prevailing. And mining and quarrying are similar kinds of investment too – extraction or temporary closure or even abandonment being obvious choices of action which will be a function of actual prices of and/or demand for the product concerned. All these examples have a big thing in common – the firm has flexibility in terms of its course of action depending upon outcomes and factors unknown at the time of the project's inception. And, of course, international investment is another example. Invariably it begins with a small commitment which may be scaled upwards should the environment prove profitable, or it may be curtailed should the host country appear to offer less attractive cash flows than anticipated. Qualitatively, the idea is fairly straightforward.

AN EXAMPLE USING DECISION TREES

Let's take the notion further and let's bolt on some numbers too. We will look at an example; it makes exposition easier. Consider a decision facing a minerals exploration company. It concerns a silver mine with a residual of two million troy ounces of silver which could all be extracted next year assuming a sufficiently attractive price. Assume that the current price is 205 pence per ounce having moved up from 180. The best estimate of next year's price is put at 200 pence which, with variable costs of 180 pence, would yield a contribution (and profit – since, at least for this example, fixed costs are put at zero) of 20 pence per ounce. Reopening the mine would involve a one-off cost of £450,000. Assuming that 12 per cent per annum is the appropriate discount rate for the project, it can be seen that the traditional discounted cash flow appproach shows it to be a no go decision. Figures, summarised in Table 7.1, indicate a negative net present value of some £94,000.

Table 7.1 Silver mine projections – base case

	Year	
	0	1
Reopening costs	–£450,000	
Contribution – silver sales		+£400,000
Discount factor at 12%	1.00	0.89
Present value	–£450,000	+£356,000
Net present value	–£94,000	

But this classic discounted cash flow appraisal is not good enough. It ignores the options to mine if the price is high enough or not to mine if the price is not sufficiently attractive to do so. Assume that the best estimate price of 200 pence per ounce has been arrived at as a mid-point of estimates of 250 pence and 150 pence per ounce: each of these possible prices has a 50 per cent probability factor associated with it. Remember that variable costs of extraction were put at 180 pence per ounce. Clearly, should a price of only 150 pence be available in the marketplace, there is no logical way that a profit orientated company would extract any silver. It would leave the mineral in the ground. At a price of 250 pence, things are obviously very different. The interesting thing is that including an allowance for the possibility of not going ahead with extraction, the project has a positive net present value on the basis of expected monetary value analysis – simply multiplying anticipated cash flows by their associated probability and then discounting. Figure 7.1 indicates that the expected net present value on this basis is £175,000.

The difference between the bottom lines in Table 7.1 and Figure 7.1 arises because the latter takes cognisance of the option not to mine should the price fail to yield a contribution when the time to consider extraction arrives. In other words, the classic, single out-turn, non-option orientated analysis ignores the tactical flexibility which every good manager tries to keep open. Perhaps this is one of the reasons why so many line managers seem to feel that DCF analysis has a lot to offer but it somehow fails to reflect adequately the reality of the world in which they operate.

What should be clear is that the ability to change tactical direction in response to new information can contribute significant increments to value. And such financial flexibility should be given due weight at the

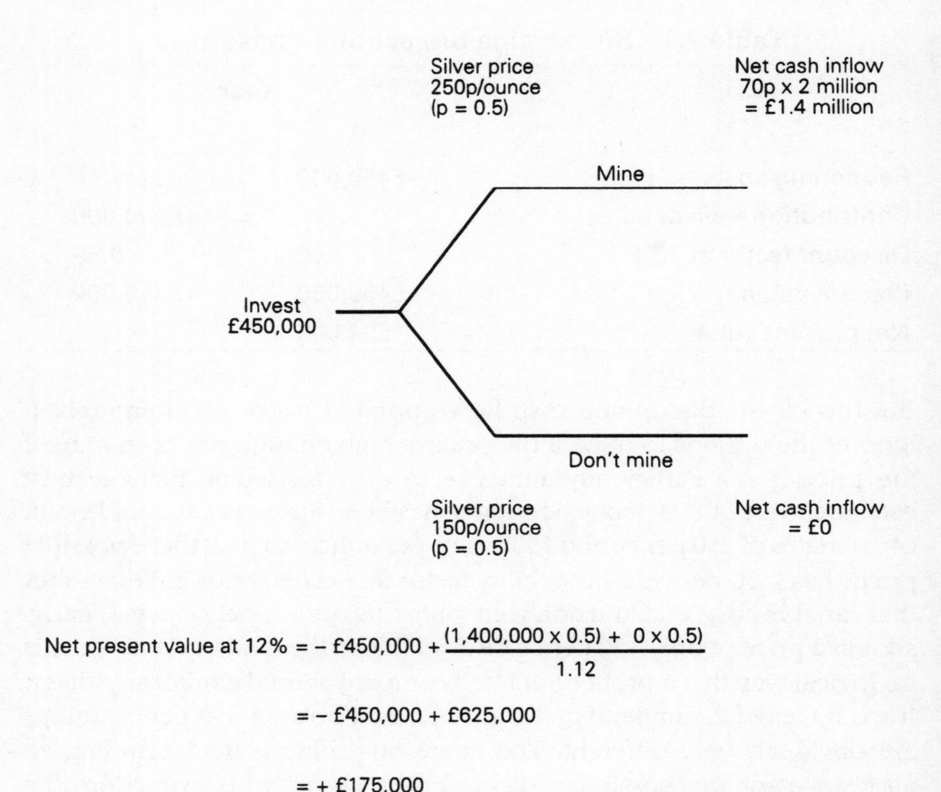

Figure 7.1 Silver mine projections accounting for option not to extract metal

gestation phase of a project's life – that is, at the quantitative appraisal stage. Investments which possess this flexibility have the characteristics of options. Research and development gives the firm the right but not the obligation to scale up from the pilot plant to the full commercial scale. Oil exploration rights or possession of mining reserves give the firm the opportunity to extract (which may or may not be a right because of planning consents and so on) but not the obligation to do so. Expansion into a foreign territory gives the firm the possibility (again it may not be a right) of scaling up should things turn out attractively, but to abandon should out-turns be less positive.

These kinds of investments readily equate to options in stock market terms or even currency options – and should therefore be valued accordingly. Remember that security and foreign exchange options give the holder the right to acquire or sell something at a particular price (the strike price) within a specified timeframe but there is not an obligation to do so. In the case of certain kinds of investment project, the firm acquires an opportunity (not necessarily a right) to do something but is not committed. The similarity is obvious.

A call option in the stock market gives the holder the right to buy shares at a fixed price over a period of time but not the obligation to do so. Similarly an investment in research and development gives the firm the potential to acquire the benefits thereof for the cost of commercialisation. The owner of a mine or oil well has the possibility of acquiring the proceeds from the mine's or oil well's output but does not have an obligation to do so and, like the stock market call option buyer, he or she may defer selling the proceeds of the asset's output. Pre-emptive (and not necessarily heavy) investment in new, including international, markets may give the firm the edge when it comes to opportunities for scaling up to a full sized production and distribution network whilst retaining the option to withdraw from that market if out-turns are unfavourable. The similarity between stock market or currency options and certain kinds of investment decisions is summarised in Table 7.2. With respect to research and development, minerals extraction projects and exploratory investments in new markets, including international ones, classic DCF techniques, unless accompanied by serious modification, fail to take into account the tactical flexibility and value-creating upside potential of subsequent add-on aspects and consequently understate true investment potential.

Various articles have appeared in the literature of capital budgeting stressing the need to extend the analysis of certain kinds of investment decisions to embrace these option-type characteristics. Reference to the put option aspect of capital budgeting – the value of the potential to abandon the project – has a long history. Robichek and van Horne (1967) were among the first to recognise this feature; they have been followed by a long list of contributions on this score. The option to expand further – the call option – has been the focus of a number of more recent papers. Kester (1984 and 1986) and Mason and Merton (1985) pioneered the way. Brennan and Schwartz (1985) and Siegel, Smith and Paddock (1987) apply the option pricing model to mining and oil exploration projects respectively and Copeland, Koller and Murrin (1990) note its relevance to minerals industries and pharmaceutical research and development. Only Shapiro (1992) and Kester and Morley (1992), so far, have applied the notion, in a mainly qualitative way, to international investment although

Table 7.2 Projects as options

Investment	Value-creating flexibility	
	Upside	**Downside**
Stock market option	Acquire shares at exercise price or sell on shares for intrinsic plus time value	Option lapses – or is sold for time value
Foreign exchange option	Acquire currency at exercise price or sell on option for intrinsic plus time value	Option lapses – or is sold for time value
Research and development	Opportunity to take project commercial	Abandon – or perhaps sell R & D rights (rather like selling for time value?)
Mines and oil exploration	Opportunity to extract ore/oil	Abandon. Or mine later. Or sell reserves
Exploratory or pre-emptive investment in new and international markets	Opportunity to scale-up locally	Abandon. Or soldier on. Or sell out (again rather like selling for time value)

Kulatilaka and Marcus (1992) refer to it *en passant* – their main focus is upon embedded options in operational flexibility. The message is that the old-style capital appraisal techniques are more than adequate in terms of dealing with cash cow investments but leave something to be desired where there is operational flexibility or contingent opportunities for growth. In these circumstances, DCF methods consistently undervalue projects due to their failure to allow for strategic flexibility. At the current time it is fair to say that far too few standard textbooks on finance or strategic management give this topic sufficient coverage – notable exceptions include Shapiro (1990), Copeland and Weston (1988) and Weston and Copeland (1992). When it is incorporated, it is frequently referred to by the letters PVGO – present value of growth opportunities.

Now, let's move on and take an R & D situation as a quantified example of an investment opportunity with a broad spectrum of flexibility. The numerical data are as follows. Bringing the research work that has already been done on a product to the marketplace is likely to involve further investment, entailing, first of all, development costs of £3 million in each of years 0, 1 and 2. In year 3, the firm would then, assuming market and other environmental conditions were favourable, build a plant costing some £40 million to go commercial. Assume that all data are net of tax and that no new working capital investment is required. The scaled-up project is expected to generate £5 million per annum for 10 years and at the end of year 13 have a terminal value of £10 million. The appropriate risk-adjusted discount rate is 12 per cent. How does such a project look in terms of its net present value? Well, we can approach this problem via traditional DCF analysis or by a more sophisticated decision-tree route involving the firm's options available. We'll take the former first of all. Whether the project is viewed from year 0 or year 3 as the first year of the series of cash flows, traditional discounting produces a negative net present value. Table 7.3 shows the relevant numbers involved. In summary, it indicates that, with year 0 as a base, the expected incremental cash flows give a net present value of minus £14.13 million. With year 3 as a base (that is, viewing the flows for years 0, 1 and 2 as sunk), the net present value of incremental flows is minus £8.53 million. The discount rate used is 12 per cent per annum and the makeup of the net present value is shown in Table 7.4.

What happens, though, if we look at this project with the help of our knowledge of decision-tree analysis? This approach takes cognisance of the fact that, when it comes to going commercial, the firm faces more than one possible demand scenario and more than one operating option. In order to give an idea of the kind of analysis necessary, assume that, rather

Table 7.3 R & D project viewed from the standpoint of traditional DCF analysis (figures in £ million)

Expected incremental cash flow in year	**0**	**1**	**2**	**3**	**4 to 13 inclusive**	**13**
Costs and revenues						
Development costs	–3	–3	–3			
Plant and equipment				–40		
Incremental inflows					+5 pa	
Terminal value						+10
Discounting cash flows @ 12% with year 0 as base	–3	–2.67	–2.40	–28.40	+20.05	+2.29
Net present value as at year 0	–14.13					
Discounting cash flows at 12% with year 3 as base (cash flows in years 0, 1 or 2 become sunk costs)				–40	+28.25	+3.22
Net present value as at year 3				–8.53		

Table 7.4 Present value of incremental flows (£ million)

Base year	0	3
Development costs	–8.07	
Plant and equipment	–28.40	–40.00
Post-year 3 operating inflows	+20.05	+28.25
Terminal value	+2.29	+3.22
Net present value	–14.13	–8.53

than facing a single incremental cash flow scenario for years 3 to 13, the firm is of the view that there are four reasonably possible outcomes, all with a 25 per cent probability associated with them. Remember that what we are trying to do is to make a decision as at time 0 about whether to go ahead with development. Unadjusted for decision-tree analysis, the four outcomes would have a sum of post-year 3 operating inflows plus terminal value of (see Table 7.4) £31.47 million (measured in terms of year 3 present values). In respect of the four possible outcomes, let us assume that the sum of operating inflows and terminal values is estimated (in year 3 present value terms) as:

- Scenario 1 + £90.00 million
- Scenario 2 + £45.00 million
- Scenario 3 + £6.88 million
- Scenario 4 – £16.00 million

With this background, and given scenario 1, the firm would clearly go ahead and build the commercial-scale plant. The same decision would hold for scenario 2 as well. But note that the present value of incremental inflows for scenarios 3 and 4 make it obvious that the firm would not build the big plant because incremental inflows would fail to recoup the £40 million outlay necessary. Table 7.5 shows these scenarios in further detail.

The data in Table 7.5 are transformed into estimated values as of year 3 by multiplying the net present value under each scenario by the probability of occurrence. This has been done in Table 7.6 where it can be seen that a value, as of year 3, amounting to £13.75 million is obtained. This figure is the decision-tree/option analysis net present value of inflows and terminal value using scenarios 1 to 4. Remember that the developmental cost of £3 million per annum through years 0, 1 and 2 gave us a present value of these outflows totalling £8.07 (in year 0 present value terms). When the expected value of £13.75 million as at year 3 is converted to year 0 terms by discounting at 12 per cent per annum, a figure of £9.79 million is obtained. This is sufficient, if all our calculations

Table 7.5 R & D project – scenarios viewed from the standpoint of decision-tree/option analysis

Value of	R & D	Plant and equipment	Incremental flows plus terminal value	Net present value
Measured in present value terms as at year	**0**	**3**	**3**	**0**
Traditional discounted cash flow analysis as in Table 7.4 (£ million)	–8.07	–40.00	+31.47	–14.13
Decision-tree approach				
Scenario 1	–8.07	–40.00	+90.00	(35.59 – 8.07)
Scenario 2	–8.07	–40.00	+45.00	(3.56 – 8.07)
Scenario 3	–8.07	–	+6.88	–8.07
Scenario 4	–8.07	–	–16.00	–8.07

Table 7.6 R & D project valued from the standpoint of decision-tree analysis

	Decision	Plant and equipment in year 3 cost terms (£ million)	Incremental cash inflows in year 3 present value terms (£ million)	Incremental inflow multiplied by probability (£ million)	Expected net present value in year 3 terms (£ million)
Scenario 1	Scale up	–40.00	+90.00	+50 (0.25)	12.50
Scenario 2	Scale up	–40.00	+45.00	+5 (0.25)	1.25
Scenario 3	Do nothing	–	–	nil	–
Scenario 4	Do nothing	–	–	nil	–
					13.75
Multiply by present value factor for year 3 at 12%					0.7118
Year 0 present value of expected incremental inflows					£9.79 million
Less development costs in year 0 present value terms					£8.07 million
Net present value according to decision-tree analysis					£1.72 million

are correct, to justify proceeding with development – the net present value is £1.72 million. The decision-tree/option analysis, then, indicates a decision to go ahead with development whereas traditional discounted cash flow suggests a no go decision.

In ignoring the option not to build the plant, traditional DCF analysis estimates a negative net present value (NPV) of £8.53 million as of year 3. Option valuation allows for the decision not to build the plant and it values only those outcomes that will follow if the plant is built. If the R & D investment fails to work or if market conditions are unfavourable, the plant will not be built. Figure 7.2 shows the probability distribution of possible outcomes of the R & D investment as of year 3 according to both the traditional DCF valuation method and the decision-tree valuation method. It clearly illustrates the contrast between the two methods of appraisal. The decision-tree/option valuation approach properly values only positive NPV outcomes, since if negative out-turns are forecast, the plant will not be scaled up. By contrast, traditional DCF analysis values all outcomes – negative as well as positive, which must logically be wrong since if negative NPV out-turns are forecast, scaling-up investment will not take place.

Of course, the example in Tables 7.3 to 7.6 inclusive is simplistic. In reality, the firm is invariably presented with a more complicated set of possible outcomes and it may be feasible to build plants of different sizes; the example simply incorporates one plant costing £40 million. These complexities would not alter the method of analysis; they would merely make the figuring more extensive. And they would make the problem an obvious candidate for computer analysis.

THE BLACK AND SCHOLES APPROACH

It is evidently the contention of this chapter that the means of appraisal suggested makes it ideal for analysing extractive industry projects, research and development investments and cross-frontier expansion of a pre-emptive nature. The basic framework can be sophisticated without too much difficulty to give it the full range of Black and Scholes features for those projects where future commodity prices form the main variable in the investment decision.

For readers requiring a very quick refresher on the mathematical model developed by Fischer Black and Myron Scholes (1973) for pricing stock market traded options, a quick summary follows. Their assumptions are:

- The option can be exercised at maturity only
- There are no transaction costs and no taxes

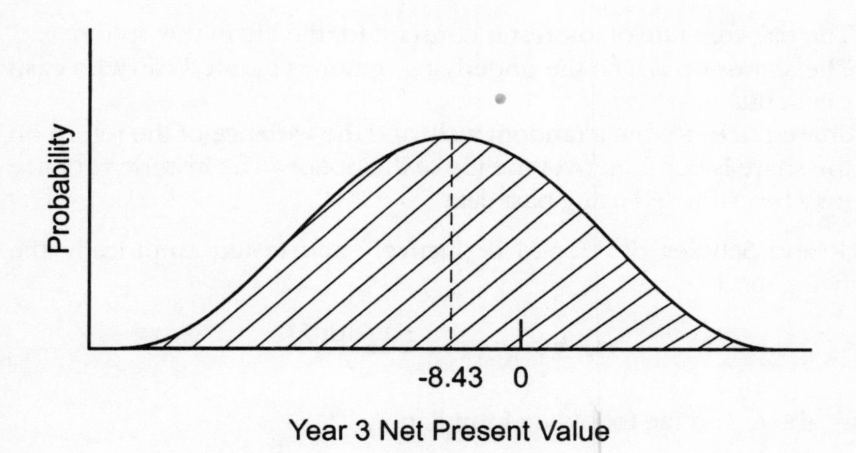

Traditional DCF valuation assumes the plant will be built and it values both positive and negative potential out-turns

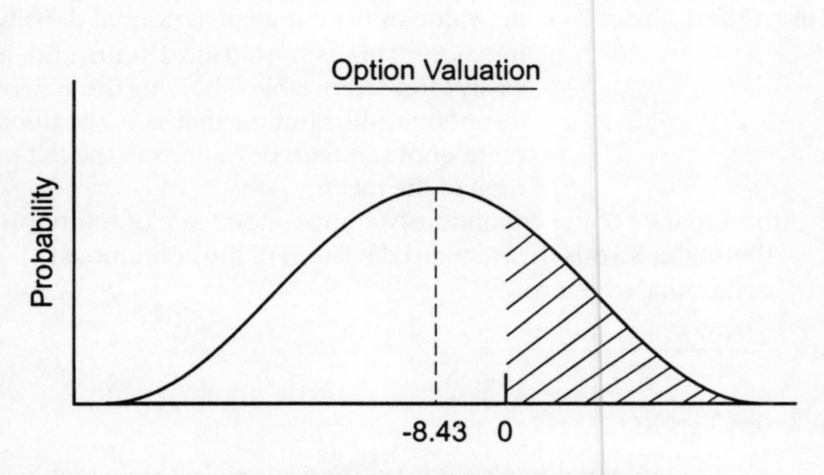

Option valuation takes cognisance of the possible decision not to build the plant. It values only out-turns that will follow should the plant be built.

Figure 7.2 Traditional DCF Valuation versus option vluation

- The risk-free rate of interest is constant for the life of the option
- The shares on which the underlying option is granted carry no cash dividends
- Share prices follow a random walk and the variance of the return on the share is constant over the life of the option. The historic variance may be estimated using past data.

Black and Scholes developed deductively and tested empirically the following model:

$$C = SN(dist\,1) - \frac{EN(\text{dist } 2)}{e^{rt}}$$

In the above and the following formulations:

C = price of the option
S = current price of the shares
E = exercise price
t = time remaining before expiration of the option, usually expressed as a proportion of a year
e = the base of the natural logarithm, or 2.71828
r = the continuously compounded riskless rate of interest
N(dist 1) and N(dist 2) = the value of the cumulative normal density function. This is a statistical term and is easily found from tables showing the area of the normal distribution that is a specified number of standard deviations to the left or right of the mean.
$\sigma 2$ = the variance of the continuously compounded rate of return on the share. So σ is the standard deviation of the continuously compounded return.

$$\text{dist } 1 = \frac{ln(S/E) + (r + \frac{1}{2}\sigma^2)t}{\sigma\sqrt{t}}$$

$$\text{dist } 2 = \text{dist } 1 - \sigma\sqrt{t}$$

The above formulation is complex. And its derivation obviously involves mathematics beyond elementary levels. But since readers may be more interested in its application than its proof, a numerical example follows. Assume that the current share price is £2.36, the strike price is £1.90 and there are 22 days of an option to run to expiration. With a risk-free rate of return of 9 per cent and a variance rate of return of 16 per cent (found by contrasting the performance of the company's shares against the market), we can now find the likely value of a call option according to the Black and Scholes model. From statistical tables N(dist 1) and N(dist 2) may be found to be 0.990 and 0.987 respectively. The theoretical value of the option in pence can be found from the formula to be:

$$236 \times 0.990 - \frac{190 \times 0.987}{2.71828^{0.0925 \times 0.06027}}$$

This simplifies to 47 pence. The answer can easily be checked in general terms. The value of the option must be at least the difference between the stock price and the exercise price, namely 46 pence (the intrinsic value). Since the option period is short, implying a low time value, the option premium should be near to this figure.

Effectively then, option pricing follows the routine summarised in Figure 7.3. What is most interesting is not the variables that are used in the formulation but those that are left out. It is important to note that in all the above models no mention has been made of market direction or bias as an appropriate input. An implicit assumption of the model is that the market moves in a random fashion. In other words, while prices change, the chances of a rise are the same as the chances of a fall, and the likelihood of large movements relative to small movements is normally distributed. Plotting daily market movements over time should, according to this assumption, result in the bell-shaped curve, the normal distribution.

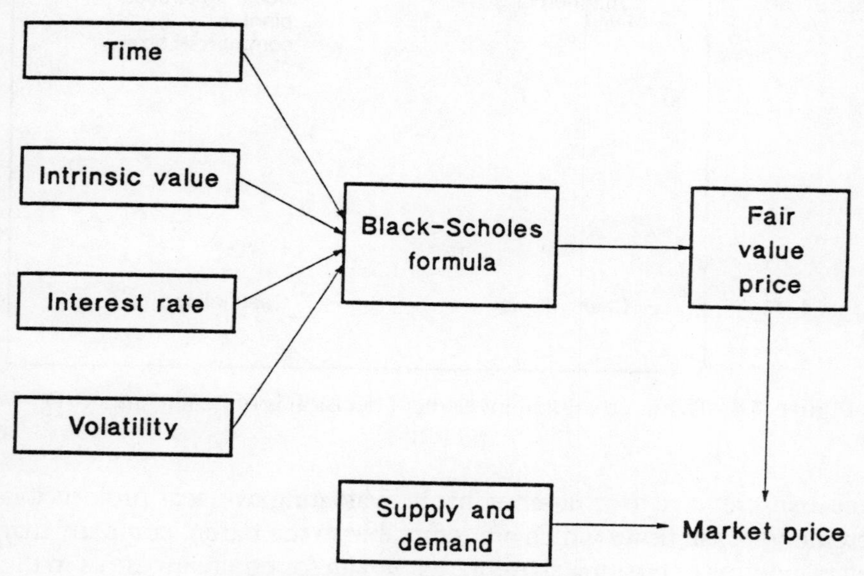

Figure 7.3 How an option is priced

THE INTERNATIONAL DIMENSIONS

The mode of appraisal so far considered would ideally suit the international investment decision. The R & D example given above could easily be adapted to suit typical pre-emptive international investment decisions because of their essential similarities. The closeness of the R & D example and a pre-emptive international project is summarised in Figure 7.4. If mining projects and R & D projects are cousins, international investments and R & D are second cousins.

	R & D Example	International Investment Decision
Years 0–2	Development costs	Pilot plant with low volume sales
Year 3	Commercial scale plant	Scale up of pilot plant to commercial size
Years 4–13	Cash inflows	Cash inflows

Figure 7.4 The international investment decision is quite like an R & D project

Of course, we have to remember that in evaluating overseas projects it is incremental cash flows which are remittable to the parent company that matter in terms of creating shareholder wealth for equity investors in the home country based parent. So this creates a further dimension of complexity, but one that is fairly readily handled, focus being upon cash generation which may legally be sent back to the home territory (where, of course, it may suffer further tax deduction which also has to be taken into account).

The kind of contingent methodology which is exemplified in this chapter would clearly lend itself readily to toe-in-the-water type investments that a lot of Western companies are undertaking in Eastern Europe or China where upside potential may be evident and, if found to be forthcoming, would involve an upgrading of relatively minor initial investment. That companies do not take this into account in quantitative appraisal terms at the present point in time may be due to the lack of publicity given, until now, to the technique of analysis which is, in all probability, most relevant. The author feels, on the basis of his experience in business, that qualitatively this mode of analysis is used by many far-sighted top managers.

It needs to be stressed that application of the Black and Scholes routine to investment projects which possess option features will yield a superior result, in terms of quality of analysis, than the decision-tree approach. Remember that the latter method merely captures a small number of all possible out-turns – in the R & D example in this chapter, only four scenarios were looked at. In reality, there is a whole continuum of possible scenarios in between the four which have been spotlighted – these are effectively ignored in a simple decision-tree approach. Using a methodology based on Black and Scholes, this deficiency is overcome. But remember that the Black and Scholes approach is only appropriate where potential out-turns exhibit a random walk. Where this is not the case, the decision-tree method would better capture the reality of the situation. Used in appropriate circumstances, calling into play the standard deviation and variance of potential outcomes, Black and Scholes captures the whole spectrum of possible payoffs. It does focus upon those would-be results between scenario 1, scenario 2, scenario 3 and scenario 4 in the example earlier in this chapter. As such, it is likely to yield a more accurate result, all other things being equal. Of course, it has to be said that building into our equation a standard deviation of potential oil prices may not be difficult. After all, we have past evidence to help us and our own views on the future volatility of prices. It is therefore not too problematical to build a Black and Scholes model in these circumstances. But what about an R & D project on building a new plant in China? Assuming that potential results display random walk characteristics, the decision-tree approach may be acceptable, but a better result would flow from an option pricing methodology, even though firm evidence or estimates on standard deviations are pretty much pie in the sky.

In practice, if we are looking at a normal distribution of returns, we may be able to use the Black and Scholes formula, with an approximate figure for the standard deviation of returns. The method to be used might first of all involve calculating the mean return. Then an estimated distribution of probable returns may be crudely approximated by asking appropriate questions of key managers involved in the potential project. This should yield an indication of subjective views on the distribution of possible outcomes prior to input to the option pricing model. Of course this approach is pretty rough and ready. And, in practice, a decision tree route may be acceptable.

THE MESSAGE

The valuation of projects that have more than one tranche of investment, with the latter a function of the former, or of market conditions, requires a form of investment appraisal which is beyond traditional discounted cash flow – it needs to take account of available options that the firm might pursue. To use the analogy of option pricing, what we need to look at is, effectively, the base case value which would be the product of traditional DCF analysis and, on top of this, the value of the discretion associated with either undertaking, or not undertaking, the scale-up scenario. To put this algebraically, we would have:

$$V = NPV + Opt$$

where V is the theoretical increment to value of the firm, NPV is the base case net present value and Opt is the value associated with the option.

Option pricing theory tells us that there are four critical variables in valuing any option. These are (see Figure 7.3) time value, volatility, interest rates and intrinsic value. To put these variables into the context of investment projects as options, it should be clear that they liken, respectively, to the following.

- The period of time during which the scale-up decision may be realistically deferred.
- The volatility of the price and demand for the key product of the project. This is substantially all to do with the risk associated with the project.
- The level of interest rates.
- The proprietary nature of the option.

Let us look in more detail at each of the above key points. Taking the deferrability of scale-up first, the ability to put off an investment gives the firm additional time to examine the course of future events and to reduce the chance of costly errors should unfavourable developments occur. The longer the time interval to scale up, the greater the odds that a positive turn of events will occur thus increasing the project's profitability. It could, of course, even transform a negative NPV project into a positive one.

We now turn to the riskiness of the project itself. Surprisingly enough, the greater the risk associated with the investment, the more valuable an option on it. This arises because of the asymmetry of gains and losses. A big upside out-turn confers a highly positive NPV. But large downside operating out-turns do not necessarily flow through to the bottom limit NPV because of the option not to scale up. This means that the riskier the project the greater the odds of a large gain without a corresponding increase in the size of the potential loss. It needs to be borne in mind, of course, that whilst an increase in the risk of the project may increase the value of the option, in the context of capital budgeting it may increase the asset beta and thus reduce the NPV of the base case scenario. So, whether increased volatility actually increases the value of the overall project cannot be immutably asserted. Sometimes the increased value of the option exceeds the reduction in the NPV of the base case scenario; sometimes the increased value of the option falls short of the reduction in the NPV of the base case scenario.

The same kind of logic applies in respect of the level of interest rates. A higher discount rate, all other things being equal, lowers the present value of a project's future cash flows. At the same time, it reduces the present value of the cash outlay needed to exercise an option. Generally, but not always, the net effect is that high interest rates raise the value of projects with expansion options.

Fourthly, there is the proprietary nature of the option itself. What do we mean by this? Very simply, that an exclusively owned option is worth more than one which is shared or competed for with others. Self-evidently, shared options are less valuable because competitors can replicate the firm's investments and, in so doing, drive down profitability. Kester (1984) observes that companies frequently commit investment funds early rather than late, despite their ability to defer. Presumably the cost of deferring exceeds the value sacrificed in early exercise. He goes on to suggest that it pays a company to exercise its growth options earlier rather than later when:

- Options are not proprietary; that is, they are shared
- The project's NPV is high

- The level of risk and interest rates are low
- Industry rivalry is intense.

Kester provides a useful guideline through a two by two matrix in respect of timing of commitment of capital. Figure 7.5 summarises the essence of his suggested decision matrix. An interesting comment by Kester is that companies generally try 'to obtain a dominant competitive position in order to achieve and protect high returns on investment. But by giving a company the right to time the investment more selectively, the growth option provides an important, though often overlooked, motive for dominating the market'.

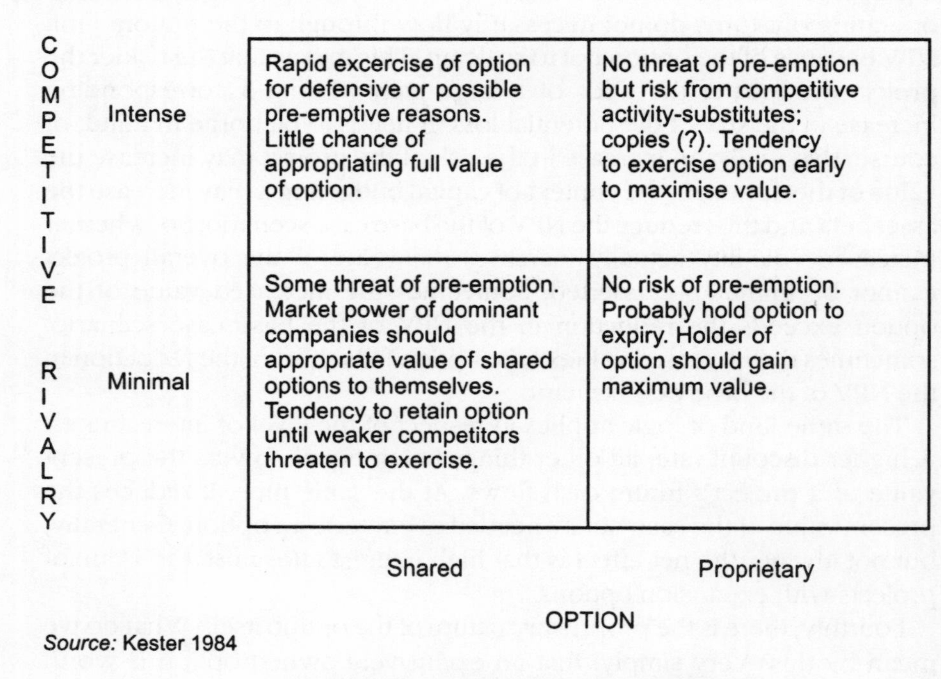

COMPETITIVE RIVALRY
Intense
Minimal
Rapid excercise of option for defensive or possible pre-emptive reasons. Little chance of appropriating full value of option.
No threat of pre-emption but risk from competitive activity-substitutes; copies (?). Tendency to exercise option early to maximise value.
Some threat of pre-emption. Market power of dominant companies should appropriate value of shared options to themselves. Tendency to retain option until weaker competitors threaten to exercise.
No risk of pre-emption. Probably hold option to expiry. Holder of option should gain maximum value.
Shared
Proprietary
OPTION
Source: Kester 1984

Figure 7.5 Investment timing matrix

Kesinger (1987) summarises the position in three operating rules:

1. The more volatile the relationship between the prices of input and output commodities, the greater the difference between the true NPV and the DCF-NPV.
2. The difference between the true project NPV and the DCF-NPV is greater the more innovative the project, and the stronger the barriers to entry for potential competitors.
3. A company which has the same uses as another company, plus

additional operating options, will gain a higher NPV. The more flexible the system, the greater the difference between the true project NPV and the DCF-NPV.

The third point above may need some clarification. It refers to the sort of operating flexibility that might be endowed by building heating capacity that could be fired by either gas, coal or oil, as opposed to any one of these individual fuels; and there is a wealth of similar examples.

Suffice to say that the potential for developing theory and practice along the lines summarised here should be self-evident and fruitful. After all, good top managers are probably looking, qualitatively, at opportunities in just this way. They ask themselves what are the potential returns, how can capital investment be controlled, and how can they pre-empt competition, limit downside risk but keep as many courses of action as possible open?

The Boston box concept of a sturdy clutch of wildcats, one or two of which will become stars and cash cows, whilst those that don't mature appropriately are culled (or capped is perhaps a better term), is a very similar idea. The wildcats are the options. Investing in new opportunities in a pre-emptive, relatively inexpensive and painless way short term (the option premium) gives the scope to increase involvement later on if successful (the exercise of the option). In managing the portfolio, the out-of-date, unsuccessful options have to be curtailed; failure to do so nurtures Boston box dogs.

The message is that structuring investment decisions in such a way as to confer option elements enhances shareholder value over and above the base case present value. In fact, the value of an investment is equal to the present value of the base case scenario, the typical NPV calculation, plus the potential associated with options to scale up, to abandon and so on.

CONCLUSION

In this chapter it is contended that many international investment decisions should be financially appraised in terms of decision-tree or option pricing model analysis. With mining projects and oil exploration, it is usually the case that the price of the commodity (and hence returns) is likely to follow a random walk, making application of the Black and Scholes methodology appropriate. This is rarely the case with R & D projects and frequently it is not so for international investment either (except mining, oil and the like). Potential returns may be vastly skewed – for example pharmaceutical research might promise a small probability of a vast pay-off versus a large probability of nothing at all. And pre-emptive investment in a concrete roof tile plant in Eastern Europe may also promise non-normal distribution potential with, perhaps, high probabilities at the low out-turn end. In such circumstances it may be entirely inappropriate to use a Black and Scholes based method since, as will be recalled from earlier mention in this chapter, one of the key assumptions of their model is that prices follow a random walk with constant variance over the life of the option.

In cases when the distribution of returns is non-normal, it is recommended that valuation of growth options in international investment and R & D situations involves a decision-tree route – maybe using fairly imprecise, but ball-park figures, for NPV and probabilities along the lines of the data analysis in Tables 7.3 to 7.6 inclusive.

If we are in a situation where the distribution of returns is normal, using a Black and Scholes methodology would be appropriate. But we may have to estimate the standard deviation of returns crudely. Thus, having determined the mean return, asking appropriate questions of key managers involved in the project should yield an indication of their subjective views on the distribution of potential out-turns. And this may be input into the option pricing model.

Applied to the total corporate business, the logic of valuing growth options is relevant. The value of the firm is given by the present value (PV) of future cash flows projected for existing operations, based upon conventional discounting algebra (plus the present value of the tax shield on debt if an adjusted present value (APV) approach is being used), plus the value of options embedded in its operations – including R & D, international investments and similar activities – and the value of put and call options which may have accrued as a result of financing the business. (Of course when debt with put or call features, warrants and so on is *initially* issued, the no free lunch theory would suggest that the company would not have any put or call gains or losses; these may accrue through the passage of time given changes to interest rates, exchange rates, share prices and so forth.) Written formally in terms of an APV equation:

APV of business =	APV	of existing operations currently in place
	+	PV of tax shield on debt
	±	PV of financing options which may have accrued
	+	PV of options on R & D, international operations, mining activities, operational flexibility etc (PVGO)

It is interesting to note that Woolridge (1988) identified significant shareholder gains accruing in pursuance of announcements of R & D advances and expenditures. This would surely be a reflection of the call option element endowed by the nature of the breakthrough.

Clearly the importance of the perspective described in this section to strategic management and to financial management cannot be overstated. It is not the contention of this chapter that traditional DCF analysis should be rejected. The argument advanced here is that it needs to be refined in appropriate cases by the application of decision-tree/options analysis. Together, and correctly used, the two are a potent force. The cricketing analogy of Pakistan's two fast bowlers Waqar Younis and Wasim Akram is obvious. Both powerful in their own right, their combination is lethal. Going back a bit, the pairings of Trueman and Statham, Laker and Lock and Miller and Lindwall also spring to mind. As a follower of football in the 1960s and '70s, the analogy of Bobby Charlton and Dennis Law (oh, and George Best too) also springs to mind. No more analogies...my age is showing!

LESSONS FOR MANAGERS

The whole point is that one of the strategies that adds corporate value is to maintain flexibility through structuring investments – and indeed a whole host of other managerial actions – in a manner paralleling options. Investments of this kind, which includes the lion's share of international commitments, should be:

- Evaluated to embrace the option characteristics
- Analysed from a standpoint beyond the traditional DCF model.

Structuring investment decisions in such a way as to confer an option element enhances shareholder value over and above the base case present value scenario. Failure to evaluate investments of this kind to allow for this option aspect can only result in an understatement of the potential shareholder value created.

REFERENCES

Barwise, P, Marsh, P R and Wensley, R (1989) 'Must Finance and Strategy Clash?', *Harvard Business Review*, Sep–Oct, 85–90

Black, F and Scholes, M (1973) 'The Pricing of Options and Corporate Liabilities', *Journal of Political Economy*, May–Jun, 637–59

Brennan, M and Schwartz, E (1985) 'A New Approach to Evaluating Natural

Resource Investments', *Midland Corporate Finance Journal*, spring, Vol 3, No 1, 37–47, in Chew, D H Jnr (ed) (1993) *The New Corporate Finance*, McGraw-Hill, New York

Copeland, T E and Weston, J F (1988) *Financial Theory and Corporate Policy*, 3rd ed, Addison-Wesley, Reading, MA

Copeland, T, Koller, J and Murrin, J (1990) *Valuation*, Wiley, New York

Kesinger, J W (1987) 'Adding the Value of Active Management into the Capital Budgeting Equation', *Midland Corporate Finance Journal*, Vol 5, No 1, 31–42

Kester, W C (1984) 'Today's Options for Tomorrow's Growth', *Harvard Business Review*, Mar–Apr, 153–60

—(1986), 'An Options Approach to Corporate Finance', in Altman, E *Handbook of Corporate Finance*, Wiley, New York

—and Morley, J (1992) 'Note on Cross-Border Valuation', Harvard Business School note 292–084 in Kester, W C and Luehrman, T A (1993) *Case Problems in International Finance*, McGraw-Hill, New York

Kulatilaka, N and Marcus, A J (1992), 'Project Valuation Under Uncertainty: When Does DCF Fail?', *Journal of Applied Corporate Finance*, fall, Vol 5, No 3, 92–100.

Mason, S P and Merton, R C (1985) 'The Role of Contingent Claims Analysis in Corporate Finance', in Altman, E I and Subrahmanyam, M G (eds) *Recent Advances in Corporate Finance*, Richard D Irwin, Holmwood, Ill

Robichek, A and van Horne, J (1967) 'Abandonment Value and Capital Budgeting', *Journal of Finance*, Dec

Shapiro, A C (1990) *Modern Corporate Finance*, Macmillan, New York

—(1992) *Multinational Financial Management*, 4th ed, Allyn and Bacon, Needham Heights, Mass

Siegel, D R, Smith, J L and Paddock, J L (1987) 'Valuing Offshore Oil Properties with Option Pricing Models', *Midland Corporate Finance Journal*, spring, Vol 5, No 1, 22–30 in Chew, D H, Jnr (ed) (1993) *The New Corporate Finance*, McGraw-Hill, New York

Weston, J F and Copeland, T E (1992) *Managerial Finance*, 9th edn, The Dryden Press, Fort Worth, Texas

Woolridge, J R (1988) 'Competitive Decline: Is a Myopic Stock Market to Blame?', *Journal of Applied Corporate Finance*, Vol 1, No 1, spring, 26–36

8

Privatisation and the International Business Environment

David Parker, University of Birmingham

INTRODUCTION

This chapter is concerned with the nature of privatisation and its impact on international business. During the 1980s many countries followed Britain's lead and introduced wide-ranging privatisation programmes embracing state-asset sales, deregulation and competitive tendering for public services. The argument for these reforms centred upon raising efficiency, although in developing countries, and after 1989 in the former communist economies, raising finance for essential investments also proved an important rationale. Elsewhere privatisation receipts provided a useful supplement to hard-stretched government treasuries and in some countries, notably Britain, privatisation provided a means of increasing share ownership or expanding 'popular capitalism'. But it has been the belief that resources are more efficiently used in the private sector which has been the most enduring argument for privatising state assets.

Privatisation alters both the internal and external environments of business and in doing so changes the agenda for management. Privatisation creates new opportunities for investment, production and trade, but at the same time it introduces new uncertainties regarding the future shape of economies and political regimes. This is especially so in the former communist economies of Central and Eastern Europe, but it is also true in the capitalist economies.

Public enterprises are said to be inefficient because:

1. Management in state industries is given vague and conflicting objectives in 'pursuit of the public interest'
2. State industries suffer from political interference leading to distorted output, pricing and investment policies
3. Politicians and civil servants fail to monitor and control management behaviour as effectively as the private capital market
4. Trade unions in the public sector succeed in improving their own

pecuniary and non-pecuniary incomes at the expense of taxpayers (in other words they pursue economic rents)
5. Where taxpayers underwrite losses and bankruptcy is not a credible threat efficiency must decline
6. Managerial salaries in the public sector are politically determined and rarely compare with equivalent salaries in the private sector, therefore the quality of management suffers (Parker 1985, Winiecki 1991).

While acknowledging the potential inefficiencies of state ownership, economists recognise, however, that simply transferring assets from the state to the private sector does not guarantee a performance improvement (Millward and Parker 1983, Kay and Thompson 1986, Vickers and Yarrow 1988, Hartley et al 1991). In other words, the act of privatisation is not a sufficient condition for better performance. Not all privatised firms have recorded higher productivity since privatisation (Parker and Martin, 1993). Such evidence suggests that ownership per se is not a sufficient explanation of performance changes. Research suggests that if performance is to improve then the incentive environment facing management must alter (Dunsire et al 1991, Parker 1993a).

Privatisation has been heavily studied from an economics perspective, while the implications for undertaking international business and for corporate strategy have been relatively undeveloped. This chapter attempts to refocus the discussion and research agenda. The first part of it provides a model for assessing the likely impact of privatisation on efficiency. This is then extended by considering the implications of privatisation for internal organisation and management. Reference is particularly made to three economies, which have been selected to represent the privatisation process in a developed economy, a developing economy and a mis-developed economy, namely the UK, Malaysia and Czechoslovakia respectively. (On 1 January 1993 Czechoslovakia split into two sovereign republics, the Czech Republic and the Slovak Republic.)

The discussion of privatisation in each of these economies is couched in terms of:

- The context
- The content
- The process
- The form of privatisation.

By context is meant the history and the social, economic and political environment in which privatisation is taking place. Content describes the privatisation and the scale of change. Process is concerned with the method by which privatisation occurs. The type of privatisation introduced and the conditions attached to it are what is meant by the form of privatisation. The chapter ends by emphasising the implications for international business.

Throughout the chapter reference is made to 'efficiency'. It is recognised that efficiency can have many dimensions. Here it is taken to embrace static and dynamic efficiencies as understood in economic theory. Static efficiency exists when a firm produces a given output at least cost in terms of resource use (this is sometimes known as productive efficiency or 'X'-efficiency). Dynamic efficiency relates to innovation in terms of outputs and production processes leading to higher consumer welfare.

A MODEL FOR ASSESSING THE IMPACT OF PRIVATISATION ON EFFICIENCY

Economists argue that privatisation can improve efficiency by altering favourably the external environment in which managers operate. It can do so firstly by changing the product market in which firms operate from monopolistic to competitive. Firms supplying in competitive markets have to be efficient to survive. Some economists have gone so far as to argue that it is competition rather than ownership which is the key to performance improvement under privatisation (eg Kay and Thompson 1986), though where the state retains ownership it has a direct pecuniary incentive to limit competition. Competition could produce losses in state firms which have to be met by the exchequer. In that sense ownership and competition are related.

Secondly, privatisation alters the 'agent-principal' relationship. Agent-principal relationships exist wherever one person or set of persons (the principals) devolve powers to another person or persons to act on their behalf. In business this is seen most clearly in the relationship between management and shareholders. The shareholders hold the ultimate property rights in the firm and appoint managers to manage their assets. The shareholders are the principals and the managers their agents. Provided the management manage the firm in the interests of the shareholders, the relationship imposes minimal transaction costs (simply the costs of information flows back and forth between shareholders and managers). However, the agent-principal relationship provides opportunities for management to 'cheat' on their shareholders by pursuing their own pecuniary and non-pecuniary incomes at the expense of returns to shareholders. To minimise this cost, shareholders must provide appropriate reward structures for management (eg profit bonuses) and undertake the costs of monitoring managerial behaviour (monitoring costs).

Agent-principal relationships exist in the public sector too. Indeed, here they are usually more complex, involving the public as principals; politicians and top civil servants as first-tier agents; and the boards of state industries and departments as second-tier agents. The more elaborate agency relationship increases monitoring costs; in addition it is generally recognised that the ballot box is an inefficient mechanism for the public to signal how it wishes its industries and services to be run. Politicians, civil servants and public boards may lack the necessary information on the principal's wants to manage public assets effectively. By contrast, the Austrian economist Friedrich von Hayek (1978) and others have questioned the incentive mechanism for public sector managers to manage in the interests of the public even when the information exists. Public sector managers may pursue their own utility. The relative efficiency of public and private operations appears to reduce to which of the two institutional forms, public or private ownership, best provides the information and incentives to agents and principals to ensure economic efficiency.

In the private sector principals can sell their shares in their firms and thus exit from the market. Selling shares depresses the share price and can lead to a takeover bid by rival management (Alchian 1965, Jensen and Meckling 1976, Fama 1980, Hartley and Parker 1991). No such mechanism exists in the public sector where shares are not tradable (indeed tangible shares may not exist at all). Moreover, in recent years the large, institutional investors (eg pension funds) have proved willing to put pressure on management to resign when returns to shareholders have proved especially disappointing. State enterprises may be supported by long-term funding from the exchequer and hence captive taxpayers. In addition, public ownership is highly diffused amongst the entire population.

A change in the agent-principal relationship caused by privatisation may therefore have an appreciable impact on a firm's performance independently of any change in the product market. Finally, objectives of firms in the private and public sectors may well differ, with a consequent impact on operating efficiency. In the private sector firms usually have short- and longer-term objectives related to the pursuit of profit (shareholders require profit); in the public sector objectives can be multifarious, diffused, confused and sometimes inadequately articulated.

The roles of competition, the agent-principal relationship and managerial objectives are brought together in Figure 8.1, which provides a simple schema for mapping organisations and their performance. This cube relationship is based on a recognition that the underlying objective of privatisation is to raise static and dynamic efficiency (Hartley and Parker 1991). Control over the firm by owners can vary between the extremes of total and minimum control, depending upon the agent-principal relationship. Total control implies that the firm's management will manage the business exactly in accordance with the objective(s) of the principals.

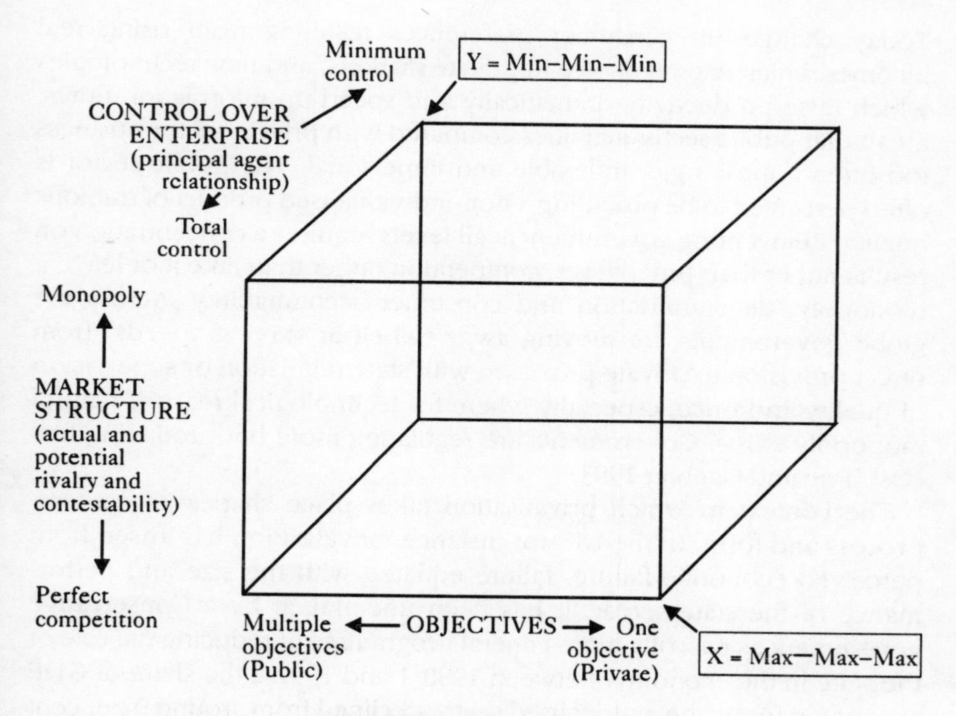

Figure 8.1 The cube model

The usefulness of this schema to an analysis of privatisation can be illustrated as follows. A firm at position X exists in a perfectly competitive product market, there is complete control of management by the owners, and the firm pursues one clear objective or compatible set of objectives. Taking profit maximisation as this objective, position X implies maximum incentives for static and dynamic efficiency. This can be contrasted with position Y. A state-owned monopolist with minimal agent control over management and multiple and conflicting objectives can be expected to have low efficiency.

The cube can be a useful tool to assess the likely scope and source of efficiency gains under privatisation. Privatisation tends to involve movements falling between the polar points of X and Y implying varying degrees of maxima and minima and hence differences in expected performance changes.

THE CONTEXT OF PRIVATISATION

Today changes in consumer preferences resulting from rising real incomes which extend choice in private markets, and new technologies which raise productivity dramatically and speed up information flows, mean that public sector activities compared with private sector business too often appear rigid, inflexible and impersonal. The public sector is often perceived to be providing a non-individualised product of dubious quality. Reinventing government at all levels requires a concentration on results rather than procedures, competition rather than take it or leave it monopoly, decentralisation and consumer accountability. Across the globe governments are moving away (albeit at varying speeds) from direct provision to private provision with state regulation or supervision of quality and price, especially where for technological reasons natural monopoly exists. Governments are regulating more but producing less (Osborne and Gaebler 1993).

The context in which privatisation takes place shapes its content, process and form. In the UK, for instance, privatisation has arisen from perceived economic failure, failure equated with the size and performance of the state sector. It has been undertaken by a Conservative government as part of a more general programme of reducing the role of the state in the economy. Between 1980/1 and 1991/2 the share of GDP accounted for by the nationalised sector declined from around 9 per cent to just 3 per cent, giving Britain one of the smallest publicly-owned industrial sectors. The origins of privatisation, therefore, lie in political realignment in the 1970s, which saw the Conservative party adopt policies based on more liberal free market economics, thus ending the post-war consensus on the role of the state. This political realignment in turn arose from years of poor economic performance, which was blamed on the growth of the state sector.

The origins of privatisation in Czechoslovakia, as in Britain, lie in political realignment following the perceived failure of state industry. But in Czechoslovakia, and now in the independent Czech and Slovak Republics, the change is of a different scale involving 'turnaround management' across the entire economy and at a time of major economic dislocation. In 1989 61 per cent of the country's exports flowed through

COMECON; by 1991 COMECON was disbanded and trade with the former communist states had collapsed. Despite seeking new markets in the West, in 1991 alone the country's GDP fell by around 16 per cent.

In the last decade Malaysia's economy has been highly successful in attracting inward investment, notably from Japan, recently producing an economic growth rate in excess of 8 per cent per annum. Unlike in Britain, therefore, in Malaysia privatisation does not arise from perceived economic failure. It does arise, however, from concern about the costs of public investments, which impose a strain on the exchequer, and from a desire to improve the performance of the state sector. The desire to develop the stock market has also been a factor.

Malaysia is a multi-ethnic society with 55 per cent of the population Bumiputra (Malay), 43 per cent Chinese and 10 per cent of Indian descent. At independence the Chinese dominated the economy, while the Bumiputra majority held political control. Following serious racial riots in May 1969, economic policy was geared to redistributing income and wealth in favour of the Bumiputra population. Directly and through banks and trust agencies, public sector investment grew at a rate of 12.6 per cent per annum in real terms during the 1970s. The existence of complex interlocking shareholdings between firms and the federal structure of state and regional authorities, both of whom have invested in firms, combines to make estimation of the precise scope of public ownership in Malaysia difficult. The World Bank concluded, however, that there were probably over 1,100 state-owned enterprises, together accounting for around 25 per cent of GDP and employment in the mid-1980s (World Bank 1989). Most of these were small-scale firms which operated in competitive markets, but others, notably the basic utilities – telecommunications, water, electricity and gas, were large and monopolistic. Since mid-1983 the government has pursued a programme of privatisation, thereby reversing the previous reliance upon public sector investments in economic development.

THE CONTENT OF PRIVATISATION

The British privatisation programme has been extensive, though limited to the industrial, transport and energy sectors. To date the welfare state has largely escaped privatisation. Between 1979 when the Conservative government was elected and the early 1990s over £41 billion of state assets were sold. Starting with shares in the oil company BP in 1979, the programme was extended to British Aerospace and Cable and Wireless in 1981, Amersham International and the National Freight Corporation in

1982, and Associated British Ports in 1983. More controversial and important for the long-term development of the programme was the decision in November 1984 to sell the public sector telecommunications provider British Telecom (BT). This was the first sale of a major public utility holding a natural monopoly position and necessitated the creation of a regulatory structure to prevent monopoly abuse. Subsequently, the gas, water and electricity industries were also privatised and similar regulatory bodies were created. In addition to the sale of state industries, Britain's privatisation programme has included compulsory tendering for certain NHS and local government services, such as cleansing, catering and more recently for some white collar activities (Parker 1990).

The privatisation programme in Britain, therefore, has amounted to a gradual and measured dismantling of the state sector. Few risks have been taken with the industries chosen for privatisation. The industries have been restructured and their balance sheets strengthened ahead of privatisation so as to ensure, as far as is possible, their long-term success. With the main exception of certain dockyards, to date there have been no embarrassing business failures amongst the privatised firms.

In Czechoslovakia a major privatisation drive was introduced in 1990 when a target of privatising over 4,000 organisations was set. Czechoslovakia's privatisation programme began on a different scale from that in Britain and has been further complicated by the division of the country into two sovereign republics. By the mid-1980s around 97 per cent of the country's value added came from the state (including cooperative) sector, hence Czechoslovakia had one of the most state-dominated economies amongst the communist countries. It is envisaged that almost all state industry, services and agriculture will be privatised over the next few years with the main exceptions of mineral resources, water and the railways (Parker 1993b).

By contrast, Malaysia's privatisation programme, while receiving considerable publicity, has so far been quite limited. To date few firms have been sold to the private sector and in relation to the objective of raising efficiency there are some worrying features. From the earlier discussion, economic efficiency is raised by introducing more competition in the product market and by the threat of a hostile takeover bid in the stock market. In the case of privatisations in Malaysia, product market competition has been little affected. Where competition has traditionally been restricted it remains restricted, for example in airlines and telecommunications. Also, few completed sales have involved the government giving up a controlling interest in the assets. In most divestitures the government has remained the dominant shareholder and has retained ultimate control over managerial decisions. Where the government retains control, directly or indirectly, the threat of a hostile takeover bid as a necessary spur to managerial efficiency is not credible.

THE PROCESS OF PRIVATISATION

In Britain the main method of privatisation has been to convert the public enterprises to private companies with the shares held by the state and then to float part or all the state's shareholding on the stock market, usually through an offer for sale and occasionally through a sale by tender or some combination of both methods. In a few cases disposal has occurred through a direct transfer of the business to another company; examples include the sale of the Royal Ordnance Factories and Rover cars to British Aerospace plc. In other cases a management–workforce buy-out has been preferred, most notably for bus companies and in the case of the National Freight Corporation.

The government has been keen to see small shareholders buy shares during privatisation and issues have therefore been skewed in favour of the small buyer. In the early years the public was seduced by the prospect of large and quick capital gains as share prices soared in the first few days of trading. For example, BT shares rose by over 80 per cent during the first day of trading in the stock market. It is questionable, however, whether large numbers of small shareholders will police managerial behaviour effectively. Recent studies have argued that corporate control is likely to be more effective where there are large blocks of shares (Shleifer and Vishny 1986, Caves 1990, Leech and Leahy 1991). Where ownership is concentrated, the benefits from monitoring management behaviour and trading in shares are more likely to exceed the transaction costs of share dealing. Where ownership is widely dispersed there may be no individual or group of shareholders with the incentive or voting power to exercise effective control over management. In which case a principal-agent problem remains, in turn raising questions about the extent to which privatisation improves the agent-principal relationship to limit managerial discretionary behaviour.

In Czechoslovakia, and now in the Czech and Slovak republics privatisation is taking place by various routes: by return of property to those dispossessed under communism; by direct sale through auctions and tenders to domestic citizens; through a voucher scheme (under which citizens purchase from the state at nominal cost vouchers to buy shares directly or through intermediary investment funds in privatised firms); and by sale to or joint ventures with foreign investors (of which a prominent example is the Volkswagen investment in Skoda). By the end of 1992 over 31,000 small businesses, mainly shops and workshops, had been sold, largely by auction, under the October 1990 Small Privatisation Act. By mid-1992 67 per cent of shares in over 1,400 state companies had been sold through the voucher method and 171 firms had been completely privatised under the Large Privatisation Act of February 1991.

In Malaysia shares have been sold in state firms, for example Malaysian Airline Systems, which are then traded in the stock market. The largest sale to date involved the telecommunications department – Syarikat Telekom Malaysia – where the disposal of an initial 7 per cent of the shares raised M$1.5 billion. (*Financial Times* 1990). The government has also turned to joint ventures, for example with Lockheed in creating a company called Airod, which in 1985 inherited the airforce aircraft repair and overhaul department, and has utilised build-operate-transfer (BOT) schemes for infrastructural investments such as highways.

In the UK and Malaysia the legal and financial systems for successful privatisation already existed prior to the introduction of their privatisation programmes. Malaysia like Britain has been able to sell shares in privatised firms through an existing and liquid stock market and private property rights are well defined and protected. In Czechoslovakia, however, the necessary financial structure and legal systems are still having to be created and are uncertain and untested.

THE FORM OF PRIVATISATION

In Britain only limited competition has been introduced at privatisation in the telecommunications, gas, water and electricity industries (though competition is now increasing in telecommunications and gas supply). Instead, an elaborate regulatory structure has been created based on operating licences incorporating public interest criteria policed by regulatory bodies (eg Oftel for telecommunications, Ofwat for the water industry). In consequence, privatisation has changed the form of state regulation of these industries. Under public ownership regulation was controlled from within the bureaucratic mechanism of the state and was flexible and reactive to political as well as economic pressures. Privatisation has brought regulation out into the open and made it more visible and structured (Parker 1993c). As yet it has not removed the state's interest in the performance of what are key industries in the economy. Most likely it never will. In deciding between nationalisation and privatisation with state regulation the choice is between two institutional forms both having potential inefficiencies (Parker 1989).

In the Czech and Slovak Republics businesses have been privatised with the minimum of reconstruction. The speed of the desired privatisation, driven by the political need to dismantle state control quickly following the fall of the communist government, has ruled out the low-risk strategies adopted in the UK and Malaysia. Consequently, failures amongst privatised businesses are predicted and indeed are desirable to remove some of the economic distortions introduced by state planning. This means, however, that some investors will be disappointed. Though former Czechoslovakia has relative political stability when contrasted with other parts of Central and Eastern Europe, widespread financial losses could undermine this stability and lead to a loss of confidence in private enterprise.

For overseas investors, investing in privatised businesses in the Czech and Slovak Republics is high risk and requires a strong nerve. At the same time, the Republics need foreign involvement in the form of straight investment and in the form of joint ventures and strategic partnerships. In general, government has welcomed Western capital. The management of change requires management with the will to tackle interest groups both within and outside the business which oppose change. It requires management with a knowledge of how to succeed in competitive markets, something often lacking amongst incumbent management used to administering according to central plans. Too many Czechoslovakian companies have suffered from low motivation at work and high absenteeism and have produced low-quality products, which have sold in Western markets on price alone. Low prices alongside low productivity have led to inadequate surpluses for reinvestment. Much of Czech and Slovak industry needs considerable injections of capital.

In addition, Western management methods, including introducing proper management information, accounting and inventory tracking systems, need to be introduced. Marketing methods need to be learned, as does relationship building with suppliers and financiers. A recent study in Poland concludes that such changes are best driven forward by a dominant shareholder with a large personal stake in the business's ultimate success (cited in McDonald 1993). Where a large number of small shareholders exist few may attend boards or take any real interest in the management of the firms. In other words, an efficient agent-principal relationship will be best secured in former Czechoslovakia by concentrating shareholding and supporting strategic investments by Western firms that can input managerial expertise. This suggests that returning property to previous owners and encouraging small-scale direct investment through the voucher scheme have political significance but are of questionable economic benefit. By investing through the new investment funds, however, shares are concentrated. These funds show signs of evolving into active institutional investors (Parker 1993b).

In Malaysia the slower pace of privatisation, as in Britain, has permitted careful restructuring of businesses to avoid subsequent failure and the inevitable political fallout. Also, the existing management has mainly remained in place. In Malaysia and Britain striking improvements in performance have tended to come during the preparation for sale rather than following privatisation (Bishop and Kay 1988, Adam et al 1992 p 251, Parker and Martin 1993). The opposite should be true in the Czech and Slovak Republics.

Earlier in this chapter we saw that, in terms of raising efficiency, important considerations are the impact of privatisation on product market competition, on the agent-principal relationship, and on the objectives of the firm. This was mapped in Figure 8.1 in terms of a cube relationship of ownership and organisational performance. Applying this schema, in the UK and Malaysia there has been very little change in terms of the market structure axis. Where competition was restricted under public ownership it remains largely restricted. By contrast, in Czechoslovakia privatisation is associated with a major increase in competition as state monopolies are broken up, new enterprises are encouraged and the economy is exposed to Western competition. Figure 8.2 illustrates the relevant movements within the cube.

In terms of the change in the agent-principal relationship, the Malaysian programme is the worst. In most cases private investors lack control over the enterprises and there is no takeover threat. Government remains, directly or indirectly, the major principal or shareholder.

In the UK the government has given up majority control of firms on sale, though a 'golden share' has been retained to protect certain businesses from undesired takeovers. It is Czechoslovakia (and now the separate Republics), however, that is going furthest in terms of pursuing complete privatisation.

Turning to objectives, privatisation is changing these in favour of more commercial goals in Britain and the Czech and Slovak Republics. In Malaysia, however, the continued existence of a dominant political shareholding implies that objectives may not be clarified.

Using the cube, it is apparent that privatisation in Czechoslovakia is likely to have the most marked effect in terms of raising static and dynamic efficiency, whereas the Malaysian programme is likely to have the least effect.

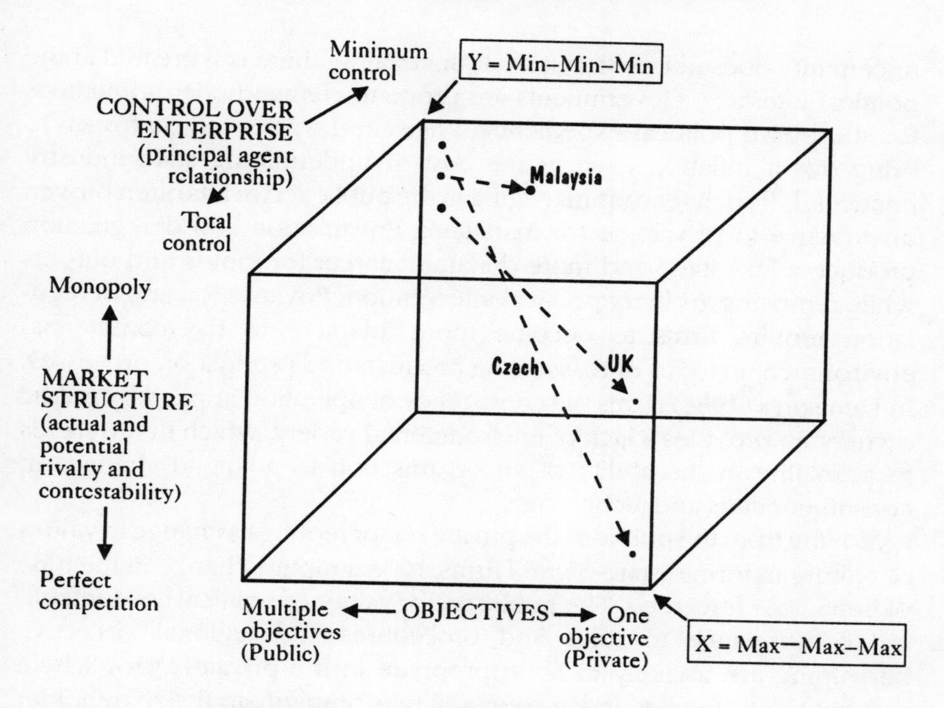

Figure 8.2 The cube model with examples

THE IMPORTANCE OF THE INTERNAL ENVIRONMENT

The response of organisations to privatisation in terms of internal restructuring appears to be central to explaining differences in performance following privatisation (Parker 1993a). This should not be surprising since changing the ownership of an organisation does not *in itself* change anything which is likely to lead to a performance improvement.

If privatisation is to produce significant changes in behaviour and performance, this implies major changes in the way the business is managed and structured. There will need to be a substantial shift in culture away from concern with rules and procedures ('how we do things') typically found in the public sector towards concern with outcomes or financial results ('what we are achieving') (Dunsire et al 1988).

Public ownership in regulated markets provides a comparatively static or stable environment for management. The competitors are known (or non-existent), the technology tends to change slowly, and prices and financing are determined along agreed lines. This is not to imply that uncertainty does not exist, but what uncertainty there is is created at the political interface. Governments are prone to change policy sometimes for short-term political expediency. Prices and wages can be frozen to bring down inflation even at the cost of undermining state industry finances. For such reasons managing in the public sector has often proven unattractive to private sector managers. Privatisation and deregulation produce a less static and more dynamic market for inputs and outputs while removing arbitrary political intervention. Privatisation and deregulation require firms to become more adaptive to the commercial environment in terms of reassessing products and production processes. In Denison's (1984) terms the consistency of operation implied by public ownership provides a lack of environmental variety, which in turn leads to a decline in the ability of an organisation to adapt to changes in consumer needs and technology.

Moving from the public to the private sector requires a change in values or culture in former state-owned firms, for example a change in the type of behaviour rewarded. The public sector values of political accountability, conformance to rules and procedures and national collective bargaining are unlikely to be appropriate in the private sector where competition is greater and accountability is primarily to the shareholder not the exchequer. What is then needed is a culture of environmental adaptability. A culture of adaptability is implied for an industry undergoing rapid and important change resulting from privatisation and deregulation. On the other hand, where privatisation does not involve deregulation and competition remains muted, the expectation would be that the previous public sector culture will continue because pressure for change coming from the external environment is significantly reduced.

Privatisation implies a rematching of the organisation to its external environment to achieve 'strategic fit'. This in turn has implications for investment, divestment, products, markets and relationships with customers and suppliers. State ownership involves a series of *negative feedback* loops which keep the organisation at an existing and essentially static equilibrium by sustaining through rules and procedures existing practices. Negative feedback loops in any organisation form organisational defence routines (Argyris 1990) which prevent the firm from moving too far from what is the given and accepted practice of doing things. Such negative feedback loops, however, are essentially destructive of organisational adaptation since they reinforce repetitive, safe and uniform behaviour. Such behaviour is unlikely to be appropriate once a firm transfers to the private sector.

Privatisation when coupled with considerable deregulation of markets implies the need for managerial imagination and innovation. It implies that the organisation must move by *positive feedback* towards a non-equilibrium state as required by the new external environment. Stable equilibrium states imply the case for bureaucratic organisations performing according to the rules. The professional bureaucracy is especially appropriate for stable environments. But the privatised firm must operate on the border between stable and unstable equilibria or what Stacey calls the 'chaos border area', encouraging and tolerating considerable innovation and change while at the same time preventing organisational disintegration (Stacey 1993). This is a considerable challenge for former public-sector management, management ill prepared by experience for dynamic change with its inherent tensions and risks.

Privatisation requires considerable changes in the internal environment of firms to accommodate changes in the external environment. These are likely to be more profound the greater the extent of privatisation and deregulation, as in the Czech and Slovak Republics. Where the change is more token in nature, as in Malaysia, the degree of internal change is likely to be much smaller (Parker 1994). More specifically, we might expect to see changes in the following characteristics of the organisations.

Organisational structure

The political structures established under public ownership are likely to need changing with privatisation. A bureaucratic or mechanistic structure may be appropriate for a stable and certain environment, but a change in status towards commercial management implies the creation of a structure which facilitates 'entrepreneurial' behaviour including quicker decision-making and local accountability (Mintzberg 1983). As experience in the 1970s in the US financial and airline markets has shown, a deregulated environment requires an organisational form which can respond quickly to changes in consumer preferences (Burton and Obel 1986 p 24). Hence, the expectation would be that privatisation will be associated with a less hierarchical, less centralised and less rule-bound organisational structure.

Human resource policies

The public sector has a tradition of formalised and often centralised collective bargaining. Unions are recognised and salaries are often based on agreed scales rather than individual merit. Privatisation may lead to performance related pay, localised over centralised bargaining to reflect ability to pay at the local level, and perhaps even de-recognition of unions (Metcalfe 1988 p 84, Ferner 1990). Also, because human resource policy can play an important part in cultural change (Burack 1991, Salama 1991), following privatisation there may be a new interest in ways of maintaining and improving staff commitment and productivity, including new training methods, management briefings, and in-house news-sheets and video presentations.

Management

Research suggests that 'leadership' is a key factor in successful adaptation to major changes in the external environment (Mintzberg 1979, Torbert 1989, Alderson and Kakabadse 1992). It is the function of top management to convey the new set of cultural values to the rest of the organisation through a clear and consistent message and, by so doing, to overcome inertia, opposition to change, and goal conflict within the organisation (Clarkson and Martin 1980, Peters and Waterman 1982).

This does not necessarily imply a management masterplan. It does, however, require management to establish and monitor the procedures and structures which enable the firm to succeed in the new external environment, and to provide strategic direction in the sense of providing and protecting a learning and adaptive internal environment. Where management remains deeply associated with the old culture, as in parts of Czech and Slovak industry, new management is required or steps must be taken, for example through managerial retraining, to produce the paradigm shift.

Nature and location of the business

The nature and location of the business in the public sector are politically defined. By contrast, the private sector is much freer to develop new lines of business and invest in new locations according to the dictates of market forces (Drucker 1990 p 8). Therefore, privatisation is likely to be associated with investing in new locations, including overseas, and the development of new markets and new sources of supplies. It may also be associated with the sale of some lines of business and the acquisition of others.

Goals

In the private sector a major goal is profitability, but in politically controlled activities objectives are commonly ambiguous and qualitative, involving legality, political accountability, equity in treatment, standardisation, accuracy, economy in resource use and probity. There tends to be a concern for conformity and consistency ('fairness') between users of the service and with avoiding mistakes that might lead to political embarrassment. The public sector is popularly associated with a concern for procedural norms or rules rather than outcomes. The move to private ownership is likely to lead to a reformulation of goals, involving a simplification of objectives in favour of commercial outcomes. This will be particularly so when the firm is no longer state regulated.

Communication and reporting systems

More commercial management, especially when coupled with a more decentralised organisational structure, requires new communication and reporting systems, including management information systems. What senior management wants to know may change as may the way that lower ranks of management and the workforce are controlled. Privatisation, therefore, is likely to be associated with a review of existing systems and the introduction of new systems including new internal accounting procedures. Where management is devolved to speed up decision-making and impose local accountability, systems will need to be put in place to ensure that failure in one part of the organisation does not produce total failure. Local management may no longer need head office agreement regarding day-to-day managerial decisions, but the centre will wish to monitor local financial performance against target.

PRIVATISATION AND GLOBALISATION

In recent years firms have been altering their corporate strategies and refocusing on core businesses; they have been 'sweating' their existing corporate assets to obtain higher returns, while at the same time acquiring under-valued corporate assets from other firms; they have been attempting to achieve economies of scale and scope and learning economies to stay one step ahead of the competition and to expand market share; at the same time they have needed to invest heavily in product and process developments. Moreover, globalised markets and industries with converging consumer tastes and rapid diffusion of technologies at a time of rising fixed costs imply a crucial need for cooperative arrangements between firms (Ohmae 1989 p 143). Similarly, the ability to transfer technology quickly and effectively across national boundaries is a critical factor for market success (Keller and Chinta 1990). The firm that is able to learn fast and adapt to market and technological changes by rapid and continuous internal reconfiguration will be the firm with the competitive lead. The concept of a world market and continuous organisational reconfiguration sits uneasily alongside state-owned monopolies, which are by definition highly defined firms operating in politically protected markets.

Privatisation with the associated deregulation of competition will add further impetus to these developments. New markets previously preserved for state monopolies are opened up, in recent years notably in the airlines and in telecommunications. New opportunities for investment often in the form of joint ventures are created, while firms can benefit from technology transfer of latest designs (product innovation) and latest design tools (process innovation).

State-owned firms often have a pressing need for new investment and new management ideas and marketing skills, especially when the umbilical cord to government funds is severed. In both Malaysia and Czechoslovakia, governments have turned to foreign investors. Increased competition for firms previously protected by state monopoly inevitably increases pressures on profit margins, leading to restructuring, divestment of loss-making activities and sometimes outright closure.

In the past, relatively few state-owned firms have ventured heavily into international investments including mergers and acquisitions (a notable exception are French public enterprises). As a rule, state corporations have accounted for less than 5 per cent of a country's cross-border acquisitions activity (Stevens 1992 p 15). Public sector firms are usually constrained in terms of international investment by political opposition to investing abroad (the 'exporting jobs' argument), by a lack of access to international financial markets, by a lack of managerial expertise, and by restrictions imposed by the founding legislation on the type of business that can be undertaken. Former state-owned firms can capture a march on their foreign counterparts. Reinvigorated by exposure to market forces, they can provide formidable competition in winning international business when firms are privatised and markets are deregulated elsewhere.

An important element of international corporate strategy today is the strategic alliance. This allows the costs of production and distribution to be shared and new skills to be learned through a process of organisational cross-fertilisation (Hamel 1991). Specific forms involve alliances to service customers, as discussed at length by Ohmae (1989), as well as equity and contractual joint ventures, manufacturing consortia and R & D agreements (Shan 1990). Since state ownership has proven to be a barrier to strategic alliances, privatisation opens up new and exciting possibilities, especially in formerly state-protected industries such as telecommunications and air travel. In recent years privatised British Telecom and British Airways have been at the forefront of developing alliances with foreign firms as well as in undertaking international acquisitions. Both companies intend to be global players in the 1990s.

There will, however, be certain constraints on the speed of all these developments. They are as follows.

- The extent to which governments continue to restrict competition and international investment in their economies even after state firms are privatised.
- The extent to which governments continue to regulate privatised industries, such as telecommunications, limiting service and price competition and the number of operators. Privatisation can occur with little if any deregulation of markets, though in such cases the potential for efficiency gains following privatisation will be stunted.
- The extent to which governments are willing to allow major firms to fail. Operation in the private sector implies business failure as well as success. Governments may be unwilling to see the national airline or aerospace firm fail, however, and can support overtly, through subsidies and licences, and more covertly, through preferential procurement terms, the national operator. In which case foreign firms may be unwilling to compete or unable to compete effectively, and efficiency incentives will be distorted.

Uncertainty regarding the reaction of governments to the financial failure of former state-owned firms may be sufficient in itself to deter competition. In Malaysia, the government's retention of a controlling interest in many 'privatised' industries acts as warning that there is no intention to create a level playing field for international investors. In Britain, government has retained a 'golden share' in some privatised companies to prevent unwelcome takeover bids, especially by foreign investors, and has regulated certain markets, such as energy and telecommunications, through operating licences. In addition, and the European Single Market notwithstanding, the privatised aerospace industry still receives 'launch aid' from government and apparent favour when government contracts are placed. Other countries do the same.

LESSONS FOR MANAGEMENT

- Understanding privatisation requires an appreciation of its context, content, process and form. The term privatisation takes on different meanings in different parts of the world. Where the state retains a majority shareholding, as in Malaysia, it is not at all clear that the term 'privatisation' is apposite. Politicians are apt to use the term privatisation like the alcoholic uses the lamppost, for support rather than illumination.
- Privatisation can lead to improved economic efficiency, but this is most likely to occur only when it is coupled with more competition and with the introduction of shareholders who monitor and restrict management behaviour.
- Privatisation to be meaningful requires a change away from the process-dominated culture of the public sector to a performance-dominated culture. This has implications for the way that business strategy is formulated and implemented.
- This in turn means the likely introduction of: new management and management practices; new organisational structures; new human resource policies; new goals; changes in communication and reporting systems; and possibly changes in the nature and location of the business, including investments and divestments, merger and take-overs, and new joint ventures.
- Increasing pressures to internationalise are incompatible with the public accountability and political constraints inherent in state ownership. Privatisation creates reinvigorated potential partners, markets and suppliers. It also creates potential new competitors. Privatisation is repositioning firms and their products and in so doing is considerably changing the international business environment.

REFERENCES

Adam, C, Cavendish, W and Mistry, P S (1992) *Adjusting Privatization: Case Studies from Developing Countries*, Currey, London

Alchian, A A (1965) 'Some Economics of Property Rights', *Il Politico*, Vol 30, pp 816–29

Alderson, S and Kakabadse, A (1992) 'Strategic Change: the Role of the Top Team', in Faulkner, D and Johnson, G (eds) *The Challenge of Strategic Management*, Kogan Page, London

Argyris, C (1990) *Overcoming Organizational Defenses: Facilitating Organizational Learning*, Allyn & Bacon, Boston, Mass

Bishop, M and Kay, J (1988) *Does Privatization Work? Lessons from the UK*, London Business School, London

Burack, E H (1991) 'Changing the Company Culture: the Role of Human Resource Development', *Long Range Planning*, Vol 24, No 1, pp 85–95

Burton, R M and Obel, B (1986) 'Environmental–Organizational Relations: the Effects of Deregulation', in Burton, R M and Obel, B *Innovation and Entrepreneurship in Organizations: Strategies for Competitiveness, Deregulation and Privatization*, Elsevier, Amsterdam and Oxford

Caves, R E (1990) 'Lessons from Privatization in Britain: State Enterprise Behavior, Public Choice and Corporate Governance', *Journal of Economic Behavior and Organization*, Vol 13, No 2, pp 145–69

Clarkson, K W and Martin, D L (1980) 'The Economics of Nonproprietary Organizations', *Research in Law and Economics Supplement*, JAI Press, Greenwich, CT

Denison, D R (1984) 'Bringing Corporate Culture to the Bottom Line', *Organizational Dynamics*, Vol 13, No 2, pp 5–22

Drucker, P F (1990) *Managing the Non-Profit Organization*, Butterworth-Heinemann, Oxford

Dunsire, A, Hartley, K and Parker, D (1991) 'Organisational Status and Performance: Summary of the Findings', *Public Administration*, Vol 69, spring, pp 21–40

Dunsire, A, Hartley, K, Parker, D and Dimitriou, B (1988), 'Organisational Status and Performance: a Conceptual Framework for Testing Public Choice Theories', *Public Administration*, Vol 66, winter, pp 363–88

Fama, E F (1980) 'Agency Problems and the Theory of the Firm', *Journal of Political Economy*, Vol 88, Apr, pp 288–307

Ferner, A (1990) 'The Changing Influence of the Personnel Function: Privatization and Organizational Politics in Electricity Generation', *Human Resource Management Journal*, Vol 1, No 1, autumn, pp 12–30

Financial Times (1990), 'Telekom Malaysia Goes Well', 17 Oct, p 31.

Hamel, G (1991), 'Competition and Inter-partner Learning within Strategic Alliances', *Strategic Management Journal*, Vol 12, pp 83–103

Hartley, K and Parker, D (1991) 'Privatization: a Conceptual Framework', in Hartley, K and Ott, A (eds) *Privatization and Economic Efficiency: a Comparative Analysis of Developed and Developing Countries*, Edward Elgar, Aldershot

Hartley, K, Parker, D and Martin, S (1991) 'Organisational Status, Ownership and Productivity', *Fiscal Studies*, Vol 12, No 2, May, pp 46–60

Jensen, M C and Meckling, W H (1976) 'Theory of the Firm: Managerial Behaviour, Agency Costs and Ownership Structure', *Journal of Financial Economics*, Vol 3, Oct, pp 305–60

Kay, J A and Thompson, D J (1986), 'Privatisation: A Policy in Search of a Rationale', *Economic Journal*, Vol 96, Mar, pp 18–32

Keller, R T and Chinta, R R (1990), 'Multinational R & D Siting: Corporate Strategies for Success', *Academy of Management Executive*, Vol 4, No 2, pp 33–43

Leech, D and Leahy, J (1991) 'Ownership Structure, Control Type Classifications and the Performance of Large Companies', *Economic Journal*, Vol 101, Nov, pp 1418–37

McDonald, K R (1993), 'Why Privatization is not Enough', *Harvard Business Review*, May–June, pp 49–59.

Metcalfe, L (1988), 'Accountable Public Management: UK Concepts and Experience', in Kakabadse, A, Brovetto, P R and Holzer, R (eds) *Management Development in the Public Sector: a European Perspective*, Avebury, Aldershot

Millward, R and Parker, D (1983), 'Public and Private Enterprise: Comparative Behaviour and Relative Efficiency', in Millward, R, Parker, D, Rosenthal, L, Sumner, M T and Topham, N *Public Sector Economics*, Longman, London

Mintzberg, H (1979) 'An Emerging Strategy of Direct Research', *Administrative Science Quarterly*, Dec, p 24

— (1983) *Power In and Around Organizations*, Prentice Hall, Englewood Cliffs, NJ

Ohmae, K (1989) 'The Global Logic of Strategic Alliances', *Harvard Business Review*, Mar–Apr, pp 143–54

Osborne, D and Gaebler, T (1993) *Reinventing Government: How the Entrepreneurial Spirit is Transforming the Public Sector*, Addison Wesley, New York

Parker, D (1985) 'Is the Private Sector More Efficient?' A Study in the Public v Private Debate', *Public Administration Bulletin*, Vol 48, Aug, pp 2–23

— (1989), 'Public Control of Natural Monopoly in the UK: Is Regulation the Answer?', in Campbell, M, Hardy, M and Healey, N (eds) *Controversy in Applied Economics*, Harvester Wheatsheaf, London

— (1990) 'The 1988 Local Government Act and Compulsory Competitive Tendering', *Urban Studies*, Vol 27, No 5, pp 653–68

— (1993a) 'Ownership, Organisational Changes and Performance' in Clarke, T and Pitelis, C (eds) *The Political Economy of Privatisation*, Routledge, London

— (1993b) 'Unravelling the Planned Economy: Privatisation in Czechoslovakia', *Communist Economies and Economic Transformation*, Nov

— (1993c) 'Privatisation Ten Years On: a Critical Analysis of its Rationale and Results', in Healey, N (ed) *Britain's Economic Miracle: Myth or Reality?* Routledge, London

— (1994) 'International Aspects of Privatisation: a Critical Assessment of Business Restructuring in the UK, Czechoslovakia and Malaysia', *British Review of Economic Issues*, Feb

— and Martin, S (1993) 'The Impact of UK Privatisation on Labour and Total Factor Productivity', University of Birmingham Working Paper.

Peters, T J and Waterman, R H (1982) *In Search of Excellence*, Harper Row, New York

Salama, A (1991), 'The Role of Top Management and Human Resource Practices in Organisational Culture Change', Conference on International Privatisation, University of St Andrews

Shan, W (1990) 'An Empirical Analysis of Organizational Strategies by Entrepreneurial High-Technology Firms', *Strategic Management Journal*, Vol 11, pp 129–39

Shleifer, A and Vishny, R W (1986) 'Large Shareholders and Corporate Control', *Journal of Political Economy*, Vol 94, pp 461–88

Stacey, R (1993) *Strategic Management and Organisational Dynamics*, Pitman, London

Stevens, B (1992) 'Prospects for Privatisation in OECD Countries', *National Westminster Bank Quarterly Review*, Aug, pp 2–22

Torbert, W R (1989) 'Leading Organizational Transformation', in Woodman, R W and Pasmore, W A (eds) *Research in Organization Change and Development*, Vol 3, JAI Press, Greenwich, CT

Vickers, J and Yarrow, G (1988) *Privatization: an Economic Analysis*, MIT Press, Cambridge, Mass

von Hayek, F (1978) *New Studies in Philosophy, Politics and Economics*, Routledge and Kegan Paul, London

Winiecki, J (1991), 'Theoretical Underpinnings of the Privatisation of State-Owned Enterprises in Post-Soviet-type Economies', *Communist Economies and Economic Transformation*, Vol 3, No 4, pp 397–416

World Bank (1989) *Malaysia: Matching Risks and Rewards in a Mixed Economy Program*, World Bank, Washington, DC

9

Logistics in Europe: Managing the Differences*

James Cooper, Cranfield University School of Management

INTRODUCTION

Logistics in Europe has entered a period of rapid change, but much will stay the same. An acceptance of this paradox is central to developing an understanding of the dynamics of logistics in European-based businesses.

To a certain extent the impetus for change in logistics is conceptual, not least in applying recently formulated logistics principles within business environments. The integrative approach of logistics to the supply chain, to both smooth the flow of products and add value to the marketing process (Christopher 1985) has already had a profound impact on European businesses, mirroring developments in the USA and Japan. And there are forces for change other than conceptual ones. The globalisation of industry (Dicken 1986) and the internationalisation of retailing (Treadgold 1988), for example, creates a much more fertile environment for logistics to flourish. Indeed, logistics underpins the successful internationalisation strategies of many major companies: hardly surprising in view of the increased emphasis on the movement and storage of goods.

Yet logistics in Europe cannot be the same as elsewhere in the world. There are major differences which separate Europe from the rest of the world and, indeed, European countries from one another. An obvious example is the completion of the Single European Market (SEM) by the end of 1992. No other region of the world has such an ambitious plan for increasing the freedom of trade between participating countries. But when we speak of logistics in Europe we must be careful to define our

* This paper was previously published in *The International Journal of Logistics Management* (1991), Vol 2, No 2. Reprinted by kind permission.

boundaries; the SEM applies only to the twelve members of the European Community. The European Free Trade Association (EFTA) and the newly emerging democracies of Central and Eastern Europe speak of continued economic fragmentation with significant implications for logistics.

What are these implications? The important point is that, while logistics concepts may have a universal application in theory, in practice many divergences occur as a consequence of major differences between countries in terms of business environment and culture, regulation and varying rates of economic development. This dichotomy between unification and diversification will be a key theme of this chapter as it discusses both the possibilities and the realities of logistics in Europe. It begins by discussing changing logistics needs, continues with a section on the related strategies of providers of logistics services (ie transport, storage and information), and concludes with an analysis of market segmentation for logistics services in Europe. In so doing, it identifies the driving forces for change, together with the barriers which slow down the pace of change for logistics in Europe.

DEMAND-SIDE LOGISTICS

There is no single model of a supply chain which is typically European. As in other economic blocs, there is a whole family of supply chains which vary according to length and complexity. Any one supply chain will have a variety of members, each of which will have a lesser or greater influence on logistics management. At one extreme there will be a very short and simple supply chain in such businesses as mail order, which gives the opportunity for very tight control. At the other extreme there are long and fragmented supply chains where producers, sales agents, wholesalers and retailers each have a key role, but where differences in interest obstruct an integrated approach to logistics management.

Over time, one or other members of the supply chain may seek to control more of the supply chain, in order to gain the benefits of logistics integration. An important example of this trend has been UK grocery retailers who have not only eliminated many wholesalers from supply chains but dictate the terms of supply to their suppliers.

Indeed, one of the key points to emphasise in any discussion of the supply chain is its dynamics; just as businesses are not static, neither are supply chains. Both manufacturers and retailers are important members of many supply chains and responsible for driving change. The following two subsections outline the major changes in manufacturing and retailing which are now taking place within Europe, and their impact on the management of the supply chain.

Manufacturing: key trends for logistics in Europe

A discussion of manufacturing in Europe needs to take as its starting point the wider trends in world manufacturing. Europe, after all, is one part of a wider picture of manufacturing activity. However, Europe is special in a number of important respects and these need to be taken into account when discussing logistics and opportunities for change. For example, despite concern about the success of automotive manufacturing in Japan, the European Community remains well ahead of both Japan and the USA in terms of the numbers of cars produced (Eurostat 1989).

An important trend which has led international business development had been increasing homogeneity and integration of the world's major economies (Levitt 1983). This has helped to accelerate the growth of 'global' companies. But it is vital to appreciate that companies have grown globally in a variety of ways, depending on the circumstances of their businesses.

Doz (1986), for example, has pointed out that factors such as market share and the proportion of government-controlled customers are major considerations in a company's strategy as it internationalises its business. In particular, multinational companies (MNCs) with a relatively small market share and a high proportion of government-controlled customers will usually have to follow a strategy of 'national responsiveness' (see Figure 9.1), where manufacturing must be developed locally to serve national markets. At the other extreme, transnational companies (TNCs) can integrate their operations, with focused production (and R & D) serving markets around the world (Dicken 1986). Considerations of this kind can greatly affect how international companies set up supply chains to serve markets (see Figure 9.2).

The future shape of manufacturing and supply to market therefore depends not just on the wishes of the international producers, but also upon geopolitical trends. If anything, we are now likely to see more transnational companies and fewer nationally responsive ones, given the move away from both command economies and the state ownership of companies. This implies a developing shift in the boundaries shown in Figure 9.1, or a migration of companies across the boundaries, or both.

Europe, being part of this process, therefore seems likely to play host to more production and assembly plants with focused production, supplying world markets rather than national ones. To a certain extent

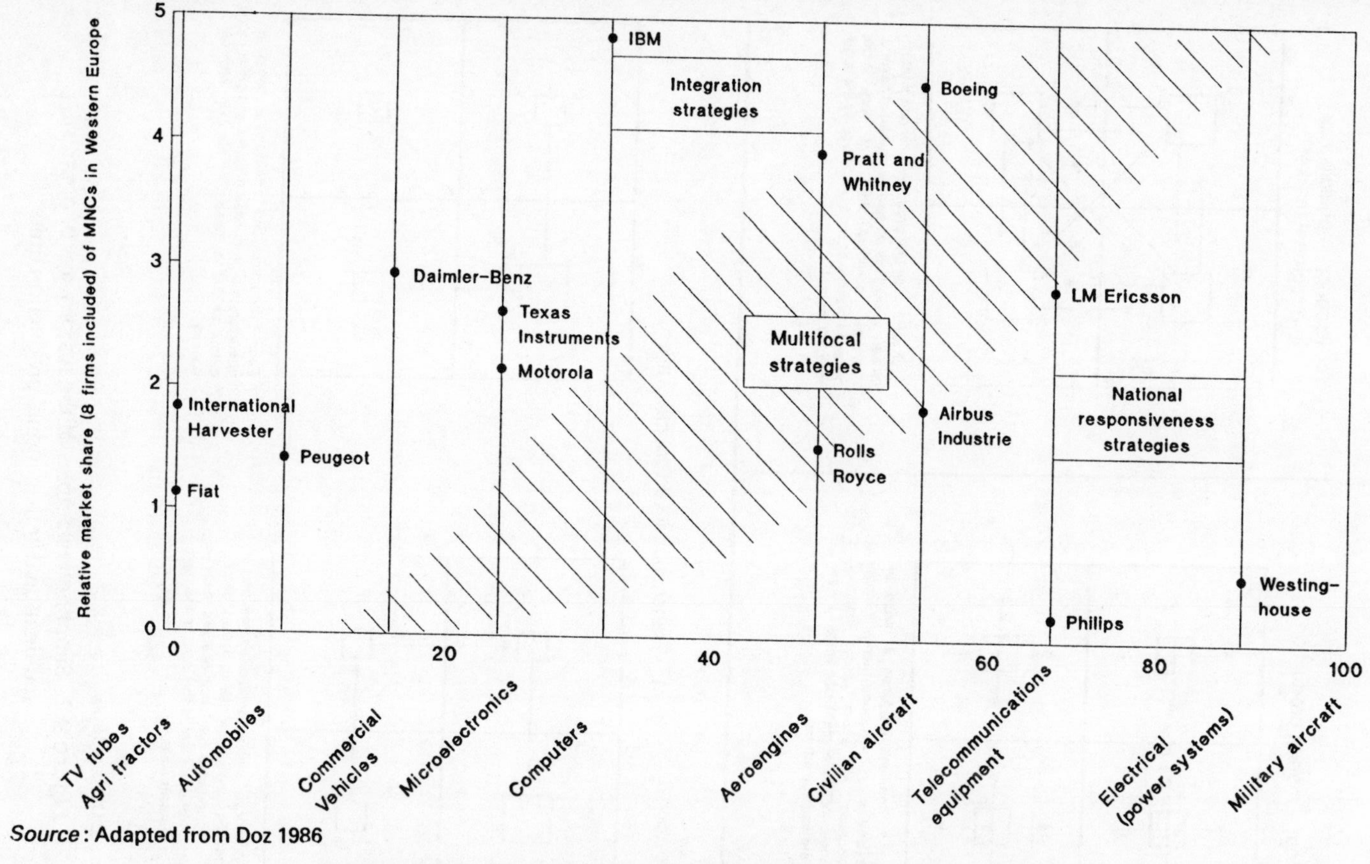

Source: Adapted from Doz 1986

Figure 9.1 Customers, market shares and multinational strategies

a) Host – market production

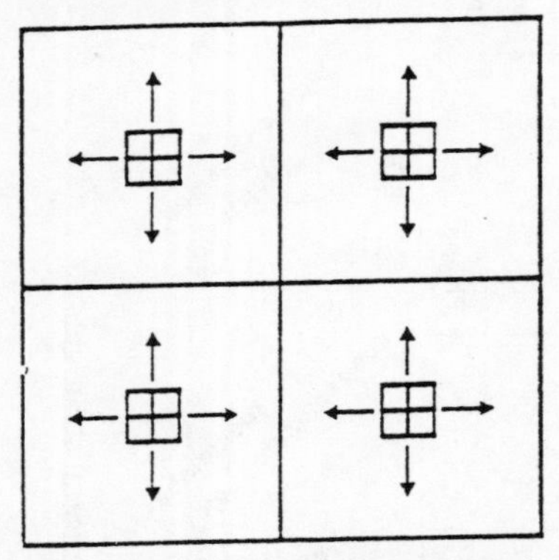

Each production unit produces a range of products and serves the national market in which it is located. No sales across national boundaries. Individual plant size limited by the size of the national market.

b) Product – specialisation in a regional market

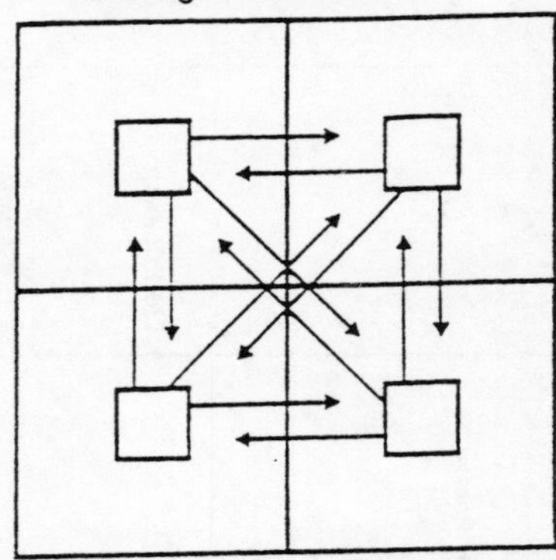

Each production unit produces only one product for sale throughout a regional market of several countries. Individual plant size very large because of scale economies offered by the large regional market.

c) Transnational vertical integration

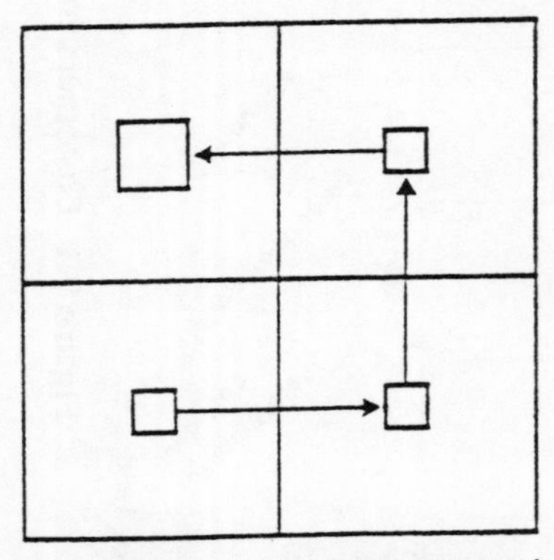

Each production unit performs a separate part of a production sequence. Units linked across national boundaries in a 'chain-like' sequence – the output of one plant is the input of the next plant in the sequence.

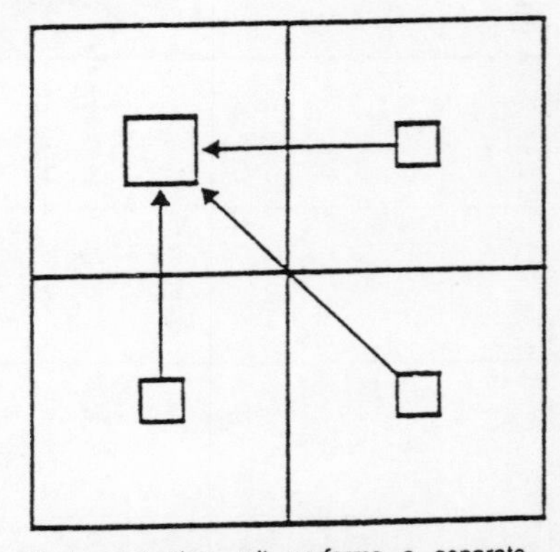

Each production unit performs a separate operation in a production process and ships its output to a final assembly plant in another country.

Source: Dicken 1986

Figure 9.2 Simplified examples of the major ways of organising multinational/transnational production units

Table 9.1 The structure of European industries (influenced by procurement)

	Value of EC market (billion ECU per year)	Intra-EC trade	Number of EC producers	Number of American producers
Boilermaking	2	Little	12	6
Turbine generators	2	Little	10	2
Locomotives	0.1	Little	16	2
Mainframe computers	10	Extensive	5	9
Telephone exchanges	7	Moderate	11	4
Telephone handsets	5	Little	12	17

Source: EC Commission (appeared in *The Economist*)

this process is already well advanced in the automotive and consumer electronics industries. The scene looks set for a similar trend to develop in other niches, such as pharmaceuticals and some high value industrial production, such as telecommunications equipment.

As Zinn and Grosse (1990) have pointed out, in order to develop a transnational strategy, a manufacturer must be able to integrate and control international operations through centralised logistics management. This is because the global approach has so many important implications for logistics, in respect of:

- Establishing specialised plants to supply regional as well as local markets
- Implementing integrated transport and order processing systems
- Responding to rapidly changing market conditions by switching products from one market to another
- Using problem-solving techniques originating in one market across all other markets
- Sharing R & D costs, not only in product design but in the logistics area (say, inventory management or electronic data interchange (EDI) implementation).

Yet there are distinctive features of European industry which set it apart from its counterparts, especially in Japan and in the USA. These factors seem likely to have a major impact on the ability of some European companies to develop their logistics along the lines proposed by Zinn and Grosse. In particular it is essential to consider the current structure of some European industries. As Table 9.1 illustrates, for industries strongly influenced by government procurement, Europe has too many companies – small by world standards – in traditional sectors of industry such as locomotive making. By contrast, in sunrise industries such as information technology (IT), it has too few of any importance. Clearly it is part of the central logic of the SEM to help create European companies with the critical mass to compete in the global marketplace. But this process will be relatively slow and cumbersome. Furthermore, it retards developments in logistics management. For example, the British computer company ICL has had to delay its planned rationalisation programme in logistics as a result of its recent merger with Fujitsu. Similar consequences can be expected from mergers between wholly European firms.

One of the crucial areas for change in logistics that must be addressed by both MNCs and TNCs concerns the organisation of logistics operations. While it is true to say that most MNC/TNCs take a pan-European approach to logistics strategy, this is much less true of their logistics operations, which continue to be organised and managed mainly on a national basis. The only industry sector to manage movement and storage operations on a pan-European basis is automotive and then only for inbound logistics (procurement of components). Yet this is likely to change over the next few years as more Europe-wide logistics networks are developed by third parties, partly in response to the economic deregulation of freight transport. As we have seen, a number of TNCs already see Europe as a unified entity in production terms, with factory production and/or component suppliers managed on a Europe-wide basis. Integrated logistics networks are clearly a logical next step in smoothing the flow of products along the supply chain.

Figure 9.3 highlights the increasing importance of logistics as a result of changes in the manufacturing environment. Many of the driving forces behind the development of logistics are global forces rather than European ones (although there may be considerable local adaptation; for example just-in-time tends to work differently in Europe from Japan). However, better use of inventory has special meaning in Europe because, on the whole, too much inventory is held in too many warehouses, as a consequence of the national organisation of operations in many companies. Now that the real cost of holding inventory is so high many companies need to eliminate unnecessary inventory from the supply

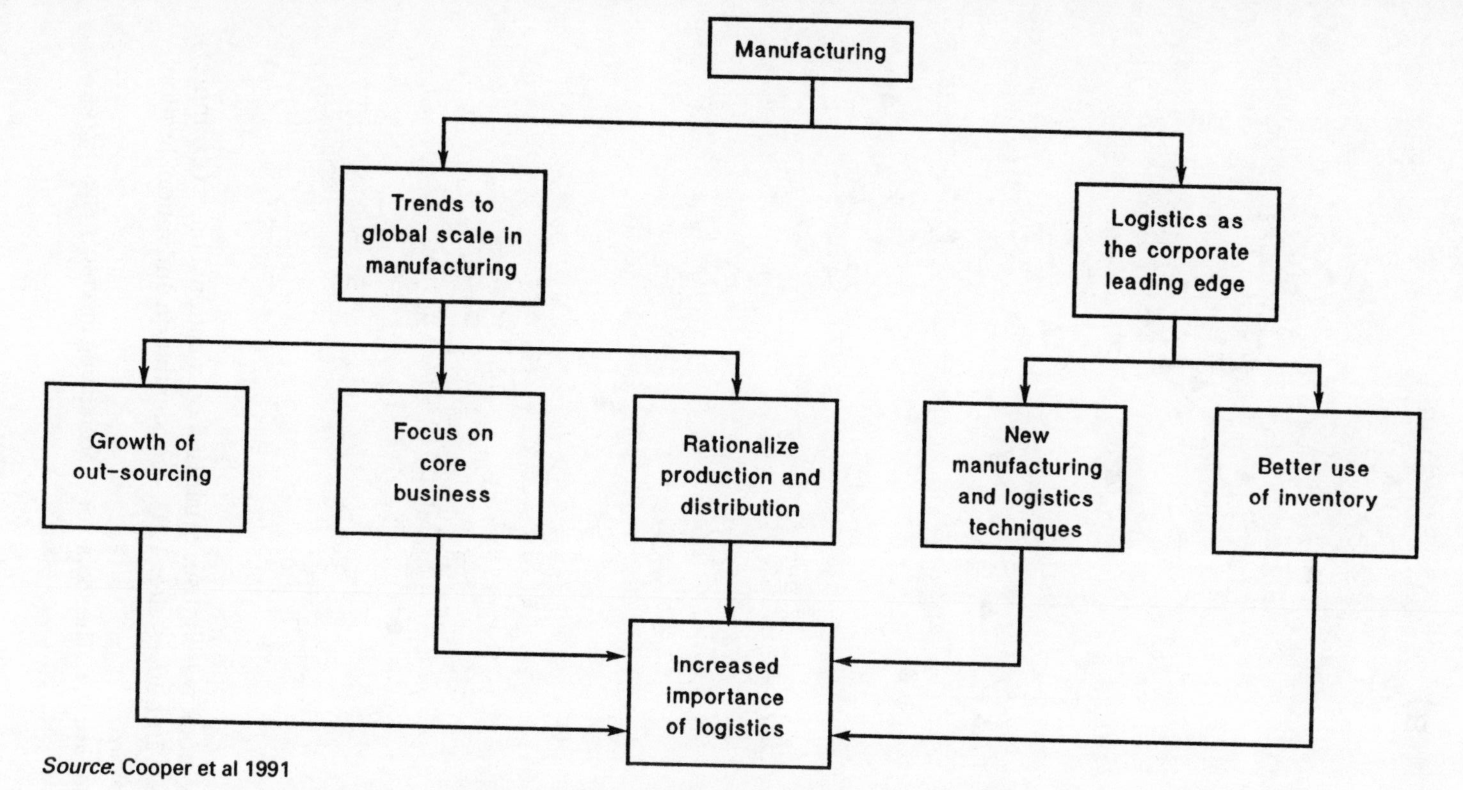

Source: Cooper et al 1991

Figure 9.3 Driving forces in manufacturing logistics

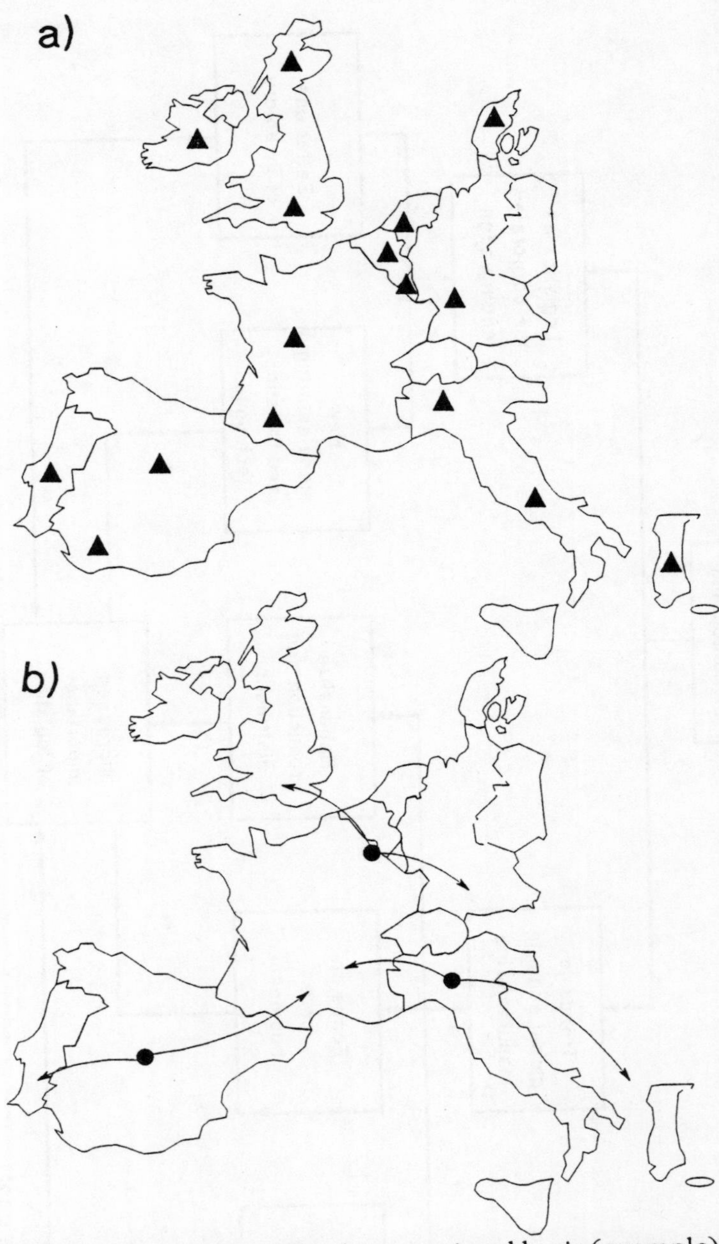

a) Philips' stock warehouses organised on a national basis (example)
b) Philips warehouses after 1993 – concentration and rationalisation
Source: Kearney

Figure 9.4 The scope for concentrating inventory after 1992

chain. Just-in-time (JIT) has already made a celebrated contribution in this direction; now the locational reorganisation of inventory is required to make a further contribution and so raise the competitiveness of European industry relative to its rivals. Companies such as Philips and Monsanto, operating in ever-more competitive markets are now committed to a radical restructuring of their inventory-holding facilities in Europe, aided by the SEM (see Figure 9.4). There should be no doubt about the wide scope of the opportunities for cost reduction by concentrating inventory into fewer, larger locations. In the UK, capital tied up in inventory amounts to over £80 billion, representing about 20 per cent of the value of manufacturing output. Waters (1990) argues that this has a potentially important impact on international competitiveness when in Japan, for example, the corresponding figure represents only 10.5 per cent of the value of manufacturing output. The process of concentrating inventory has a number of major cost implications, including the following.

- Greater concentration of inventory implies a smaller overall inventory requirement. Using the square root law applied to inventory (Maister 1976), it can be argued that under ideal conditions a single warehouse handling, say, 1 million units per annum should require only half as much stock as a system of four warehouses, each handling 250,000 units a year.
- If inventory is concentrated in fewer warehouses, the overall cost of operating the warehouses may fall because of economies of scale in warehousing (Williams 1974).
- The administrative costs (eg order processing, invoicing and rate negotiations) sustained by users of freight services are likely to decline as inventory is held in fewer places. Not only are users likely to reduce the number of freight companies working on their behalf, but there will also be more opportunities to use IT in tasks which support logistics.

Apart from the above cost implications, there are also customer service implications that arise from the concentration of inventory. In general, concentration means that customers become physically more remote from the goods they have ordered. Steps need to be taken to ensure that customer service levels are not eroded; indeed, there may be a marketing need for even better levels of customer service as companies continue to compete more aggressively for sales. This implies a reassessment of logistics channels with an emphasis, perhaps, on faster and more reliable delivery.

It is important to recognise, however, that the European business environment does not readily favour the swift reshaping of logistics systems. In particular, it should be noted that many companies wishing to develop pan-European logistics systems with fewer, larger storage points for inventory are not making rapid progress towards this goal. As already discussed, the only industry sector which is well ahead in pan-European logistics is automotive, and then only for inbound supply of components to factories.

Here lies the key to the problem. In the automotive industry, companies such as General Motors and Ford represent single purchasers of many components. Given the large volumes of automotive components in the logistics pipeline and the wide geographical spread of suppliers, it makes good sense to organise as much as possible on a pan-European basis. The commercial power of automotive TNCs makes it possible for them to convert wishes into reality.

But for outbound logistics (ie the physical distribution of finished products) the key considerations are often somewhat different. Above all, the importance of national sales and marketing teams must be recognised. For reasons of language and cultural differences it is unlikely that there will be any change to the national basis for most sales and marketing operations in Europe for a long time, if ever.

Significantly, sales and marketing teams have a naturally close relationship with outbound logistics which, as we have seen, is still organised on a national basis by most MNC/TNCs in Europe. In many companies, sales and marketing departments are fundamentally opposed to pan-European organisation of outbound logistics because it breaks this close relationship; they fear poorer levels of service when they have to depend on order fulfilment from another country. Top on the agenda of sales and marketing fears are the following.

- There will be more misunderstandings between company staff, particularly as a result of different languages being used. This can readily lead to a worse performance in order fill, especially for sales and marketing teams which have to order from a neighbouring country (eg Spanish sales and marketing ordering from a regional warehouse in south-west France).
- There may be preferential treatment for the local sales and marketing team by staff based at regional European warehouses. It is normal practice for sales and marketing staff to become well acquainted with the people who control delivery to their customers. Outbased sales and marketing teams will clearly feel at a disadvantage compared with their colleagues based at a regional European warehouse, when competing for products in short supply.

There are, of course, ways of getting round these obstacles. EDI, for example, means that normal replenishment can take place without language being a barrier. Nonetheless, the fears of sales and marketing are presenting a considerable obstacle to the rationalisation of systems for outbound logistics in Europe. The result is that many companies with plans for pan-European systems are having to implement them much more slowly than they first thought. This is causing some problems for builders of third-party logistics systems in Europe (see below).

Retailing – key trends for logistics in Europe

Retailing provides a dramatic contrast with manufacturing in the extent to which it has become internationalised. Whereas manufacturing has gone through several stages of internationalisation, from simply exporting to the development of transnational companies, retailing has typically stayed at home. This is not to say that there have not been adventurous retailers. Some retailers, such as F W Woolworth, embarked on an ambitious programme of retailing throughout the world many decades ago (although this company has now substantially divested itself of its overseas interests). Typically, however, many retailers have had little experience outside their home countries.

Yet there is new evidence of a trend towards greater internationalisation, not just in Europe, but throughout the world. Treadgold (1988) suggests that the crucial difference compared with the past seems to be that retailers are becoming increasingly active in identifying and exploiting opportunities in other countries before opportunities at home are exhausted.

Internationalisation in retailing puts an increasing emphasis on achieving excellence in logistics. In clothing, Benetton has used innovative approaches to logistics to develop and sustain its position as a 'world power' in retailing (Montgomery and Hausman, 1985). Similarly, in furniture retailing, Ikea would have been unable to expand world wide from its Swedish home market without a sound grasp of the importance of logistics in developing new business.

At the European level, we have also seen a growing interest in developing across borders, not least in grocery retailing which, by revenues, represents the largest retailing segment of all. One of the most important cross-border moves has been by French companies into Spain. Around 19 per cent of Carrefour's turnover comes from its 24 hypermarket Pryca operation. Similarly, Alcampo is owned by Auchan, and Continente/Saudisa is owned by Promodes.

Belgian, Dutch, German and UK grocery retailers have also entered into the process of internationalisation but are rather less focused on European expansion than their French counterparts. The USA is a favourite destination. The notable exception to this expansion programme is one of the 'Big Four' countries in the EC, namely Italy. As yet, it is neither an origin nor destination country for grocery retailers engaged in greater internationalisation. This is because Italy is characterised by small independent retailing businesses. Figure 9.5 shows the extent to which the level of fragmentation in grocery retailing varies considerably between European countries.

The key point here, of course, is that fragmentation limits the ability of retailers to exert control of the supply chain. So while Dutch, German and UK grocery retailers have been active in promoting logistics innovation in various ways, this is much less of an option for their Italian counterparts.

The main logistics innovations developed by leading grocery retailers in Europe are as follows:

- Using IT to maintain better control over the supply chain
- Releasing more sales space in retail outlets by eliminating storage space
- Contracting out to specialist companies those logistics activities such as transport and storage which are not 'core' business. (Cooper et al 1991).

Clearly, then, grocery retailing in Europe comprises two sets of countries with respect to their ability to promote logistics innovation in grocery supply chains. First, there are those countries where there is a high degree of concentration of grocery retailing. Companies in countries such as Germany, the UK and the Netherlands are in a good position to use logistics for competitive advantage. Second, there are a number of other countries where, for reasons of national regulation and/or consumer preferences, retailing remains a small-scale (mainly family) activity. Most of these are Mediterranean countries and include Italy, Greece, Spain and Portugal.

In non-food retailing it is less easy to generalise about fragmentation and its impact upon logistics innovation. For example, the ownership of shoe shops may be concentrated, which tends to favour innovation. But this is usually countered by the typically small size of outlet in shoe retailing. Information systems are more demanding to instal in thousands of small shops, and there is little opportunity to release more sales space by eliminating storage space. All the same, as a generalisation about retailers, there does seem to be something of a north–south split in

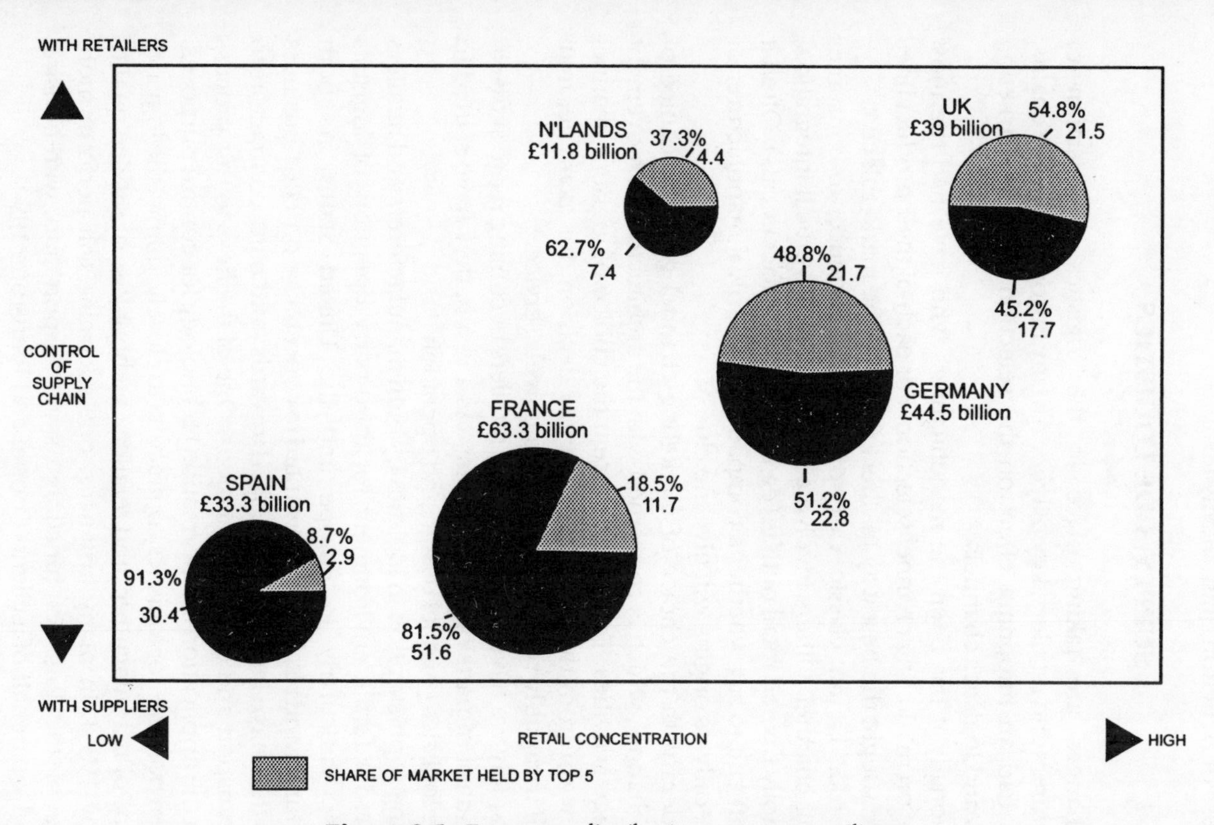

Figure 9.5 European distribution: grocery retailing

Europe, with northern retailers more active in controlling and shaping parts of the supply chain. However, there will always be exceptions, as the success of Benetton dramatically testifies.

SUPPLY-SIDE LOGISTICS

Many changes are taking place in the logistics organisation of manufacturers and retailers, key players in many European supply chains. This has had an important effect on the selection of both marketing channels and logistics channels.

Traditionally it has been the manufacturers who have had the most influence on marketing channel selection. For each of their product lines they have sought the best way to direct goods to the marketplace.

Mail order is the classic case of a direct producer-to-consumer marketing channel. Others involve a high degree of vertical integration, using wholly owned retail outlets (eg Boots in pharmaceuticals). Often it can be difficult to say whether a company is primarily a manufacturer or a retailer; only its origins will give the clue.

In tandem with the choice of marketing channel goes the choice of logistics channel, which is concerned with the architecture of movement and storage activities. To a certain extent the choice of logistics channel will follow on from the marketing channel decision; for example, mail order will invariably require the use of a parcels service.

Increasingly we have seen European retailers becoming more active in taking control of parts of supply chains. As a result, they have started to influence logistics channel design and operation.

Growing sophistication in logistics by both manufacturers and retailers has created a fertile environment for third-party operators of logistics networks, particularly in Europe and the United States. As both manufacturers and retailers have wanted to concentrate on 'core' business activities they have increasingly looked towards third party contractors to handle transport and storage operations. One of the keys to this process has been the application of information technology for control purposes. It has been possible for logistics contractors to closely 'mimic' the logistics operations of manufacturers and retailers, without loss of service quality (Quarmby 1985). In many instances, one specialist will perform more than one of the logistics functions, say transport and warehousing combined, on behalf of a client (Cooper and Johnstone 1990).

Many logistics contractors have responded with alacrity to the new demands of their clients. Most of these contractors will have originated in haulage (trucking), a business noted for its poor profitability while owner-operators are allowed easy entry to (and exit from) the market. Becoming a logistics network operator gives niche positioning which is more defensible.

In Europe, a number of logistics network operators are embarking on ambitious plans for expansion, to meet the developing needs of manufacturers and retailers. In part, this process has been triggered by economic deregulation of the road freight sector in many European countries. No longer are providers of road freight services so constrained by the availability of operating permits. Instead, they are able to expand or adapt to meet the changing needs of client companies (Cooper et al 1991).

The expansion of third-party logistics networks is based on two main features of the changing pattern of demand exhibited by manufacturers and retailers.

- There will be more one-stop shopping for logistics services. As the logistics needs of users become ever more complex, many realise that it is cumbersome and expensive to employ a large number of service providers. Eventually this may result in a preference for one-stop shopping where one provider of logistics services can meet all the needs of a user. Already, many manufacturers can be seen to be rationalising the number of providers of logistics services that they use. General Motors, for example, is in the process of halving the number of its European providers of logistics services. In a four-year period, one division of Monsanto will have reduced its number by about 75 per cent.

  The rationalisation of storage points is often a spur to reducing the number of logistics service providers. For example, Albert Heijn in the Netherlands and Kaufhof in Germany are in the initial stages of making a single contractor responsible for storage and transport at a new generation of larger warehouses.
- Manufacturers and retailers have multiple service needs in their chosen logistics channels. Logistics network operators therefore must develop a multi-service portfolio. For example, a retailer may prefer to send goods to some stores using a dedicated logistics service. For other stores, often more inaccessible and requiring lower volumes, a shared service will be preferred. One-stop shopping would therefore imply that a logistics network operator has capabilities in providing a variety of services, not just in transport, but also in storage. Companies such as Nedlloyd have been building up their multi-service portfolio with a number of acquisitions (eg the parcels carriers Van Gend en

Loos in the Netherlands and the spedition company Union in Germany.)

The greater geographical spread of companies, as demonstrated by overseas acquisitions, points to the development of mega-carriers. These can be defined as companies with multiservice logistics networks operating over a wide area (Cooper et al 1991). The evidence seems to suggest that several kinds of company are in the running to become the first European mega-carriers. As Figure 9.6 shows, there are a number of potential mega-carriers arising from a number of different origins. A key point about many potential mega-carriers is that they may not wish to undertake all activities within their networks; some will be subcontracted but controlled by information technology. This is especially true of services such as line-haul transport which has little value added.

Rapid attainment of mega-carrier status may, however, not be possible (or even desirable) for many larger freight companies. Enormous financial resources are required and unforeseen difficulties can place companies under great pressure. Nedlloyd is just one example of a company which is feeling the financial strain of its expansion programme.

Indeed, there is a variety of difficulties and pitfalls that face the potential mega-carrier. Among the most significant are the following.

- It can be difficult to develop successful strategic alliances across different business and management cultures.
- Apparent synergies may in reality be more difficult to exploit than anticipated (eg the acquisition of Flying Tigers by Federal Express has failed to deliver the expected returns).
- It can be difficult to integrate information systems following mergers, joint ventures and strategic alliances.
- There may be problems of control with rapid growth (such as Rockwoods' difficulties, which led ultimately to the company going into receivership).
- Retreat is difficult – once a carrier starts to offer one-stop shopping then to step back from this strategy and try to select only higher revenue earning activities can result in the loss of key customers (Cooper et al 1991).

And added to this list is the special difficulty faced by the aspiring European mega-carrier. Just how quickly can manufacturers and retailers translate their desire for pan-European networks into reality? As we have seen, there are a number of organisational obstacles in their path, not least the wish of many in sales and marketing roles to preserve a national basis for logistics operations. Timing will be crucial. There is no point in

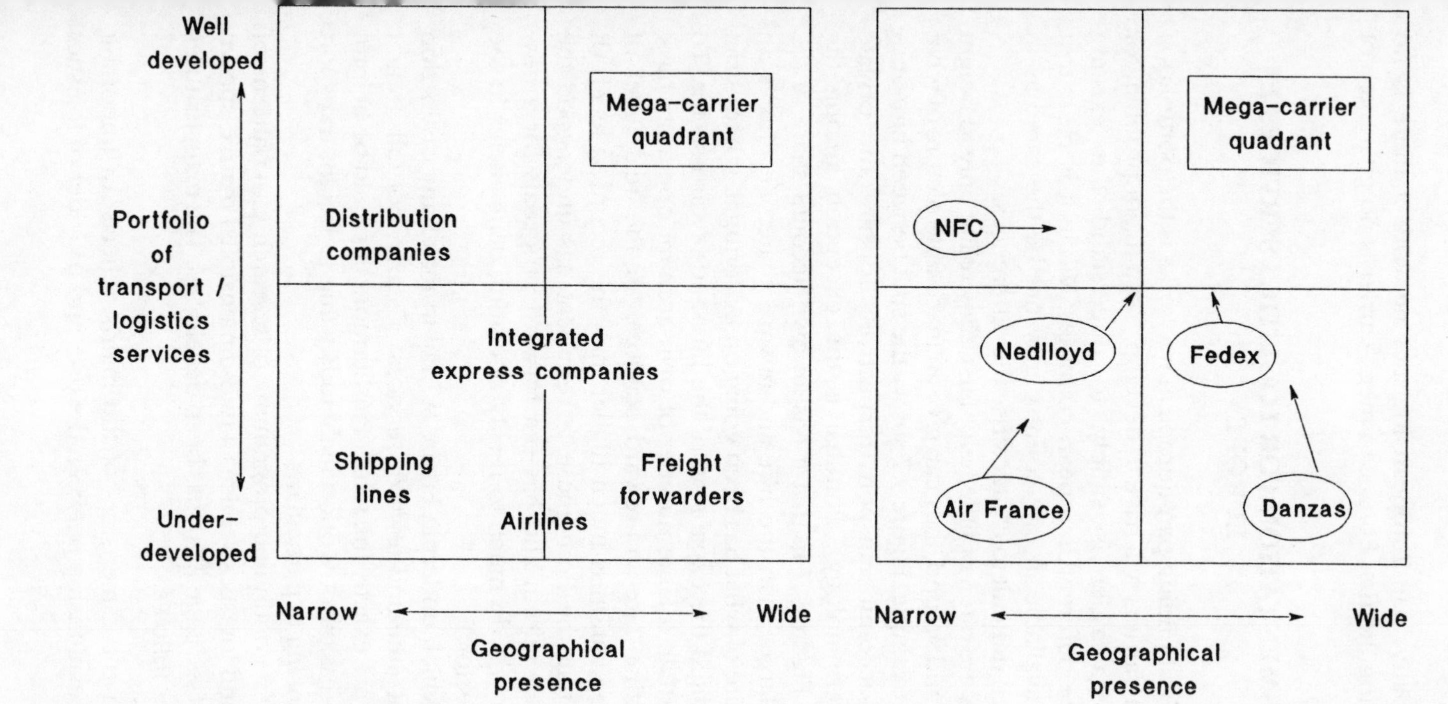

(a) Carrier and logistics taxonomy
(b) Current positioning of selected players

Figure 9.6 Mega-carrier clssification

building a third-party, pan-European logistics network if there is no demand for it. Being the first European mega-carrier is no guarantee of success.

MARKET SEGMENTATION FOR LOGISTICS SERVICES IN EUROPE

A crucial element in building pan-European networks is the portfolio of services that mega-carriers will have to develop. Yet a major problem for any aspiring mega-carrier is simply to understand the existing marketplace in the different European countries. While it is clear that logistics services available in one country may not be the same as in another, it has been difficult to characterise the differences.

Official statistics are often of little help. First, they relate only to freight transport services and second, they can give an inaccurate picture of what is happening. For example, Figure 9.7 shows the split between hire-and-reward and own-account transport (respectively for-hire and private trucking in US terminology). Portugal is the exception among the countries cited in Figure 9.7 in that it has an own-account share of the market which is larger than the hire-and-reward share. Yet this is an entirely false picture of what has been going on in Portugal, where strict regulation has limited the expansion of the hire-and-reward sector. To make up the shortfall, a large number of own-account operators have provided clandestine hire-and-reward services, so the real level of hire-and-reward operation is much higher than the recorded level. (It should be noted that the Portuguese government has understood the need for regulatory reform and has put forward proposals for a new framework which will do much to rectify operating deficiencies in the freight transport sector.)

Also, the data which underpin Figure 9.7 fail to make any distinction between different hire-and-reward services. Clearly not all freight transport services are exactly the same. Furthermore, it would be helpful to gain some impression of work which adds value to freight transport services – warehousing in particular.

In the course of a continuing programme of research into patterns of freight transport and logistics services a two-dimensional matrix, shown here as Figure 9.8 (see page 218), has been developed. The main features of the matrix are as follows.

- The 'management' dimension' of the matrix reflects an important aspect of the relationship between the user and provider of logistics

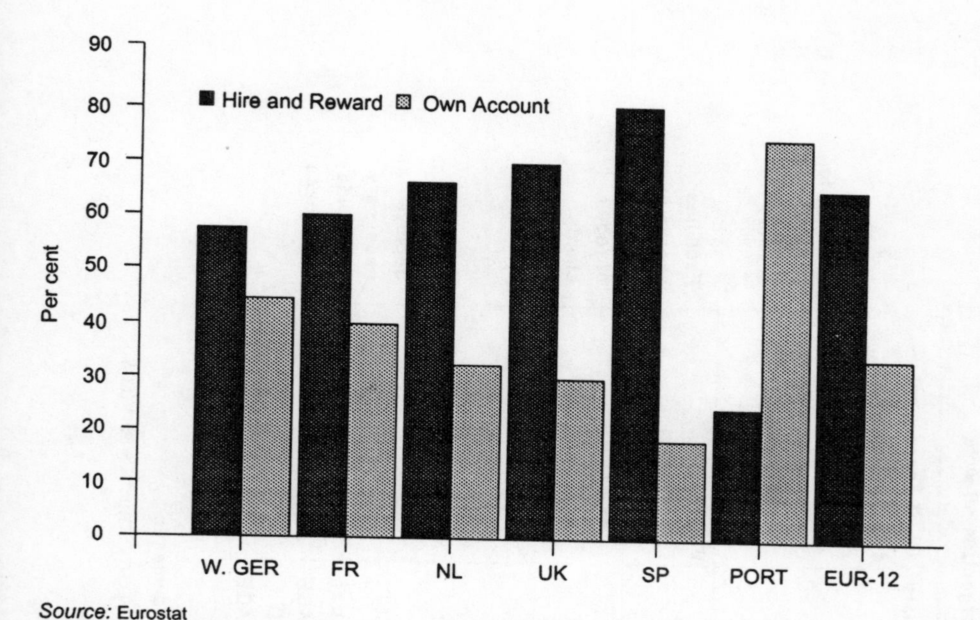

Source: Eurostat

Figure 9.7 Hire-and-reward and own-account shares of freight markets in selected countries

services; namely, does the provider organise the work or does the user?

- The 'capacity dimension' represents how capacity can be shared among users.
- The matrix makes a distinction between the two mainstream activities of transport and distribution (ie transport and storage with associated information systems).

Development of the matrix arose from the need to segment markets for logistics services in a variety of different European countries. This means using the definitions of services rather than their descriptions. In other words, it is clearly unsatisfactory to translate the English description of a service (eg dedicated contract transport) into, say, German and expect to maintain understanding. (In fact, the German term for this service is 'Massgeschneiderte Transporte', which translates back into English as 'tailor-made transport', a description which would not immediately be recognised as being synonymous with 'dedicated contract transport'.)

The value of the matrix is that it allows the definition of a service, rather than its description, to become the semantic currency. So, the notion of

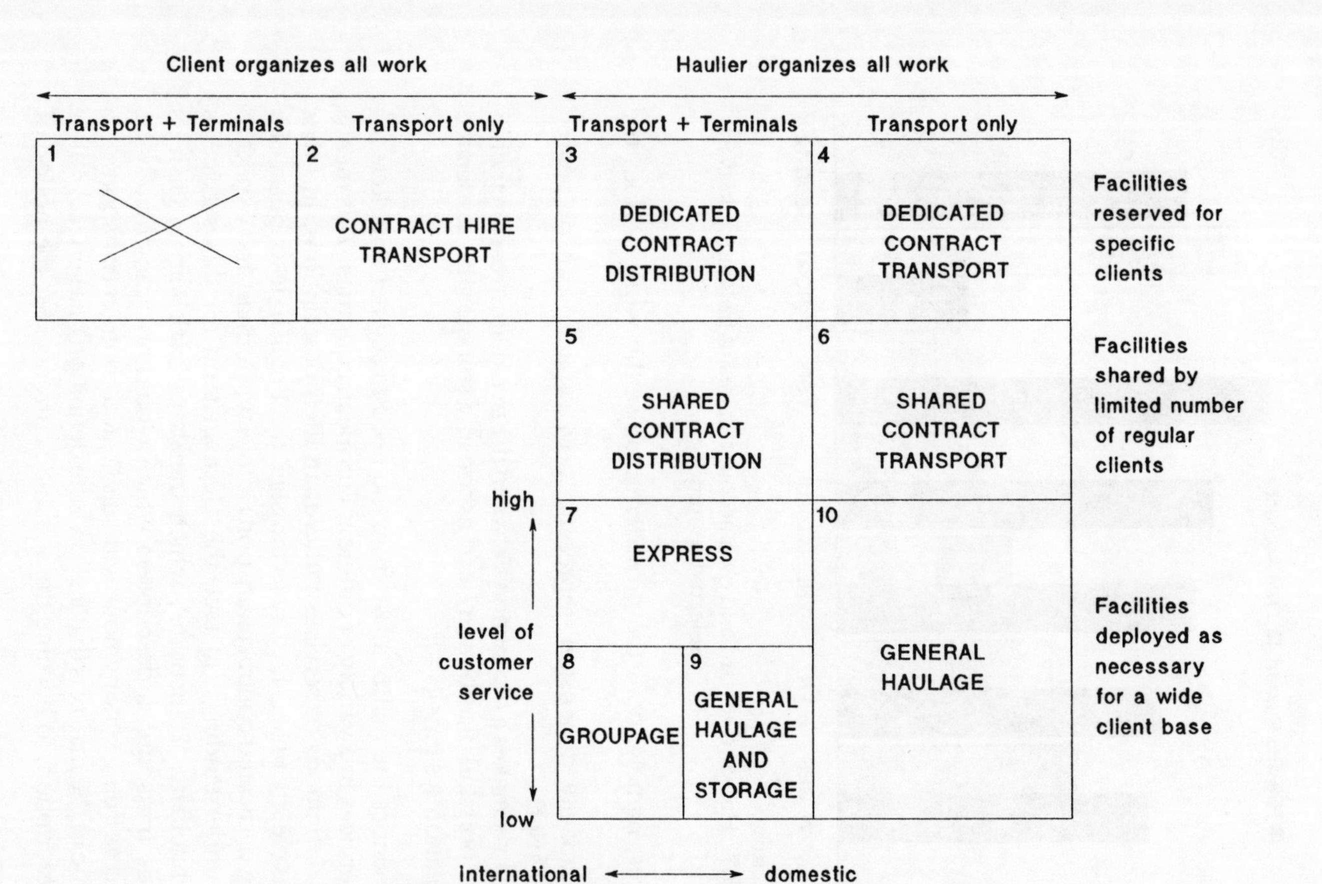

Figure 9.8 Classification of third-party logistics services

dedicated contract transport can be better conveyed by explaining that it represents a service where:

1. Transport capacity is divided into 'client sets' with each set reserved for use by a specific client
2. The operator organises all the work according to customer service standards agreed with the client.

The matrix therefore offers the opportunity to identify with some clarity the existence of particular logistics market segments.* It avoids having to translate and interpret names of services, which invariably leads to considerable misunderstanding and a failure to classify accurately the separate parts of national markets for logistics services.

In conjunction with the matrix, which allows the identification and naming of logistics services, a questionnaire (not reproduced here) was used to establish both the present scale of a particular service, and whether it was growing or declining relative to other services. Both the matrix and the questionnaire were then sent out or taken to correspondents across Europe for completion.

An important point to note about the questionnaire is that it was designed largely for judgemental use. Very little data exist to describe, for example, expenditure on general haulage services in the various European countries. Correspondents (about ten in most countries) were asked to use their judgement to rank the scale of a service relative to others. Although this is an undeniably imprecise way of judging scale we were impressed by the degree of consensus among correspondents from any given country. Experts in the field of logistics can have an encouragingly similar view of what is going on.

Moreover, the purpose of the exercise was not so much to judge the absolute scale of a logistics service in any one country, but rather to establish a service profile for each country. In broad terms, services 2–7, as represented by the cells in the matrix (see Figure 9.8 and Box 9.1) represented the more advanced services. The remaining services 8–10 (groupage, general haulage and storage, and general haulage) are altogether more traditional. By establishing a service profile, some basic comparisons, appropriate to the precision of the study could be made between countries.

The study, which fundamentally aims to build up a picture of logistics

---

* For example, use of the matrix revealed a complete absence of contract hire transport in Germany. Confusion over its legality in that country has halted its development.

Box 9.1 Definitions of logistic services

Cell 1: Use of the matrix Figure 9.8 allows for the existence of a service of this type, where ownership of both transport and warehousing rests with the third party but where all control is exercised by the customer. However, the existence of this theoretical possibility for a service has not been confirmed through the market segmentation study.

Cell 2: Contract hire transport. Here a haulier/distributor provides vehicles and (usually) drivers, which are put at the disposal of the client. All maintenance and vehicle replacement responsibilities fall to the haulier. However, it is the client that organises the work of the driver and vehicle. In particular, the client's responsibility will be to allocate consignments for delivery and decide upon routes.

Cell 3: Dedicated contract distribution. Services of this kind involve both transport and warehousing capacity, which is divided into 'client sets' with each set dedicated to one specific client. This compartmentalisation of the contractor's capacity between clients means that the service needs of any one client will not be compromised by the conflicting needs of other clients, such as may occur when capacity is shared. Dedicated contract distribution is, in effect, a third-party replication of own-account operation, and contracts generally have a 2–5 year duration. As a comprehensive, 'tailor-made' service for clients, dedicated contract distribution offers good scope both for the application of logistics concepts and the advanced uses of IT systems.

Cell 4: Dedicated contract transport. This is directly analogous to dedicated contract distribution (cell 3 above), but involves only a transport service.

Cell 5: Shared contract distribution. This service arises when several clients of a distributor have specialised needs in common (eg in packaging, handling, storage or even common destinations, such as hospitals). The client benefits from the distributor being able to consolidate consignments which have these specialised needs in both transport and warehousing.

Cell 6: Shared contract transport. This type of service is a variant upon shared contract distribution, but involves only transport.

Cell 7: Express. Most express services are sophisticated versions of a common-user service involving transport and warehousing (for sorting rather than storage). Companies offering express services accept only relatively small consignment sizes (say, up to 25 kg) but offer a high level of service in return, often with next-day delivery. Tracking and tracing systems often contribute to a high level of customer service.

Cell 8: Groupage. The main difference between groupage and express is that groupage services will accept larger consignment sizes, but delivery will invariably be slower. Overall, levels of customer service are not as high as in express.

(continued)

Cell 9: General haulage and storage. This is a common-user service where the haulier provides not just transport services for a variety of customers but also storage facilities.

Cell 10: General haulage. This is yet another common-user service but the haulier only performs a transport operation. There is no warehousing dimension to the work, unlike cell 9.

market segmentation in Europe and then form a view on the future shape of logistics services, was conducted during 1989 and 1990. Other points which relate to the conduct of the study are as follows.

- Geographical coverage. The matrix was used for a selected number of national freight markets in Europe, including Germany, the UK, the Netherlands, Greece, France and Sweden (for the purposes of comparison with non-EC countries). The aim was to establish any difference that might exist between particular countries or regions (eg Northern and Southern Europe).
- *Validation of matrix cells*. In addition to respondents providing local descriptions of matrix cells, it was requested that they should also give examples of companies providing any one service. This helped to validate the existence of a cell in the country for, if a respondent cannot identify a company providing the service, then it is unlikely that the service exists.
- *Analysis of the results*. Completed matrices and questionnaires from respondents in each country were centrally analysed, for the purposes of consistency, in the UK. Continuing dialogue with selected respondents helped to clarify potential anomalies and correct prospective errors.

The full results of the study are presented in a recent book (Cooper et al 1991). Here are shown two examples of the output which have been modified in Figure 9.9 to incorporate the size of the market for third-party logistics in terms of expenditure. (Most of the correspondents assessed the significance of the market segments in terms of perceived expenditure rather than, say, tonnes-kilometres.)

A striking feature of Figure 9.9 is the extent to which the market for third-party services is segmented quite differently in the UK and Sweden.

Of all the countries surveyed, the UK has the widest developed range of services according to the market segmentation results, a result confirmed by another recent study (Kearney 1990). The weakest is shared

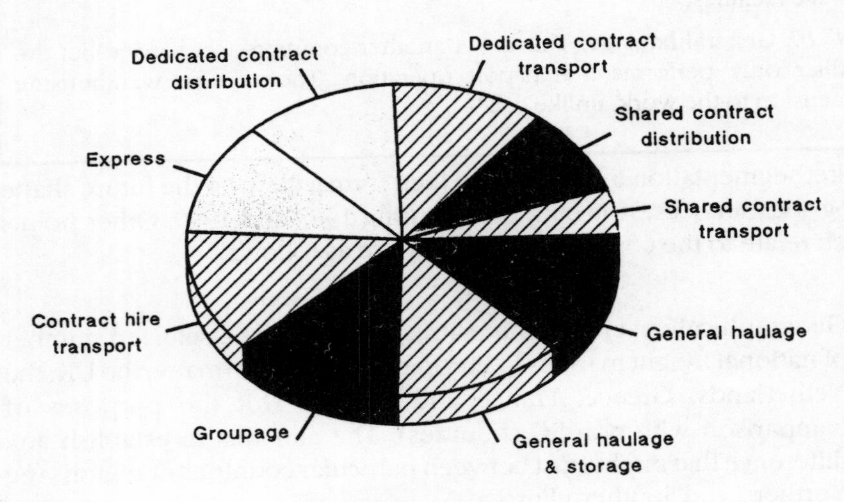

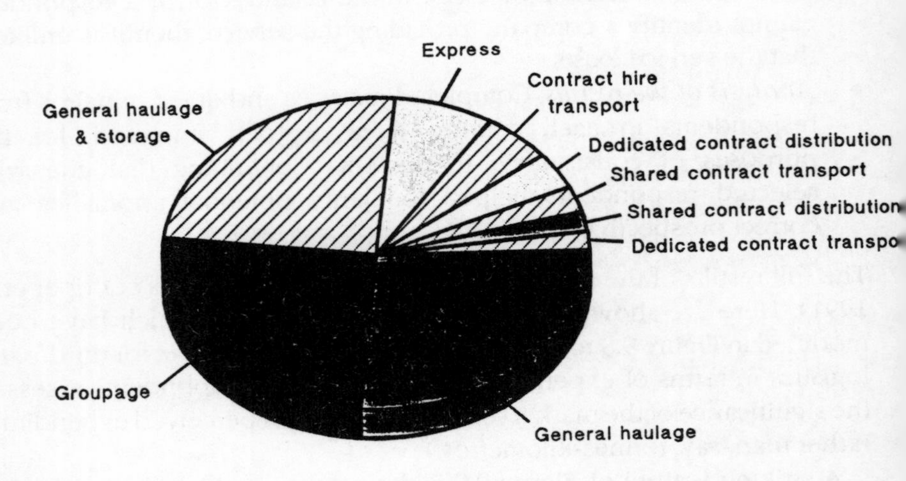

Figure 9.9 Third-party logistics services: market segmentation in the UK and Sweden

contract transport (from cell 6), which seems to have lost its market share to dedicated services (from cells 3 and 4). The main reasons for this pattern of services are:

- Deregulation in 1968 leading to rapid innovation through increased competition
- Oligopoly in grocery retailing creating demand-led changes to distribution practice
- A high geographical concentration of economic activity.

The market-segmentation results for Sweden show a concentration on common-user services (from cells 8, 9 and 10). This most probably reflects the limited opportunities for specialist services afforded in a relatively small economy. Long distances, both within Sweden itself and to major markets overseas, also make common-user services the preferred option for many shippers.

As discussed above, respondents to the market segmentation survey were asked about change in services; which ones are growing, which were static and which ones were in decline. Their responses to the question are summarised in Figure 9.10, and the key trends identified are discussed and amplified in the following list.

- *Growing.* The services most consistently marked out as very strongly 'growing' are dedicated contact distribution (3) and express (7). Groupage (8) is also relatively strong, possibly reflecting the increasing demand for international services with Europe. The trend is also generally upward for dedicated contract transport (4), with the exception of the Netherlands which sees it as static. Contract hire transport (2) is also upwardly mobile, except in Germany, where doubts about its legality have strangled its prospects.
- *Static.* Overall, shared contract transport (6) is seen as a 'static' performer. There is no perceived movement in market share in either Germany or the Netherlands. A small rise in Sweden is counterbalanced by decline in the UK. Shared contract distribution (5) is also reasonably static, with growth being confined mainly to the Netherlands.
- *In decline.* Without exception, general haulage (10) is in substantial decline across Europe. The position is similar for another common-user service, general haulage and storage (9): only Greece is experiencing growth in this service.

Overall, therefore, it appears that there is a shift in Europe from common-user services (such as general haulage, and general haulage and

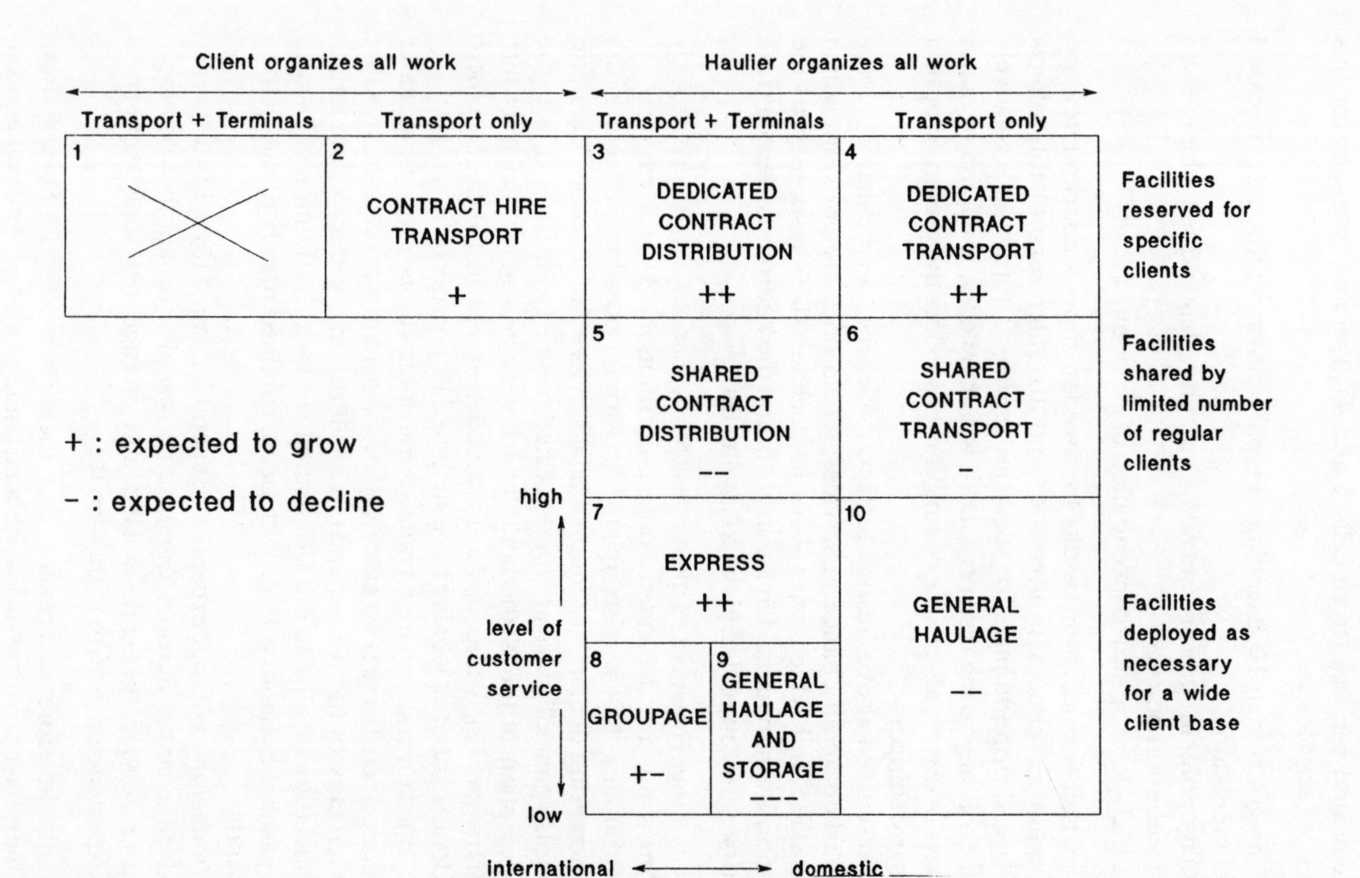

Figure 9.10 Expected changes in segment sizes

storage) to more specialised freight services, which have enhanced potential for logistics development. Dedicated contract distribution and express seem to be in particular demand.

The results from the market segmentation study are, of course, imperfect from a data point of view. Future work in the area can bring a number of refinements. However, the important point is that it is better to see a complicated picture in soft focus than not to be able to see it at all. This applies particularly to strategists working for freight companies with the ambition to build pan-European networks. It would be a dangerous undertaking to extend networks into a country with no knowledge of its market segmentation in logistics services.

LESSONS FOR MANAGERS

- Logistics in Europe is in a state of considerable flux. Increased competition, notably from Pacific Rim countries, and the new demands of the Single European Market, are making many manufacturers realise that they need new competencies in logistics.
- Yet, to achieve success, European companies face the paradox of simultaneously having to accommodate powerful forces for change and continuity when devising their logistics strategies. The challenge for managers is to achieve the right balance in logistics between radical and conservative approaches. There is no one 'golden mean' for all companies. Each must respond according to its unique competitive positioning and strategic intent.
- A major goal for many companies operating in Europe is to reconfigure their logistics systems for the distribution of finished products. The Single European Market offers the opportunity to serve customers from regional European, rather than national, distribution centres. A significant benefit is the saving in inventory holding costs through operating fewer, but larger, distribution centres. Logistics managers must be aware, however, that a number of important issues need to be resolved to secure the potential benefits. For example, the greatest inventory savings will occur with products which are standardised across Europe. To what extent is this achievable, or even desirable, for a company?
- A further major issue relates to the structure of the organisation. Regional European distribution centres invariably involve a realignment of relationships between marketing and distribution operations. Great care must be taken to ensure that the change management

process in this realignment is carefully planned at the earliest possible stage.

- The reorganisation of final distribution in Europe also offers new opportunities in the contracting out of logistics services such as warehousing and transport. Deregulation in the freight transport sector has given transport operators the opportunity to expand geographically within Europe and develop new value-added services. Some operators are creating pan-European refunds for potential customers in manufacturing and, to a lesser extent, in retailing. For logistics managers there are pros and cons to be weighed in electing to use these networks. While there are potential benefits in the 'bulk buying' of services from a single operator, and a reduction in transaction costs, there is also the danger of becoming too committed to one operator.
- Managers must also be aware in their future planning of new challenges in logistics, such as the environment and how to incorporate Eastern European markets and production sites into existing logistics systems designed according to Western European needs. Here we have what is possibly the key point about logistics management in Europe; namely, in a highly complex and dynamic environment, flexibility will be the key if companies are to maintain or achieve success.

REFERENCES

Christopher, M (1985) *The Strategy of Distribution Management*, Gower, Aldershot

Cooper, J, Browne, M and Peters, M (1991) *European Logistics: Markets, Management and Strategy*, Blackwell, Oxford and Boston

Cooper, J and Johnstone, M (1990) 'Dedicated contract distribution: an assessment of the UK market place', *International Journal of Physical Distribution and Logistics Management*, 20, (1)

Dicken, P (1986) *Global Shift: Industrial Change in a Turbulent World*, Harper and Row, London

Doz, Y (1986) *Strategic Management in Multinational companies*, Pergamon, Oxford

The Economist (1988) 'Europe's Internal Market', 9 July

Eurostat (1989) *Europe in Figures: Deadline 1992*, EC, Luxembourg

— (periodical) *Basic Statistics*, EC, Luxembourg

Kearney, A T (1990) *Uitdagende Ontwikkelingen in Europese Transport Distributie Sector*, Amsterdam, Dec

Kearney, A T Inc (1991) *Road Transport after 1992*, A T Kearney Ltd, London

Levitt, T (1983) 'The globalization of markets' *Harvard Business Review*, May–June.

Maister, D H (1976) 'Centralisation of inventories and the square root law', *International Journal of Physical Distribution*, 6, (3)

Montgomery, D and Hausman, W (1985) 'Managing the marketing/manufacturing interface', *PA Journal of Management*, 2, (2)

Ohmae, K (1985) *Triad Power: the coming shape of global competition*, Free Press, New York

Quarmby, D (1985) 'Distribution, the next ten years – the Market-place', *Focus*, 4, (6), Nov–Dec

Treadgold, A (1988) 'Retailing without Frontiers', *Retail and Distribution Management*, Nov–Dec

Waters, C D J (1990) 'How efficient is UK inventory management?', in Cooper, J C (ed) *Logistics and Distribution Management: Strategies for Management*, revised edn, Kogan Page, London

Williams, J (1974) 'Food Distribution Costs – Results of an Interim Study of Wholesale Transportation and Warehousing Costs', Monograth 3, National Materials Handling Centre, Cranfield

Zinn, W and Grosse, R E (1990) 'Barriers to globalization: is global distribution possible?', *International Journal of Logistics Management*, 1, (1)

10

Managing the Global Pipeline*

Martin Christopher, Cranfield University School of Management, and Alan Braithwaite, Logistics Consulting Partners

> Time has ceased, 'space' has vanished. We now live in a *global village*...a simultaneous happening. (McLuhan 1967)

Over twenty years ago these words might have been considered hyperbole, an exaggeration to underline the point that McLuhan wanted to make about the growing interdependence of the world community. However, today we accept such statements as fact and we have come to recognise the necessity of considering markets from a global perspective when formulating production, distribution and marketing strategies.

Global brands and companies now dominate most markets. Over the last two decades there has been a steady trend towards the world-wide marketing of products under a common brand umbrella – whether it be Coca-Cola or Marlboro, IBM or Toyota. Not only is the brand common across individual country markets but also the product has moved towards standardisation. At the same time the global corporation has revised its previously localised focus and now instead will typically source on a world-wide basis for global production.

The logic of the global corporation is clear: it seeks to grow its business by extending its markets whilst at the same time seeking cost reduction through scale economies in purchasing and production and through focused manufacturing and/or assembly operations.

However, whilst the logic of globalisation is strong, we must recognise that it also presents certain challenges. Firstly, world markets are not homogeneous; there is still a requirement for local variation in many product categories. Secondly, unless there is a high level of coordination, the complex logistics of managing global supply chains may result in higher costs.

---

* This paper was previously published in *The International Journal of Logistics Management* (1991), Vol 2, No 2. Reprinted by kind permission

These two challenges are related: on the one hand, how to offer local markets the variety they seek whilst still gaining the advantage of standardised global production and on the other, how to manage the links in the global chain from sources of supply through to end-user. There is a danger that some global companies in their search for cost advantage may take too narrow a view of cost and only see the cost reduction that may be achieved by focusing on production. In reality it is a total cost tradeoff where the costs of longer supply pipelines may outweigh the production cost saving. Figure 10.1 illustrates some of the potential cost tradeoffs to be considered in establishing the extent to which a global strategy for logistics will be cost justified. Clearly a key component of the decision to go global must be the service needs of the marketplace. There is a danger that companies might run the risk of sacrificing service on the altar of cost reduction through a failure to understand fully the service needs of individual markets (Christopher 1989).

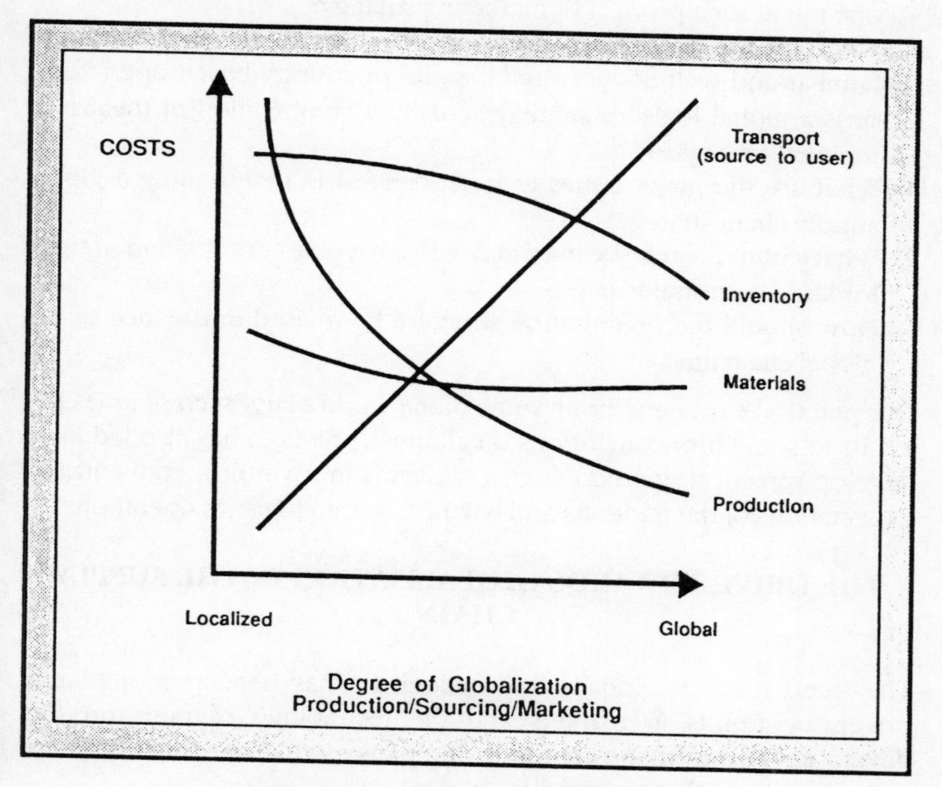

Figure 10.1 Tradeoffs in global logistics

THE GLOBAL CHALLENGE

The trend towards global organisation of both manufacturing and marketing is exposing the organisation of logistics and the supply chain as a critical success factor. The complexity of the logistics task appears to be increasing exponentially, influenced by such factors as the increasing range of products, shorter product lifecycles, marketplace growth and the number of supply/market channels.

There seems to be a number of questions which need to be answered in the process of understanding the challenge of global logistics.

1. Why are companies looking to global management of their supply chains?
2. What does a global supply chain strategy consist of? Is it actually possible to articulate a global strategy in logistics for a corporation as one might for a product or marketing strategy?
3. What are the differences between global operations and the more familiar and well-documented theatre- or country-based operations; or is a global logistics strategy actually a combination of theatre or regional strategies?
4. What are the major issues to be addressed in determining a global supply chain strategy?
5. What techniques can be used in devising a global supply chain strategy for large corporations?
6. How should the organisation structure be revised in the face of the global challenge?

Our practical experience with some of the world's largest companies has led us to some firm conclusions on all these points. It has also led us to develop practical methodologies which can overturn conventional expectations of the tradeoffs and balances within logistics operations.

THE DRIVE TOWARDS GLOBALISATION IN THE SUPPLY CHAIN

The trend towards globalisation in logistics has been predominantly driven by trends in markets and the technology of both product development and manufacturing. Companies which need to organise globally fall into three categories.

- First are commodity companies where the task is the well-developed one of moving bulk raw material from countries with surplus natural resources to those with the markets to consume them and/or the labour to process them.

- Secondly there are companies who are taking advantage of low regional labour costs to maximise profitability on labour intensive manufacturing. An example here would be Far Eastern production of sports footwear or the use of typesetting and printing services in India.
- Finally, and probably the most significant group in terms of the rate of change of the global economy and the trends for logistics, are the companies who have elected to concentrate their investment in R & D and manufacturing, focusing each of their sites on specific product-technology combinations.

The latter is sometimes referred to as a 'centre of excellence' strategy for manufacturing and product development. Almost all the major technology companies have moved in this direction. We are now also seeing consumer packaged goods companies organising this way within the European theatre of operations.

The thinking behind this approach has been well documented (Porter 1986). Firstly the increasing emphasis on substantial investment in manufacturing automation and robotics means that 'best manufacturing practice' is simply too expensive to be duplicated in each of the organisation's major markets; the skills to operate the technology are often concentrated in just a few people and they function best by working as a tight-knit team.

The focus of product development in terms of production engineering, if not in terms of more fundamental research, can benefit enormously from being close to the plant. A major source of concern in the boardrooms of corporations throughout the world is the tendency towards shortening product lifecycles simultaneously with extending lead times for product development and introduction (time to market) (Stalk & Hout 1990). The centre of excellence approach as well as having sound economic drivers is also an organisational device designed to accelerate product development cycles and increase product-market competitiveness. The observation has been made that it is becoming untenable to position a company as a full-range full-service supplier (Hamel and Prahalad 1989); the only way to respond to competition from smaller focused companies is to create strategic business units with high levels of autonomy.

The indications are that many companies who have followed this course of action have not registered the benefits to the degree anticipated. There appear to be two reasons for this.

1. The process of focusing production and concentrating on unit cost reduction has actually inhibited flexibility because of the emphasis on economies of scale.
2. The mechanics of managing an extended global supply chain have not yet been satisfactorily understood and implemented on a wide scale, and corporate organisation structures have not adapted to the radically different pressures imposed by a global strategy.

In conjunction with reduced flexibility in manufacturing and extended supply lines and lead times, corporations are finding themselves exposed to a number of consequential threats. These threats are:

- Higher inventory levels
- Increasing levels of product writeoff or markdown
- Failure to keep the markets supplied and hence lost revenue and market share
- High emergency logistics costs incurred as managers try to stay alive today, this week, this month.

In response to these pressures the leading edge companies are questioning decisions that previously were thought sound. For example, one of Europe's leading computer companies, ICL (now owned by Fujitsu), has reviewed its earlier strategy of Far East sourcing of commodity components because it believes that manufacturing cost gains are not sufficient to overcome the high transportation and inventory costs and the longer lead times that this entails (Roberts 1990). We believe that many other high-tech companies will also look again at their off-shore production and sourcing strategies for this same reason. Typically less than 10 per cent of a high-tech company's costs are direct labour. Hence the decision to source off-shore simply to save on labour costs makes little sense if penalties are incurred elsewhere in the supply chain.

According to our observations, the increasing focus of the supply chain is a response to these threats. Logistics has finally moved centre stage, placed there by the failure of the piecemeal implementation of policies within other functions in the organisation.

THE ELEMENTS OF A GLOBAL LOGISTICS STRATEGY

Logistics is pretty simple in its basics. It is about making things and getting them to their markets at the right time, in the right quantity and at the right cost. Thus a basic principle does not change whether the scale of operation of a company is just a single region or the entire world. The essential differences become ones of mode, transit time, lead time, cost controls and organisation. The ingredients remain the same, only the mix and complexity change.

Indeed, the elements of a global logistics strategy are quite well understood, They are summarised in Figure 10.2 which shows how corporate goals are 'unbundled' into operational areas and the specific operational dimensions are addressed within each. Finally the bottom line result needs to be fed back to be tested against the goals of the business; management then need to review the goals in the light of what is achievable, or pass back through the planning loop to produce a strategy with a more consistent result.

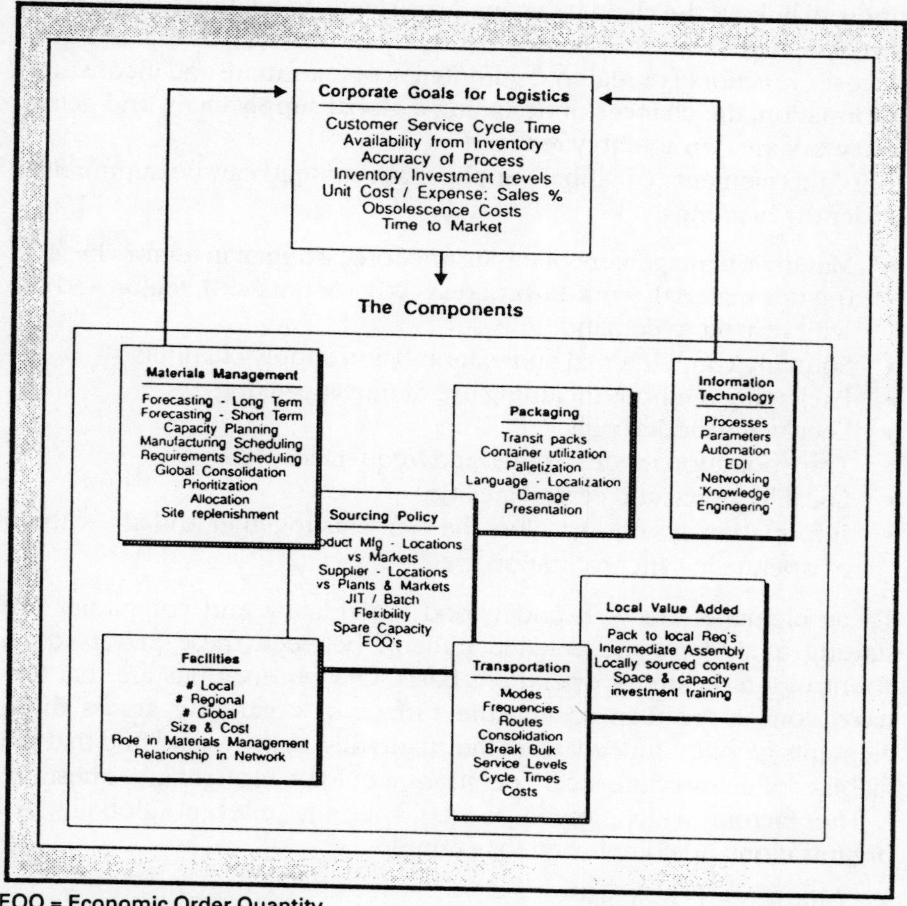

EOQ = Economic Order Quantity

EDI = Electronic Data Interchange

Figure 10.2 The elements of global logistics strategy

The reality is that this process is so complex on a global basis that the components of strategy are developed in relative functional isolation. Companies can only expect to 'iterate' towards successful global supply chains.

Without a formal logistics approach the 'ownership' of the individual dimensions of the supply chain is dispersed across the business. This is not so serious if all the executives responsible are housed in the same building or even in the same country or theatre of operations. When they are dispersed across the world with different languages and local priorities it is a major problem. Successful supply chains are dependent upon all links of the chain behaving consistently in relation to each other; if cooperative behaviour is constrained by factors such as the allocation of costs, functional or regional self-interest or inaccurate and inconsistent information, the chances of designing a global supply chain and getting it to work are considerably reduced.

So, the elements of global supply chain strategy can be summarised under the headings:

- Materials management planning and forecasting of inventory by level (eg raw material, work-in-progress (WIP) or finished), region and site with respect to demand
- Sourcing (both internal and external) and supply channels
- Packaging methods including use of transit packing
- Local value added policy
- Transportation modes, routes and frequencies
- Local, regional and central facilities
- Information systems to 'glue' the elements together and allow them to operate in synchronisation.

These elements are well understood individually and companies are starting to address the detailed tradeoff between these factors on a country or a theatre of operations basis. Our observations are that few have done more than scratch the surface of organising across these elements *globally*. Indeed, were they to do this, many would find that the viability of many of the local operations would be brought into question.

The factors which appear to be specially relevant globally are organisation and complexity; for example:

- Culture and language
- Local interest versus corporate interest
- Extended and unreliable transit and lead times
- The sheer complexity of compiling global corporate information in

order to define/refine global strategy, complicated by a track record of unreliable data

- Behavioural factors, eg 'not invented here' and 'not in my back yard'.

Our view is that managing the global supply chain involves most of the same dimensions of logistics management that we have become accustomed to considering on a local scale; it is just bigger and more complex to develop and implement. Hence the need for bold and imaginative corporate management to take responsibility and force through what may not be welcome decisions at a local level.

THE DIFFERENCE BETWEEN GLOBAL AND REGIONAL LOGISTICS OPERATIONS

Having said that the components of global supply chain operations are similar, albeit bigger and more complex than local or regional, it follows that the global supply chain is in fact the compilation and integration of a number of regional strategies.

It appears to us from our experience that managing the global pipeline from a total cost viewpoint consistent with the market requirements in the various theatres of operation is the essence of global logistics strategy.

The interdependency is clear; global supply chain management cannot exist in a vacuum. It is dependent upon consistent and coherent theatre based strategies and, of course, the reverse is simultaneously true.

We have identified six factors which are critically important to global supply chains as against those with smaller horizons. These factors exist in the planning of all supply chains but are relatively more important in terms of mix and extent in a global context; they create the need for different solutions.

1. Extended lead times of supply

The consolidation of global demand into a single manufacturing site creates contention in terms of the demands of the various markets, possibly demanding local product variations. Manufacturing management has tended to impose long lead times as a mechanism to get sales and marketing 'off their backs'. They have also been constrained by the operation of large, sophisticated and often irrelevant Materials Resource Planning systems (Fry 1990). Leading edge practice shows that the imposition of long manufacturing lead times is a largely artificial constraint. It is possible to make to order on very short timescales for specific customers in contrast to supplying from inventory. Toyota and

Nissan are both recognised as moving in this direction in Japan. Linn Electronics in the UK is a lesser-known example (Land 1990).

It is generally essential for the global chain to hold a level of intermediate inventory between manufacturing and the customer; this is required to buffer against extended transit times. However, if the size of the buffer reflects inflexibility in manufacturing or poor materials management procedures, then the size, role or need for facilities and stockholding in specific markets may well be suspect.

2. Extended and unreliable transit times

In Europe we have become accustomed to lengthy transit times for shipments from and to the Far East, Australasia and the USA. Sea freight from Japan has a transit time to Rotterdam of about five weeks. In contrast the total elapsed time from despatch to receipt of air freight if used is about five days (although faster tracks can be arranged). The use of sea freight can represent considerable investment in inventory on the high seas; it also seriously constrains the application of the basic logistics principle of postponement: that is, delay shipping decisions until the last possible moment.

We believe that as true supply chain costs become more clearly understood, the use of air freight will grow. Such are the penalties of high inventories and inflexible response to marketplace needs that the tradeoff will increasingly swing towards shorter transit times and hence swifter transit modes.

Shipping, consolidation and customs clearance all contribute to delays and variability in the lead time of global supply chains. This is well documented by van Amstel (1990) and is highlighted in Figure 10.3. Our experience confirms this as a major issue for most companies operating globally. It has two consequences

- Practice by local managers tends to compensate for this unreliabilty by over-ordering, double buffering, and competitive pressure on manufacturing and the central allocation organisation.
- Distrust that any improvement can be implemented successfully. It is ironic that lower performance standards in international freight are acceptable, whereas that would not be the case in carriage and freight within a local theatre of operations.

3. Multiple consolidation and break bulk options

The options for the management of international freight are several and

Invoice >>> Date	Depart Far East	Arrive N'lands	Arrive De-Groupage Centre	Arrive Central W/House	Booking in System	Σ of all Segments
Maximum	6	1	5	3	7	22
Average	4.5	1	2.3	1.4	2.4	11.6
Minimum	3	1	1	0	1	6
Variation						16

Figure 10.3 Range of pipeline lead times by function and in total

the tradeoffs will be complex and may be different for different product-market channels. Figure 10.4 shows the European options for shipment from the Far East from multiple source points for different products. They can be summarised under four main headings:

- Direct ship from each source to final market in full containers
- Consolidate in the supply region for final market in full containers
- Consolidate from each source for each theatre of operation with break bulk/intermediate inventory in the theatre for specific markets
- Consolidate in the supply region and also break bulk in the theatre of operations.

Obviously the inventory holding, warehousing, customer service and freight costs balance will be different for each of these and will be determined by the characteristics of the product and the profile of demand.

Multiple freight mode and cost options

The mix of freight methods which may be practical in the context of the required lead time must be overlaid on the point above. Shipping companies offer mixed sea/air services, different container sizes, scheduled and unscheduled services. As we have previously observed, the extended lead times involved in long sea passages are forcing companies to use air freight to an extent which appears costly but which, in the context of inventory holding costs, potential lost revenue and market flexibility, may be a worthwhile expense.

Negotiating through the maze of freight options is a highly specialised

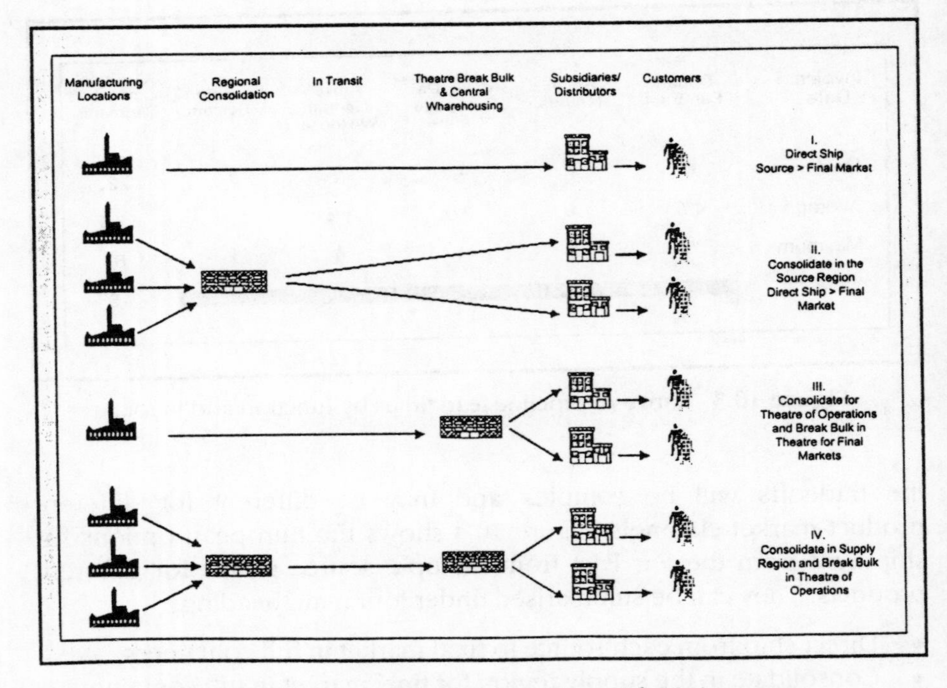

Figure 10.4 Options for Far East/Europe logistics system

skill; as is persuading a corporation to spend apparently more and more on one mode versus another

An increasingly attractive option is the use of 'door-to-door' transport providers, or the so-called 'integrators' of which DHL is probably the current market leader, with companies like Federal Express, TNT and UPS also very active. The benefits that door-to-door can provide are typically in the form of shorter and more reliable transit times, swifter and less complex procedure for customs clearance and, usually, a world-wide tracking and tracing system.

5. Intermediate component shipping with local added value

This option is beginning to move on to the agendas of the more sophisticated operators (Braithwaite 1990). These companies have re-examined their entire value chain to seek out opportunties for delaying or 'postponing' the final configuration of the product until it is as close to the customer as possible. It is often possible to achieve lower costs and improved flexibility to demand with lower inventory by shipping generic subassemblies in intermediate ship packs.

The local operation then provides:

- Localisation and finishing
- Kitting to different product options
- Local language packing
- Central inventory holding for the theatre of operations
- Deferral of the despatch to final markets
- Direct customer delivery for all the markets within the theatre without further handling.

6. *The acquisition and use of information*

The major problem for companies trying to determine a global supply chain approach is tracking down the information and reducing it to a usable form for planning. For instance, none of the companies with which we have worked has been able to offer a completely clean database of packaging specifications with channel/freight mode volumes or tonnages. Few companies have the ability to look at their data at an appropriate level of detail on a global basis in terms of either product movement or costs. Those that have moved in this direction are finding that the data are of poor quality and the accounting systems in use do not assist in seeking to evaluate throughput-related costs.

While the need has been recognised to compile and collate this type of data there appears to be a huge 'implementation gap' between the identification of the requirement and the usability of what actually gets delivered some time later.

Companies like Digital are now talking in terms of 'data warehousing' as a means of consolidating corporate-wide information, and 'knowledge engineering' as the process by which useful competitive advantage can be secured from the company's data.

Assuming that the data platform for 'knowledge engineering' has been established, the next issue for companies is developing and communicating solutions within the business. Our experience is that some or all of the following then occur.

1. Managers fail to recognise the results of the data reduction exercise as being a valid basis for planning, while the full data set is so complex that it is possible to prove almost anything is cost effective!
2. The conclusions are so radical that managers find they are being asked to consent to the dismantling of their entire function, or their power

base in terms of headcount or budget. It is not surprising that they commit reluctantly, if at all.

3. Managers are transfixed by the labels applied to the role and function of sites or channels; for example, Transhipment centre, Distribution centre. They apply their own understanding to the operating concept and role and the strategy becomes distorted in its communication and understanding.
4. The strategy is launched into a complete organisational vacuum in which ownership and accountability are undefined. We have yet to observe a supply chain strategy being successfully implemented where the benefits depend upon actions which are outside the direct control of the team carrying out the implementation.
5. Managers seek to impose unreal organisational and systems dependencies upon the plans which are then used to modify the strategy. In one example, the argument ran as follows: 'This approach requires a distributed systems strategy: distributed systems strategies are not compatible with our computing architecture and we cannot make them work, therefore we must centralise rather than decentralise'.

The truth is that people play a major role in the formation and operation of global supply chains. Lining up the troops, all facing the same way and putting the same foot forward, is the big challenge.

It is for this reason that we have concluded that planning and implementing the global supply chain is an evolutionary process in which corporations should pick the plums first in terms of cost and customer service. The key dependency is getting a platform of corporate information from which to launch the evolution of a global supply chain and from which to retrain and reorganise the structure.

DEVELOPING GLOBAL PIPELINE STRATEGIES

The burning issue for organisations is how to organise to take advantage (or alternatively reduce the dissipation of the advantage) of reduced set-up costs, more flexible manufacturing, and, where possible, economies of scale. The reality is that few companies have either the mechanism to redesign the supply chain or the systems to manage it. Just a few have organised to address these issues and have adopted a multidimensional logistics architecture.

The ability to engineer the performance of the supply chain is a crucial requirement in the context of the increasing rate of change in markets combined with operating conditions which are broadly adverse to reducing, or even containing, cost.

The key is to examine the processes which drive the logistics operations. These are all time based. The cycles of time by which we typically control our businesses are the key to attaining the goals for customer service, return on inventory and unit cost. A company with zero lead time delivers 100 per cent customer service and holds no inventory. This may seem absurd but there are companies that have radically reorganised their manufacturing and supply chain to minimise the time to respond to real demand and, as a direct result, minimise their inventory. Most managers believe that there has to be a penalty to pay in operating costs to achieve such improvements in lead time. Our research has shown that this is not necessarily the case. There is substantial advantage to be gained by looking at the supply chain as an integrated process, evaluating the individual lead time components within it and 're-engineering' the organisation to reduce cycle times and improve market focus. We have called this 'strategic lead time management' (Christopher and Braithwaite 1989).

The aim is to compress the global supply chain in an orderly, logical and progressive manner to reduce dwell time and the ratio of cost-added time to value-added time. This can only be achieved by viewing the business as a total system. The 'driver' of a company's logistics performance is the sequence of administrative and control processes through which customer service is achieved and inventory is acquired and distributed.

Getting a clear 'front to back' view of the processes involves many people; valuing and predicting the consequences of procedural redesign on customer service achievement and asset management can be contentious.

The basic principle of strategic lead time management is that organisational process creates cover and delay. The individual elements of lead time and the way in which they interact within and between the different process stages in the supply chain can materially affect the performance of the business. Our approach has been devised to address this very real need to 'engineer' process in an integrated way for the business. It is a two-stage methodology. Firstly, data modelling is carried out, using large-scale sampling and analysis techniques. This highlights the areas where non-value added time is high so that the organisational processes and lead times can be investigated with a view to reducing or eliminating them.

Armed with this understanding, a time-based simulation of the global supply chain can be constructed using on-screen computer techniques. When this model has been constructed to reflect current performance, detailed 'what if?' analyses on the design of the supply chain, its processes and lead times can be carried out. It is like performing computer aided design on an organisation.

Using time-based simulation we have been able to synthesise the organisational processes and physical operation of a complex supply chain. It is, in essence, an expert systems approach with a full predictive capability of both inventory levels and customer service performance (Horscroft and Braithwaite 1990).

With the rate of change in supplier and customer locations, product mix, markets and services, the opportunity to be able to predict supply chain performance is extremely valuable. The ability to identify the value of the costs and benefits of the various components of change is an enormous support to global supply chain management, as is the chance to focus on real business value and to tailor solutions in shorter timescales.

ORGANISING FOR GLOBAL LOGISTICS

The companies that we have studied and worked with in the recent past have all been forced to confront the issue of how to structure the global logistics organisation. In their different ways these companies have moved towards the same conclusion: effectiveness in global logistics can only be achieved through a greater element of centralisation. This in many respects runs counter to much of the conventional wisdom which tends to argue that decision-making responsibility should be devolved and decentralised at least to the strategic business unit (SBU) level. This philosophy has manifested itself in many companies in the form of strong local management, often with autonomous decision-making at the country level. Good though this may be for encouraging local initiatives, it tends to be dysfunctional when integrated global strategies are required.

Clearly there will still be many areas where local decision-making will be preferable; for example, sales strategy and, possibly, promotional and marketing communications strategy. Likewise the implementation of global strategy can still be adjusted to take account of national differences and requirements.

How then can the appropriate balance of global versus local decision-making be achieved in formulating and implementing logistics strategy?

Because specific market environments and industry characteristics will differ from company to company it is dangerous to offer all-embracing solutions. However a number of general principles are beginning to emerge.

- The strategic structuring and overall control of logistics flows must be centralised to achieve world-wide optimisation of costs.
- The control and management of customer service must be localised against the requirements of specific markets to ensure competitive advantage is gained and maintained.
- As the trend towards out-sourcing everything except core competencies increases then so does the need for global coordination.
- A global logistics information system is the prerequisite for enabling the achievement of local service needs whilst seeking global cost optimisation.

i) *Structure and control.* If the potential tradeoffs in rationalising sourcing, production and distribution across national boundaries are to be achieved then it is essential that a central decision-making structure for logistics is established. Many companies that are active on an international basis find that they are constrained in their search for global optimisation by strongly entrenched local systems and structures.

ii) *Customer service management.* Because local markets have their own specific characteristics and needs there is considerable advantage to be achieved by shaping marketing strategies locally – albeit within overall global guidelines. This is particularly true of customer service management where the opportunities for tailoring service against individual customer requirements are great. The management of customer service involves the monitoring of service needs as well as performance and extends to the management of the entire order fulfilment process – from order through delivery.

iii) *Out-sourcing and partnerships.* One of the fastest moving trends in the global business today is the trend towards out-sourcing. Not just out-sourcing the procurement of materials and components but also out-sourcing of services that traditionally have been provided in-house. The logic of this trend is that the organisation should focus on those activities in the value chain where it has a distinct advantage – the core competencies of the business – and everything else it should out-source. This movement has been particularly evident in logistics where the provision of transport, warehousing and inventory control is increasingly subcontracted to specialists or logistics partners.

To manage and control this network requires a blend of both

central and local involvement. Our view is that once again the strategic decisions need to be taken centrally with the monitoring and control of supplier performance and day-to-day liaison with logistics partners being best managed at a local level.

iv) *Logistics information.* The management of global logistics is in reality the management of information flows. The information system is the mechanism whereby the complex flows of materials, parts, subassemblies and finished products can be coordinated to achieve cost-effective service. Any organisation with aspirations to global leadership is dependent upon the visibility it can gain of materials flows, inventories and demand throughout the pipeline. Without the ability to see down the pipeline into end-user markets, to read actual demand and subsequently to manage replenishment in virtual real time the system is doomed to depend upon inventory. To 'substitute information for inventory' has become something of a cliché but it is essential nevertheless. Time lapses in information flow are directly translated into inventory. The great advances that are being made in introducing 'quick response' logistics systems are all based upon direct information flow from the point of actual demand. On a global scale we typically find that the presence of intervening inventories between the plant and the marketplace obscure the view of real demand. Hence the need for information systems which can read demand at every level in the pipeline and provide the driving power for a centrally controlled logistics system.

LESSONS FOR MANAGEMENT

To summarise, the implementation of global pipeline control is highly dependent upon the ability of the organisation to find the correct balance between central control and local management. It is unwise to be dogmatic but our experience suggests that certain tasks and functions lend themselves to central control and others to local management (see Figure 10.5).

Much has been learned in the last ten years or so about the opportunities for cost and service enhancement through better management of logistics. Now organisations are faced with applying those lessons on a much broader stage. As international competition becomes more intense and as national barriers to trade gradually reduce, the era of

Global	Local
• Network structuring for production and transportation optimization	• Order fulfilment and customer service management
• Information systems development and control	• Inventory management and control
• Inventory positioning	• Warehouse management and local delivery
• Sourcing decisions, profitability analyses	• Customer and channel cost control
• International transport mode and sourcing decisions	• Liaison with local sales and marketing management
• Tradeoff analyses and throughput cost control	

Figure 10.5 Global co-ordination and local management

the global business has arrived. Our view is that increasingly the difference between success and failure in the global marketplace will be determined not by the sophistication of product technology or even of marketing communications, but rather by the way in which we manage and control the global logistics pipeline.

References

Braithwaite, A (1990) 'Managing European Logistics Assets', *Logistics Today*, Sep/Oct

Christopher, M (1989) 'Customer Service Strategies for International Markets', Council of Logistics Management *Annual Conference Proceedings*, Oct

—and Braithwaite, A (1989) 'Managing Strategic Lead Times', *Logistics Information Management*, Vol 2, No 4

Fry, T D (1990) 'Controlling Input: The Real Key to Shorter Lead Times', *International Journal of Logistics Management*, Vol 1, No 1

Hamel, G and Prahalad, C K (1989) 'Strategic Intent', *Harvard Business Review*, May–Jun

Horscroft, P and Braithwaite, A (1990) 'Enhancing Supply Chain Efficiency – The Strategic Lead Time Approach', *International Journal of Logistics Management*, Vol 1, No 2

Land, D (1990) 'Is This the Best Place to Work in Britain?', *Sunday Times – Business World Supplement*, Mar

McLuhan, M (1967) *The Medium is the Message*, Bantam, New York

Porter, M (1986) *Competition in Global Industries*, Harvard Business School Press

Roberts, J (1990) 'Formulating and Implementing a Global Logistics Strategy', *International Journal of Logistics Management*, Vol 1, No 2

Stalk, G and Hout, T (1990) *Competing Against Time*, The Free Press, New York

van Amstel, Ploos M J (1990) 'Managing The Pipeline Effectively', *Journal of Business Logistics*, Vol 11, No 1

Index